SPEAKING TO THE HEART:

OR,

Sermons for the People.

BY

THOMAS GUTHRIE, D.D

NEW EDITION,
WITH MUCH ADDITIONAL MATTER.

New York
E. B. TREAT & COMPANY
Office of THE TREASURY MAGAZINE

241-243 West 23d Street

CONTENTS.

4403

CONTENTS

I.

NEGLECTED WARNINGS.

"Gray hairs are here and there upon him, yet he knoweth not."
—HOSEA vii. 9.

FIRE low—the order which generals have often given to their men before fighting began—suits the pulpit not less than the battle-field. The mistake common both to soldiers and speakers is to shoot too high, over people's heads; missing, by a want of directness and plainness, both the persons they preach to and the purpose they preach for. So did not the prophet Nathan, when, having told his story of the little ewe lamb, and kindled David's indignation, he fixed his eyes on the king to say, Thou art the man. So did not the Baptist, when, recognising in the crowd Pharisees swollen with pride and rich with the spoil of orphans, he cried, O generation of vipers, who hath warned you to flee from the wrath to come? And, though with speech less blunt and rude and un-polite withal, as some might say, so did not the great apostle of the Gentiles, but directed his addresses, like an arrow, to the hearts and habits, the bosoms and business of his audience. In Athens, full of false

gods, he proclaimed the true one ; in Corinth he de-
nounced the vices which made her name so infamous.
Before the Hebrews, who clung so tenaciously to the
sacrifices of lambs, bulls, and goats, he set forth the
Lamb of God, which taketh away the sin of the
world—like an expert physician applying to each
disease its own direct and appropriate remedy.

Arraigned at a judgment bar, it furnished him with
a topic of discourse.   He proclaimed the judgment to
come, and, with the skill of an orator and the courage
of a martyr, preached to an intemperate and unright-
eous judge of temperance and righteousness, till, as
the captive flashed and thundered from the bar, the
judge on the bench grew pale and trembled.   In this
he followed the example of Him, the Prince of
Preachers, whom the common people, enchanted and
enchained with his speech, heard gladly—speaking,
in the judgment even of his enemies, as never man
spake.

With matter divine and manner human, our Lord
descended to the level of the humblest of the crowd,
lowering himself to their understandings, and winning
his way into their hearts by borrowing his topics from
familiar circumstances and the scenes around him
Be it a boat, a plank, a rope, a beggar's rags, an imperial robe, we would seize on anything to save a
drowning man ; and in his anxiety to save poor sinners, to rouse their fears, their love, their interest, to
make them understand and feel the truth, our Lord

pressed everything—art and nature, earth and heaven —into his service. Creatures of habit, the servants if not the slaves of form, we invariably select our text from some book of the Sacred Scriptures. He took a wider, freer range; and, instead of keeping to the unvarying routine of text and sermon with formal divisions, it were well, perhaps, that we sometimes ventured to follow his example; for may it not be to the naturalness of their addresses and their striking out from the beaten path of texts and sermons, to their plain speaking and home-thrusts, to their direct appeals and homespun arguments, that our street and lay preachers owe perhaps not a little of their power?

Illustrating the words of the great English dramatist—

" Finds tongues in trees, books in the running brooks,
Sermons in stones, and good in everything,"

our Lord found many a topic of discourse in the scenes around him; even the humblest objects shone in his hands as I have seen a fragment of broken glass or earthenware, as it caught the sunbeam, light up, flashing like a diamond. With the stone of Jacob's well for a pulpit, and its water for a text, he preached salvation to the Samaritan woman. A little child, which he takes from its mother's side, and holds up blushing in his arms before the astonished audience, is his text for a sermon on humility. A

husbandman on a neighbouring height between him
and the sky, who strides with long and measured steps
over the field he sows, supplies a text from which he
discourses on the Gospel and its effects on different
classes of hearers.   In a woman baking; in two
women who sit by some cottage door grinding at the
mill; in an old, strong fortalice perched on a rock,
whence it looks across the brawling torrent to the
ruined and roofless gable of a house swept away by
mountain floods—Jesus found texts.   From the birds
that sung above his head, and the lilies that blos-
somed at his feet, he discoursed on the care of God
—these his text, and Providence his theme; and
with gray hairs on our own head and hoary heads
around, we feel that his practice justifies us in making these our text; and addressing you, as I proceed
to do, from these words—" Gray hairs are here and
there upon him, yet he knoweth not."

I. Gray hairs are a sign of decay.

Giving a mane to the lion, antlers to the hart, to
the males among birds a brighter plumage, and among
four-footed beasts a bolder carriage and a bigger form,
God, the maker of all, has distinguished the sexes,
not only among mankind, but among the higher orders
of the lower animals.   He had a wise purpose in this.
A God of order and not of confusion, he has for wise
purposes also given distinctive features to the different periods of human life, from the cradle onwards

to the grave. In roaming over the mountains, we often find on the tops of all but peaked and picturesque ranges, a level space—a table-land, as it is called, between the ascent from one valley and the descent into another, where the water, having no run, gathers into lonely tarns, or stagnates in a black morass. Human life between the ages of forty and fifty presents such a level. Travelling onward with little change in our appearance, in our powers of body or of mind; after growth has ceased and before decay has begun; ere the signs of youth have entirely left us or those of age have come; arrived at full maturity, with waste and supply in perfect balance, it were hard to say whether we are yet ascending from the cradle, or, having turned the hill-top, are on our way down to the grave. It is a solemn position that culminating point, where we see the cradle we have left on this side, and the grave where we shall lie on that! Yet it is not of much practical consequence to know whether we are going up or down hill, since there are in disease and the chapter of accidents many causes which make it the lot of few to number the appointed threescore years and ten. Death strikes down his victims at all ages; and of the crowd that started together, but two or three stragglers reach the natural term of life. Many more die young than old: and death so extends his ravages over the whole period of life, that, whether with buoyant steps we are pressing up or are tottering down hill beneath a load of years, we tread on graves; the road, if I may say so, is paved with burial stones; and on every side the tombs of all ages, each with its *memento mori*, tell the young not less than the old to prepare to die.

> " Leaves have their time to fall,
>   And flowers to wither at the north wind's breath ;
> And stars to set ; but all—
>   Thou hast all seasons for thine own, O Death ! "

Still, as where no river flows, or mountains rise to divide one kingdom from another, though the border land between life's growth and decay is not often very clearly marked, our Maker, for wise and kind ends, has given very distinct and distinguishing features to infancy, to youth, to manhood, and to old age. Infancy, in which man of all creatures is most dependent on others, requires constant help and care ; besides needing these, old age, marked by its gray hairs, has sacred claims on our sympathies and respect. Nature herself teaches us to look with reverence on age, even in the pages of an old book; in the leafless branches of an old tree; in the silent, deserted halls of an old roofless ruin : still more in one whose head is white with the snows of fourscore or a hundred winters ; still more in yon aged pilgrim who sits on Jordan's bank, straining his eyes to catch a glimpse of the shining ones that wait to welcome him beyond death's dark flood. "The hoary head is a crown of glory, if it be found in the way of righteousness," as

seen in Simeon in the temple, where, with Jesus
held in arms that trembled with joy more than age,
he bent his hoary head to gaze with awe, and affection, and adoration on the infant's face; and raised
it to astonish the bystanders—admiring only in them
the beautiful conjunction of age and infancy, of
life's rosy dawn and evening gray—with this ardent,
heavenly, this death-defying and death-desiring wish,
Lord, now lettest thou thy servant depart in peace,
according to thy word: for mine eyes have seen thy
salvation.

Gray hairs, what tender authority do they add to
the law, "Honour thy father and thy mother: that
thy days may be long upon the land which the Lord
thy God giveth thee!" I care nothing for the religion of man or woman who, neglecting aged and
venerable parents, leaves them to the care of strangers;
casting those on the cold charities of the world whom
they should have protected and nourished, in return for the kindness that watched over their feeble
years, and bore with the foibles and follies of their
youth. Although the deserted, dying savage, beating
the withered breasts at which a son drank in life, has
complained of him who forgot even in the pressure
of sorest want a mother's kindness and a mother's
claims, yet for those wandering tribes that, pressed by
hunger, and ever on the verge of famine, feel the old
men who cannot hunt and the old women who cannot walk to be burdens, and throw them off, there is

some excuse ; but for those of us who neglect the claims of parents—none. In such men's profession there is no reality or truth. He who does not revere a father he has seen, cannot love a Father whom he has not seen.

Other gray hairs besides those of parents have claims on our respect. "Thou shalt rise up before the hoary head, and honour the face of the old man," is a command that speaks to our hearts, and is in harmony with the best feelings of our nature. Nor in public assembly have I ever seen a feeble old man, bending under the weight of years, or, perhaps, ot sorrow, left standing, while stout youth and manhood sat lounging at ease, but the spectacle has recalled the words of that noble Greek who, seeing an aged man left to stand a butt for youths to jeer at, rose in in-dignation to rebuke the crime, and tell his degenerate countrymen how, in the better days of the republic, on an old man entering an assembly all rose to their feet to do him reverence. Gray hairs mark the decay of man ; but contempt for gray hairs, and want of re-spect in children to parents, or in youth to age, is a sign that virtue, society, and the Church of God decay. There is no worse or more evil-omened feature in American society than the forwardness and preten-sions of its youth ; nor, for we have our own faults, is there a greater social evil in this old country than the growing indifference that children shew to the feelings or comfort of their aged parents. To cast them, with·

out strong necessity, on public charity, however agreeable it may be to law, is contrary to nature, to the dictates of the gospel, and to the blessed example of him who from his dying cross cast looks of love on Mary, and committed her with most touching tenderness to the care of John.

In my text, however, gray hairs are not associated either with parental honours, or with the ripe wisdom of age, or with the piety of the venerable Simeon. They are here but the tokens of decay, marks of age, the premonitory symptoms of dissolution ; and so the truth it announces is that men, many men, live in ignorance, and act in disregard of signs that should warn and alarm them.

In illustration of this, I remark—

1. It appears in the history of States.

These words were first spoken of the kingdom of Israel. In the oppression of the poor and the sighing of the needy, in the corruption of morals and the decline of true religon, the prophet saw the signs of his country's decay—these the gray hairs that were here and there upon them, and they knew not. Nor is that uncommon. Fell consumption wears roses on her cheek, nor parts with hope but with life ; and kingdoms, as well as men and women in decline, stricken with a mortal malady, have descended into the grave, blind to their dangers and their doom. What an example of this the disruption of Rehoboam's kingdom ! The dissolute habits of his father's court, with such a tendency as water has to seek a lower level, had extended to the community, and corrupted its morals; the palace, from which religion had been scared by the introduction of idolatry and strange women, had forfeited all claim to public respect; the crown, associated with open profligacy and the basest selfishness, had lost its brightest gems; the throne that David had left to his descendants, with none to rally round it but men enervated by luxury and debased by vice, was ready to fall at the first shock; while the people, restive under their burdens, were ripe for rebellion. Such were the circumstances in which, at Solomon's death, his son was called to the helm—breakers ahead; breakers on the lee bow; white roaring breakers on this side and on that! But the pilot was blind. When circumstances called for the most skilful seamanship, reckless, he ran his ship ashore; straight on ruin. Insensible to his dangers, he had not even the discretion to return a civil answer, a decent refusal, to his people's petitions; telling those who asked that their burdens might be made lighter, the yoke less grievous, "My little finger shall be thicker than my father's loins. And now whereas my father did lade you with a heavy yoke, I will add to your yoke: my father hath chastised you with whips, but I will chastise you with scorpions." What man ever so played the fool on a royal stage, or more plainly illustrated the words of the heathen moralist —The gods first make mad those whom they intend to destroy? Such was his answer. The result was not long to wait for. In less than four and twenty hours the country was in arms; what, well guided, had resulted in reform, exploded in a revolution which hurled this madman from the throne of Israel, and left him but a fragment of his father's kingdom. Gray hairs were here and there upon him, and yet he knew not.

May his fate be our warning! We boast of our wealth; that our commerce extends to every region; that our manufactories are the workshops of the world; that our armies have pushed their conquests to the ends of the earth; that our Queen rules an empire on which the sun never sets; that the slave who touches our shore is free, and the beaten patriot who flies to its refuge is safe; how, beneath the ægis of Liberty, Peace sits crowned, while Plenty pours a full horn into her lap; and best of all, how the Bible is open, and its preaching free; and that religion, while it commands the respect of all, is enthroned in the hearts and rules the lives of many. We think that our mountain stands strong; and that we are as safe amid the revolutions that shake other countries as this island, guarded by its rocky cliffs, amid the storms that agitate the sea. I am not sure of that; there are gray hairs on us. What do you say to an amount of illegitimacy that disgraces our Christian name, and calls on masters and parents to guard the virtue of their homes? What say you to the drunkenness which costs us, year by year, vast millions of money and whole hecatombs of human lives? What do you say to the loose morality which, imported from the Continent, is fast destroying the claims which the upper classes of society have on the respect of the lower? What to the altars that stand in ruins in so many households, to the multitudes that take their pleasure on God's holy day, and to the audacious attempts made to turn our Sabbaths into days of worldly pleasure? What to the thousands in our large, the tens of thousands in our larger, and the hundreds of thousands in our largest cities, that have thrown off the profession of religion, and from year's end to year's end never enter a house of God? In these I see gray hairs, signs of national decay ; nor could I, but for one thing, anticipate any other fate for our country than that which has entombed Egypt and Assyria, Babylon and Persia, Greece and Rome— first birth, then growth, then decay, then death, then the grave. With gray hairs here and there on us, we do know it. Thank God, we know it ; and that thousands of earnest men and devoted women, fired with love to God and souls, animated by piety and the truest patriotism, are alive to our evils and working hard to cure them. There is balm in Gilead and a physician there ; and though I do not know that hair once gray ever turns black again, our country, like an eagle, may renew its youth, and mounting as on eagle's wings, rise higher and higher still. To America, could my voice reach her shores, or be heard above

the rage of passions and the roar of battle, and to our
own country also I would address the words of the
prophet: If thou take away from the midst of thee
the yoke, the putting forth of the finger, and speaking
vanity ; and if thou draw out thy soul to the hungry,
and satisfy the afflicted soul, then shall thy light rise
in obscurity, and thy darkness shall be as the noonday;
and the Lord shall guide thee continually, and satisfy
thy soul in drought, and make fat thy bones ; and
thou shalt be like a watered garden, and like a spring
of water, whose waters fail not.

2. My text applies to the false security of sinners.

It is a dreadful thing to see the happiness of a
human being, like a brittle vase, shattered at a blow,
the fair fabric collapse in an instant into a heap of
ruins. It is more painful still to have to strike the blow.
With reluctant steps I have approached the house of a
young wife to communicate tidings of her husband's
death. There is not a cloud in that summer's sky; nor,
as she thinks, in hers. The air rings with songs of happy
birds, and the garden amid which her home stands is
full of smiling beauty ; and fair as the flowers and
happy as a singing bird comes that bride forth, rushing
out to bid me welcome to her sunny home. With
such tidings I felt like an executioner. I thought of
victims going with garlands to the sacrifice. With
Jephthah, when his child came forth with dances and
delight to meet him, I was ready to cry, " Alas ! my
daughter ;" and when the truth was told, the knife

plunged into her heart, and she, springing to her feet, with one wild, long, piercing shriek, dropped on the floor at mine, a senseless form, I felt it hard to have such offices to do. I could not give her back her dead, nor at her wild entreaties unsay the dreadful truth, or admit, poor soul! that I was but playing with her fears. But how happy would I esteem myself to break in on your false security? Here to dream is death, but to wake is life ; as yonder, when you break in on the baseless visions of a prison, and shewing an open door to the felon who has woke to the miserable consciousness of his doom, bid him rise and flee—saying, Behold, I have set before thee an open door! But, perhaps, you have no fears, at least are not much alarmed; counting yourselves rather certain than otherwise of escaping hell and finding heaven at death. On what grounds, may I ask? Have you been converted? Is Christ precious to you? Have you washed in the fountain of his blood? Have you waited at the gates of prayer? Have you made your calling and election sure? Have you the witness of God's Spirit and the testimony of your conscience within you, that in simplicity and godly sincerity you have your conversation in the world? No : then be assured that gray hairs are upon you, the greatest dangers beset you, and, alas, you know not.

Frequenting the church, repairing so many times a year to the Lord's table, assembling once a day, or perhaps oftener, your household to prayers, you make a becoming profession. There were more hope of some if they did not. Harlots and publicans who feel that they have nothing, and none but Christ to trust to, press into the kingdom, leaving scribes and Pharisees at the back of the door. A plausible profession, like false hair worn to hide the gray, may but conceal the signs of our danger. Take away from some their profession, and what remains? The outside religion subtracted, nothing; or only what might suggest the unwrapping of yon tenant of a dusty tomb on the banks of the Nile. Once it was a man or lovely woman; but now, these painted, odorous, gilded cerements, fold by fold, removed, we reach a blackened mummy—a withered skeleton. Hidden from view by a fair profession, the world, the devil, hideous and unholy passions lodge within the heart, where God and Christ should be.

Be our profession what it may, if we have habits of sin—these are the gray hairs that, unless grace convert and mercy pardon, foretell our doom. Thick as these on the head of age, some men's lives are full of sin; they are going to hell as plainly as one whose form is bent and whose head is hoary is going down to his grave. But you may have abandoned many sins! Ah, but what is this? Here is a sin, small indeed, and secret, and unknown to the world, of which no man even suspects you; yet, like the one gray hair among her golden or raven tresses, which the vain beauty sees with dismay, it points to the

grave. Oh, trust to no Saviour but Christ, nor to
any evidence of a gracious state other than an entire
abstinence from all sin ; or, at least, godly sorrow for
it, and daily resistance to it ! So long as you see one
star in the sky, the sun is not risen ; so long as one
leak admits the water, the ship is not safe ; so long as
one sin reigns in a man's heart, and is practised in
his life, Jesus is neither his Saviour nor his King. The
Jews have no dealings with the Samaritans.

3. This appears in men's insensibility to the lapse
and lessons of time.

It is one of the most beautiful and beneficent
arrangements of Providence, that children, if sensible
of their helplessness, are not ashamed of that which
awakens our love and sympathy ; it gives them no
pain. Nor less kind on God's part is it that our
minds are formed to adapt themselves to the circumstances of advancing years. Indeed we often glide
so gently, so gradually down the decline of life, as to
be little disturbed with the premonitions of its close.
I remember the saying of a venerable lady, who had
seen the changes of fourscore summers : " Let no one
trust to this, that they will turn to God, and seek
a Saviour when they feel old ; I don't feel old."
And though the young perhaps will hardly credit
it, men with furrows in their brow, and gray hairs
on their head, often find it difficult to remember
that they are old ; to believe it ; to realise the approach of their end ; how near they are to the

grave. Death seems to flee before us, like the horizon which we ever see, and never reach. The river that springs like an arrow from its rocky cradle, to bound from crag to crag, to rush brawling through the glen, and, like thoughtless youth, to waste its strength in mere noise, and froth, and foam, flows on smoothly, slowly, almost imperceptibly, as it approaches its grave in the bosom of the sea. And so is it often with man. The nearer we draw to our end, through a natural callousness or otherwise, the less sensible we grow to the evils and approach of age. And when a man has not left his peace with God to seek in old age, his greatest work to a time when he is least fit to do it; when a man, having made his calling and election sure, has left nothing for a dying hour but to enjoy the comforts and peace of piety; in such a case it is a most blessed thing that old age does not make our hearts old, or benumb our feelings—that gray hairs are on us, and yet we know not.

But where, in such a case, is the hope of those who have trusted to turning religious when they turn old, and attending to the concerns of a better world when they have ceased to feel any interest in this? Death and a man, so runs the story, once made a bargain— the man stipulating, lest he might be taken unawares, that Death should send him so many warnings before he came. Well, one day, years thereafter, to his great amazement, the King of Terrors stood before him. He had broken the bargain, so said the other, who

B

clung to life. Death, he alleged, had sent him no warnings. No warnings? His eyes were dim; his ears were dull; his gums were toothless; and spare and thin were the hoar locks on his bent and palsied head; these, Death's heralds, had come, not too late, yet all in vain. Amid warnings, but unnoticed or despised, his salvation was neglected; his soul lost; gray hairs were on him; and, so far as any practical effect was concerned, he knew not. Literally, or not, they are on us. Every setting sun, and every nodding hearse, and every passing Sabbath, warn us that days of darkness come, and opportunities of salvation go. Be up, therefore, and doing—asking yourselves such questions as these: Am I saved? Have I been born again? Have I embraced the Saviour? If not, oh, seize this flying hour!

He taught a solemn truth who painted Time as an old man, with wings on his shoulders, scythe and hour-glass in his hands, and on his wrinkled forehead one lock of hair. All bald behind, and offering us no hold when it is past, let us seize Time by the fore-lock. Be saved this hour! That hoary preacher addresses you, as he shakes a glass where the sands of some of us are well-nigh run, and points his finger to the grave which, a few years hence, shall have closed over all this living assembly. Like other preachers, he shall die. Death himself shall die; but we never. Blessed or cursed with immortality, we shall live to wish we had never lived, or to rejoice that we shall live for ever. And, whether they **fall late or early**, happy then and happy now, such as, not ignorant that there were gray hairs on them, guilt in their lives, and sins on their consciences, sought salvation in Jesus Christ—washing their stains away in that atoning blood which both cleanseth from **the vilest sins, and is free to the worst of sinners!**

II.

FEAR, THE FRUIT OF DIVINE FORGIVENESS.

"There is forgiveness with thee, that thou mayest be feared."—
PSALM CXXX. 4.

WERE we told that the worm that crawls, wriggling across our path, would one day rise a winged form to soar aloft and glitter in the sunny air like a living gem; were we told that a dry, husky, sapless, dead-like thing, if buried, would spring from its grave, changed in colour and form, to become a flower of fairest hues, or a tree with tough timbers to form the ribs, or tall stem the mast of a mighty ship; were we told that water may be made as hard as stone, or that, before the smoke of its last gun has melted into air, the news of a battle may be borne hundreds of miles away, along an iron wire, through the bowels of mountains, or over the bed of the sea; which of us, if previously ignorant of them, would not be filled with wonder, if not with incredulity? We meet much to startle us, much that is unlikely, unexpected in the works of God. No wonder, therefore, that we should stumble on passages to startle us here and there in his Word; statements of duty, of fact, of doctrine, to surprise us, and prompt the exclamation of Nicodemus, when, hearing from our Saviour that man must be born again, he exclaimed, How can these things be?

Take, for example, such duties as these: "Whosoever shall smite thee on thy right cheek, turn to him the other also. And if any man will sue thee at the law, and take away thy coat, let him have thy cloak also." "If thine enemy hunger, feed him; if he thirst, give him drink." "Love your enemies, bless them that curse you, do good to them that hate you, and pray for them which despitefully use you, and persecute you." How natural for men, ignorant of the power of grace, as some are of those powers in nature that change a creeping worm into a winged insect, or water which a breath can ruffle into a pavement as solid as stone, and deeming such heights of virtue impossible, to exclaim with the Jewish ruler, How can these things be? So also might they have said, who listened with astonishment to the opening sentences of our Lord's first and of the world's greatest sermon— "Blessed are the poor in spirit," "Blessed are they that mourn," "Blessed are the meek," "Blessed are ye when men shall revile you and persecute you, and shall say all manner of evil against you falsely for my sake." This was a flight as high above the style of common preachers as that of the eagle disturbed in her mountain solitudes, and, at that moment, soaring

in the blue heavens above their heads. Accustomed
to shrink from poverty in every form, from loss and
grief, from persecution and calumny, as evils to be
avoided, I can fancy the people casting on each other
looks of surprise, doubt, and amazement, which said,
as plainly as spoken words, How can these things
be?

Then there are doctrinal statements in the Word of
God where the two parts of the sentence do not seem
to hang well together. For example, " Hearken unto
me, ye stout-hearted, that are far from righteousness."
God here brings a charge of guilt against his people ;
and how does he wind up the sentence ? Imagine a
trial for murder, for instance ! Arrayed in his robes
of office, the judge, amid solemn silence, receives their
verdict from the jury. It is, Guilty. And in what
terms does he now address the pale, wretched, trembling felon at the bar ! Fixing on him eyes full at once
of pity and of horror, he says, You have been charged
with the crime of murder, and, after a fair, full, patient
trial, have been found guilty ; and now the sentence of
the law is, that you be taken back to prison, and from
prison to the place of execution, and there be hanged
by the neck till you are dead. Where man begins
with a conviction, he ends with condemnation ; a judgment of guilt is followed up by a sentence of death.
Not so God in this case. Hearken unto me, ye stout-
hearted, ye guilty, bold, bad, daring sinners, that are
far from righteousness—what follows ? Not, I will

beat your stout-heartedness out of you, breaking you
with a rod of iron, dashing you in pieces like a potter's
vessel ; but, "I bring near my righteousness." Had
this address—calling up the pictures of the prodigal
kneeling at his father's feet, of Peter without, weeping bitterly and filling the ear of night with long-drawn
sobs, of the woman washing Christ's feet with tears,
and wiping them with her golden tresses—begun differently ; had it begun thus, Hearken unto me, ye bleeding, broken-hearted ones, that are far from righteousness, I bring near mine, its conclusion had been less
surprising. But it is as if a great, black, lurid, leaden
cloud, on which we have been gazing with silent dread,
expecting it each moment to burst in thunders, were
to dissolve itself in a shower which cools the sultry air,
and refreshes the thirsty ground.

Such another example of apparent incongruity is
afforded by the first and second members of the text,
"There is forgiveness with thee, that thou mayest be
feared !" That thou mayest be feared ! we are ready
to ask, How does that follow ? How can these things
be ? There is forgiveness with thee ! a blessed truth
that ! one we gladly assent to ; nay, hail, as the Israelites, on that night when the sea roared in their front
and Egypt pressed on their rear, hailed the path
which, stretching from shore to shore, opened them a
way of escape. But for that they must have all been
drowned ; but for this we must have all been damned—
for were God to mark iniquity, or enter into judgment

who could stand? who could answer for one of a thousand?

In opening up the subject of my text I observe,

I. That there must be something peculiar about God's forgiveness that it leads to fear.

"Honour thy father and thy mother," says the law, "that thy days may be long upon the land which the Lord thy God giveth thee." But how can this be done when parents, ever threatening, and hardly ever punishing, set their children an example of weakness, if not of wickedness? "Foolishness is bound in the heart of a child," and must be separated from it by beating, as the husk from the grain ere it is fit for the oven, or the woody fibre from the flax ere it is fit for the loom. Hence Solomon says, He that spareth his rod hateth his son. It is the forked lightning which, leaping from the clouds with a roar, rends the stoutest oak, men dread; not the sheet lightning, which, though startling us at first as it glares on the darkness of night, we have learned to regard with indifference. It shines, but does not strike; it flashes, but does not fall. No parents are less revered by their children than those who deal in empty threats, and reverse, if I may say so, the exclamation of Isaac, The voice is Jacob's voice, but the hands are the hands of Esau. So to threaten and not to punish is about as fatal to the well-being of a family, as to promise and not reward. An act of forgiveness following on every offence slacks the bonds of obedience ; and a constant repetition of acts of forgiveness on the part of a weak parent, encourages a constant repetition of acts of offence on the part of a wicked child. By and by the hand that has sown the wind reaps the whirlwind. Disobedience in the child grows into a habit ; its nature becomes thoroughly perverted ; its regard for parental authority dies ; and in the indulgent parents, whose gray hairs their children treat with contempt and probably bring with sorrow to the grave, in the wretchedness of their homes and the utter wreck of their families, we have an illustration of this grand law of domestic life, that where parents will not punish their children, their children, the least guilty party and most sinned against, will punish them. There must, therefore, be a very essential difference between the forgiveness of our heavenly and that of many an earthly father, else were these words not true, " There is forgiveness with thee, that thou mayest be feared."

Had my text run thus, There is power, justice, anger, vengeance with thee; or, in accordance with such statements as these, " Cursed is every one that continueth not in all things which are written in the book of the law to do them," " The soul that sinneth, it shall die ;" had my text said, There is truth with thee, who would not have seen this to be the plain, natural, solemn conclusion, " that thou mayest be feared !" Let God arm himself with terrors, and we feel that he is to be feared.

On the deep, where giant billows, rushing on with foaming crest, threaten instant destruction; beneath the lurid sky when, bursting in thunder peals, every bolt threatens instant death; when the pestilence, wrapped in folds of poisonous vapours, walks the streets of an alarmed city, and funerals are met at every turn, and friends and neighbours seized in the darkness of the night are dead before morning, stubborn knees bend in prayer, and terror sits on the faces of stout-hearted men; ah, then "the perpetual hills did bow, ... the mountains saw thee, and they trembled;" or in the words of another prophet, "The lion hath roared, who will not fear?" And so, had my text in connexion with God introduced scenes of terror — the great white throne; the books of judgment; the falling heavens; the dying sun; the departing earth; the pit; the smoke of torment; the worm that never dies, and the fire that is never quenched; the solemn scene that shall wind up the close of all things, a God in judgment, and a world in flames—all hearts would have responded like an echo, to the text, and this question had trembled on our lips, "Who shall not fear thee, O Lord, and glorify thy name? for thou only art holy."

But this is not the way. And how is it, that while the parents who constantly forgive are not feared, God, with whom is forgiveness, is? why is it that forgiveness does not in his case, as in theirs, breed insolent presumption? What is that strange and potent element in divine forgiveness which makes the forgiven fear—making me more afraid to sin beside the Cross of Calvary, with its quiet, pale, dead, bleeding burden, than if I stood at the foot of Sinai amid the thunders, lightnings, and trumpet peals that made Moses himself exceedingly fear and quake? In other words, how is it that, because there is not power, nor judgment, nor terror, but forgiveness with God, he is therefore to be feared, and is feared?

II. Let me explain those peculiar characters in the forgiveness of God which breed fear, not presumption, in the forgiven.

1. The manner of the forgiveness sets forth the holiness of God and the evils of sin in the strongest light.

The heathen have little fear of their gods. How should they fear them? They can make a god out of a piece of wood, or buy one for a shilling. With how little reverence some treat their divinities is related by a missionary who saw what he relates with his own eyes. The country had been suffering from long and severe drought; and unless rain came, the fields must wither, and the people die of famine. Prayer was made to their gods, with whom their worshippers, having received no answer, got very angry; and as I have seen a child beat the table on which, falling, he had hurt his head, or with little hands beat the nurse who, refusing some request, had crossed his temper, the missionary saw these simple, ignorant, blinded pagans drag their idols from the temple, and, pouring on their heads a torrent of reproaches, whip them soundly. And when we turn from such rude barbarians to the polished heathens of Greece and Rome, how little reverence did they entertain for their gods! and, though possessing a code of moral laws in some respects not much inferior to our own, how did the great mass of them live impure and unholy, in flagrant violation of all morality! Observant of the ceremonial parts of their religion, they allowed its moral laws to be no check on their vices. By the masses these laws were openly, systematically, and shamelessly violated. It is so still among heathens, who, though pagans, are not barbarians—among, for example, both the Buddhists and Hindoos of the East. Read the moral precepts of Buddha, and you will be astonished at their purity. Their correspondence with our own ten commandments, which is as startling as it is pleasing, presents a most remarkable illustration of the fact that the law which God wrote on the granite tables of Sinai was a copy of the old law that he had written on the fleshy tables of man's heart, where you may still trace the original writing, like the mutilated inscription on a shattered and weathered stone. Yet what effect have these admirable laws on the habits of the people? None, or almost none, in restraining them from the practice of the grossest vices; exerting as little influence on their lives as do the stars on our destinies.

How do we account for these facts? Nothing

more easy. These nations, like ourselves, believe in a future state and a judgment to come; their world beyond the grave, no less than ours, has its heaven and hell; and human fancy, under an awakened and alarmed conscience, has pictured nothing more dreadful than the punishments of their Tartarus, the torments of their damned. But what blunts the edge of all this, neutralising its power over their hearts, and making it practically of little, or rather of no avail, is the fact that, according to their creed, sin is forgiven on very easy terms. That is the dead fly in all systems of salvation by works. Pagan or popish, they are immoral in their tendency. This explains why those who have been most taught to seek salvation through good works have been least distinguished for the practice of them; and why the more these, substituted for the Cross, have been preached on the Sabbath-day, the less they have been practised throughout the week. For, to return to the case of the heathen, how could they think sin to be exceedingly sinful, or, holding their gods in reverence, fear to offend them, when, according to the terms on which forgiveness was granted, it was safer to offend God than men?—man requiring his debtor to pay the uttermost farthing, but God requiring of one who sought to escape the wrath and curse due to him for sin, only some words of prayers, or the performance of a religious ceremony, or the blood of some brute creature. The natural, logical, inevitable conclusion which men

drew from such views was, that the gods attached
little importance to their own laws, else they would
not be so easily appeased by the transgressors of
them.   There was forgiveness with them, but it was
not of a kind to deter their worshippers from sin—
filling their hearts with godly fear.

Turn now to the cross of Calvary, to that august
and awful spectacle on which angels, suspending their
songs, are gazing in silent wonder.   By that bloody
tree, under that frowning sky, the earth trembling
beneath our feet and the sun darkened above our
heads, does sin seem a light and little thing?   In
God's words to Ezekiel, while I point to that cross,
I ask, "Hast thou seen this, O son of man?   Is it a
light thing to the house of Judah that they commit
the abominations which they commit here?"   A little
thing?   Sin a little thing?   You think so ; and you
are right, if, as my breath blows out a candle, or a
drop of water quenches it, a prayer, a penitent sigh,
or a few dropping tears can extinguish the wrath of
God.   It is so, if the mere expression of our sorrow,
a slight repentance, can pay our debts to God, though,
as you know well, they would be accepted as payment
of them by no one else.   It is so, if that blinded
Papist, who embraces a life of poverty, who leaves a
pillow of down for a bed on the cold ground, who
wears a shirt of sackcloth, who, summoned by the
convent bell, rises at midnight to prayer, or, fleeing
the haunts of men, seeks the desert and the society

of beasts, can, by such self-denial, make atonement to God for the sins of his soul. Great as his sufferings may be, an eternity of happiness is cheaply purchased by a whole lifetime of pain—as a lifetime of pleasure is certainly a dear bargain if enjoyed at the expense of eternal pains. But if, ere one sin could be pardoned or one sinner saved, heaven must give up the Lord of Glory, and the Son of God must die; if justice accepts no cheaper sacrifice; if "there is none other name under heaven given among men whereby we must be saved but the name," nor other blood whereby we can be washed but the blood of Jesus, sin is no light and little thing.

"Wherewith," asks the prophet, "shall I come before the Lord, and bow myself before the high God? Will the Lord be pleased with thousands of rams, or with ten thousands of rivers of oil?" Thousands of rams! The smoke of such a sacrifice ascending to the skies, and rolling its murky clouds over the face of heaven, might blot out the sun; but it hides not the smallest sin from the keen eyes of God. Ten thousands of rivers of oil! Pour them on the stormy sea when our bark is battling for life, and they lay its roughest waves; but it needs the form and feet, the presence and the voice of our Redeemer, to turn the storm within my soul into a calm, and say to a troubled conscience, Peace, be still. But the prophet speaks of a sacrifice more costly than flocks of rams or rivers of oil. "Shall I give my first-born for my transgres

sion, the fruit of my body for the sin of my soul?"
Well, fancy *that* the price demanded by God for sin,
and that you see a father about to pay it. With down-
cast head, and slow, reluctant steps, he approaches the
altar where his first-born lies, ready bound. You see
him kneel to embrace and kiss his boy; to beg delay;
to pray the stern heavens for pity or for strength to
do this stern duty. He rises, and while the mother
in anguish covers her eyes, he slowly bares the steel
and raises his arm to strike; and when your sight
grows dim, your ears catch a dull stroke and a deep
groan, followed by a gush of blood; now, as you fly
a scene where the father lies fallen, fainting, on the
bloody corpse, were such the price God required for
sin, how would you exclaim, It is not a light and
little thing to sin against the Lord—Great is the
Lord, and greatly to be praised: he also is to be
feared above all gods—Holy, holy, holy, is the Lord
of hosts!

It is by an altar and through a victim that there is
forgiveness with God; pardon flows to men in a stream
of blood. But here the altar is a cross, and its victim is
the Son of the Highest. "Hast thou seen this, O son
of man?"—God incarnate hung between two thieves:
the Author of all life yielding up his own; the conqueror of death dying; the feet that walked the billows, the hands that raised the dead and burst the
fetters of the tomb, nailed to a bloody tree—for thee
—all for thee—that thou mightest be forgiven? With

his dying eyes fixed on you, within sound of his
dying groans, and of that cry that startled the heavens, My God, my God, why hast thou forsaken me?
does not sin, only to be atoned for by so great a
sacrifice, appear exceeding sinful? There is forgiveness, but after a fashion that should teach us to fear,
and, in life's lightest hours, to join trembling with our
mirth. Our pardon is written in letters of blood; the
hand that bestows the crown bears the marks of a
cross; it is a wounded form, a "Lamb as it had been
slain," that fills the throne of the universe. Looking
at these things, "Who shall not fear thee, O Lord?"
If such things were done in the green tree, oh! what
shall be done in the dry? If God did not spare his
only-begotten and well-beloved Son when he took our
sins on him, how shall he spare those who prefer
their sins to their Saviour—neglecting this great salvation?

2. The manner of forgiveness sets forth not only
God's hatred of sin, but his love to sinners in the
strongest light.

Parents are often moved to forgive, or at least not
to punish, their children from selfish motives, over-
looking the offences not so much because they love
their children as that they love themselves—themselves better than their children. Of a tender and
sensitive nature, the parent in punishing often feels
more acutely than the child who is punished; the
strokes that fall on its flesh fall on his bleeding heart.

And it inflicts such distress on many to see the tears standing in a child's eye and to hear its cries, that they, to escape this pain, allow their children to go unpunished; and since, in Solomon's judgment, this is practically to hate the child, how much did we owe those who, having, in the days of their flesh, not for their own pleasure, but with much self-inflicted pain, corrected us for our good, have left us to regret that when we had them we did not prize them more and pay them greater reverence! It may be no proof of parental love for a parent to forgive.

Besides, to forgive man in any circumstances costs us nothing. Say that he has defrauded me; injured my reputation; attempted my life; and suppose such an enemy in my power; what does it cost me to forgive him? Let us see. To reduce him to poverty would make me no richer; to destroy his peace would not restore my own; to hurt him would not heal me; to break his heart would not bind up mine; to cast a blot on his reputation would restore no lustre to my name; to take his life, saying with the bloody Papist and persecutor of God's saints in France, "Nothing smells so sweet as the dead body of an enemy," would not insure me against the stroke of death, nor lengthen my life by a single hour. It is no great proof of love after all for you or me to forget an injury and forgive the injurer. To pardon a criminal may smooth the cares and soothe the sorrows of a royal pillow, but adds none to them; it may augment but cannot diminish the lustre of a crown. It is a happy memory that remembers kindness, and forgets offences. It is a far nobler thing to conquer one's passions than to crush a foe; and sweeter than gratified revenge are his feelings who, when his enemy hungers, feeds him; when he thirsts, gives him drink. In so doing, man exhibits somewhat of the nature, and tastes something of the happiness, of God.

From the forgiveness of man turn to that of God. It is hard to say whether it most illustrates his hatred of our sins or his love of ourselves. It costs man nothing to forgive, but it cost God his Son. His Son? How painful it is to look on a dying son— even a dying infant; to watch life's sad and solemn ebbings; to see the last quiver of the little lips; to lay the pale, cold, dead body we have so often carried in our happy arms, in the coffin and the cold grave? I dare not say that God bent over his dying Son with feelings corresponding to ours; that he hung over the cross as we have hung over the cradle; or that the strange perturbations in nature, a trembling earth and rending rocks, heavens palled in darkness, and the sun turned pale with terror, though they may perhaps have extended to worlds beyond our own, reached up to the throne of nature's God. I cannot fathom, and I dare not fancy the feelings of the eternal Father, when he saw the Son whom he loved with infinite affection spit upon, scourged, reviled, bleeding, dying on the accursed tree. But how must he have loved you for whom he gave a Son so loved? and how will the love this breeds in you make you fear to dishonour or displease one who has so loved you—securing your forgiveness on such an immovable foundation and at so great a price.

To believe yourselves forgiven, while you love sin and live in the practice of it, is to believe a lie—a monstrous lie. Whom God justifies he sanctifies, and the sense of forgiveness which is inwrought by his Holy Spirit, cannot fail to produce holy fears and strenuous efforts after new obedience—such an effect as resulted in a case which not inaptly illustrates both the way in which God deals with sinners, and the obedience that springs from a sense of forgiveness. A soldier, whose regiment lay in a garrison town in England, was about to be brought before his commanding officer for some offence. He was an old offender, and had been often punished. Here he is again, said 'he officer, on his name being mentioned; everything —flogging, disgrace, imprisonment—has been tried with him. Whereupon the serjeant stepped forward, and apologising for the liberty he took, said, There is one thing which has never been done with him yet, sir. What is that? was the answer. Well, sir, said the serjeant, he has never been forgiven. Forgiven! exclaimed the colonel, surprised at the suggestion. He reflected for a few minutes, ordered the culprit to be brought in, and asked him what he had to say to the charge? Nothing, sir, was his reply; only

I am sorry for what I have done. Turning a kind and pitiful look on the man, who expected nothing else than that his punishment would be increased with the repetition of his offence, the colonel addressed him, saying, Well, we have resolved to forgive you! The soldier was struck dumb with astonishment; the tears started in his eyes, and he wept like a child. He was humbled to the dust, he thanked his officer and retired —to be the old, refractory, incorrigible man? No; he was another man from that day forward. He who tells the story had him for years under his eye, and a better conducted man never wore the Queen's colours. In him kindness bent one whom harshness could not break; he was conquered by mercy, and, forgiven, ever afterwards feared to offend. Shall the goodness and grace of God have less effect on us? Shall we continue in sin, that grace may abound? God forbid. Let the forgiven fear; and, oh, let none offered a greater forgiveness, a pardon which cost God his Son, refuse so great a boon! Weigh well, I pray you, these solemn words, He that despised Moses' law died without mercy under two or three witnesses; of how much sorer punishment, suppose ye, shall he be thought worthy, who hath trodden under foot the Son of God, and hath counted the blood of the Covenant, wherewith he was sanctified, an unholy thing, and hath done despite unto the Spirit of grace?

III.

THE UNDECAYING POWER AND
GRACE OF GOD.

"Behold, the Lord's hand is not shortened, that it cannot save; neither his ear heavy, that it cannot hear."—ISA. lix. I.

THE face of nature never seems to change. The strongest arm grows old and feeble; raven locks turn gray; wrinkles deform the finest face; the once graceful form bends tottering to the grave; and the mind itself not unfrequently seems to partake in the general decay, as if this immortal spirit were to perish with its mortal tenement. But the years which work such change on us roll over our world, like successive waves over a rock, leaving no trace behind. Each returning spring is welcomed with songs; every summer decks our meadows and gardens with the old flowers; and, as if her powers could suffer no decay, in crops of fruit and in fields of golden corn autumn year by year renews the bounties of Nature.

We revisit our birth-place after an absence, say of fifty years; and finding, with the exception of a few in whose wrinkled and withered faces we begin to recognise some features of our old, noisy, rosy, laughing companions, all our friends dead and gone, new faces in the school, a new tenant in every farm, a new peasant in every cottage, a new minister in every pulpit, and a new congregation in the pews, we might almost doubt whether we had been there before. But when we turn to look on nature, we might fancy that we had never left home, and that the last fifty years were nothing but a dream. The sun rises over the same hill, the moonbeams glitter on the same lake, the skies resound with the same songs, moorland and mountain are clad in the same flowery verdure, and the gray rocks look down as of old on the stream, that, as it winds its way, snake-like, through the valley, here brawls over the same stones, and there sweeps into the same swirling pool. And so is it everywhere with nature! The Pharaohs sleep in their stony sepulchres, and Moses in his lone mountain grave, but the Nile rolls on as in the day when the Hebrew mother committed her child to its waters, and to the providence of her God. David's harp is broken, and his skilful hand is dust, but the snows of Salmon shine as white as when he sang their praises; Kedron runs murmuring through the valley of Jehoshaphat as on the night our Saviour waded it to enter on his agony in the garden; Capernaum, Chorazin, Bethsaida! the place that once knew them knows them now no more; but the mountains of Galilee stand around her lake as they presented themselves to Jesus' eye. There we gaze on the very scenes which were familiar to him; we tread the very shores along which he often walked in lone and lofty meditation; we look on the very waters that bore up his blessed feet; and yonder, where a boat battles with the storm, and men are pulling for their lives, we might almost fancy we should see his form rise, and, by a word or wave of his hand, turn that tumbling sea into a scene of calm repose.

Yet, fixed as nature seems to be, on examining the matter more closely, we find there is nothing fixed: and that it is not her prerogative to say, "I change not." Change not! The snows of winter and the rains of summer are, however slowly, constantly altering the form and features of this great world; and by means of their ten thousand streams are carrying it off to its grave in the depths of ocean. Nor is there in Alps or Andes a mountain that pierces the clouds with its snow-crowned head, which, to parody the words of Scripture, time may not thus address, What art thou, O great mountain? before my hand and power thou shalt become a plain. Change not! It is by constant, perpetual change that nature maintains that appearance of sameness which strikes us as so remarkable—just, to use a plain but expressive illustration, as it is by constant revolutions a spinning top keeps itself from falling. The fortunes of a Moses, a Joseph, an Esther, present no vicissitudes so sudden or remarkable as those which may be traced in an atom of matter. Loosed from the rock by the hand of the frost, swept by a mountain stream into the valley, and left by a flood on the bank, it enters into a blade of grass. Emblem of our mortality, the grass withers and dies, and feeding the heather by its decay, our atom next blooms in its purple bell. Cropped by the moor-cock, it is next whirring along the hill-side, when the eagle, stooping from the clouds, strikes down his prey, and our atom now rises in wings which cleave the sky. Death at length lays low this monarch of the air : falling from his cloudy realm, he dies ; and, rotting on the soil, feeds the pastures where a lamb crops the flower into which our atom has passed. In time the lamb falls to the knife ; and now, becoming the food of man, it enters into the hand that wields a sceptre ; or curls in the tresses that lend grace to beauty ; or speaks in the tongue that in the senate-house sways the councils of a nation, or from the pulpit invites sinners to the arms of the Saviour, and with proclamation of the mutability both of the heavens and earth, thus addresses the unchangeable Jehovah · Thou, Lord, in the beginning hast laid the foundation of the earth ; and the heavens are the work of thine hands : they shall perish ; but thou remainest ; and they all shall wax old as doth a garment ; and as a vesture shalt thou fold them up, and they shall be changed ; but thou art the same, and thy years shall not fail.

On going forth by night, and fixing our attention on the heavenly bodies, we observe that every hour changes their position. The star that at its first ap-

pearance shone above our heads is now sinking in the
west, while those we saw rise from the bosom of the
deep, have climbed to the top of the sky—the whole
host of heaven appears to be marching on, one orb
only, the pole star, excepted.   Around that they seem
to roll, as the pivot on which the whole firmament
turns.   Bright guide of the mariner on the deep, in
summer and winter nights, it alone appears to remain
immovable, unchangeable, and unchanged.   What it
appears to be, God is.   Among all beings animate and
inanimate, of earth or heaven, there is but one in the
universe fixed, immovable, unchangeable.   He alone
can say, " I am the Lord, I change not ;" and therefore, speaking of him, the prophet says, " Behold, the
Lord's hand is not shortened, that it cannot save ;
neither his ear heavy, that it cannot hear."

I. The case of the Jews, to whom these words were
first addressed, does not shake our confidence in God's
willingness or power to save.

I admit that the fortunes of that people do not at
first sight appear to correspond with this very confident and comforting declaration.   For where is Jerusalem ?   Where now is she that was once called " the
joy of the whole earth," " the perfection of beauty,"
" the city of our God ?"   Insulting their captives, and
persecuting instead of pitying those whom God had
smitten, the men of Babylon bade the Hebrews take
their harps from the willows, saying, Sing us one of

the songs of Zion. It is base to hit a man when he is down; but were I to insult a Jew, the Bible would furnish me with keener sarcasm than the Babylonian's. Jerusalem's towers and palaces and temple have been devoured by fire; the very foundations of the city were turned up by the Roman's ploughshare; and the site of her holy sanctuary is at this day profaned by a Moslem mosque. She retains no vestige of her glory but some old colossal stones, beside which, like wall-flower clinging to a ruin, some poor Jews may be found weeping—kissing them with the affection that regards her very dust as dear. How taunting, insulting were it simply to repeat in their ears the words of that old, proud, patriotic psalm, Walk about Zion, and go round about her: tell the towers thereof. Mark ye well her bulwarks, consider her palaces, that ye may tell it to the generation following. What other answer theirs, but the touching, broken-hearted cry, Ichabod, the glory is departed! Yet on the day when the Roman legions beset her walls, the Lord's hand was not shortened, that it could not save; neither his ear heavy, that it could not hear. He heard the din of battle, he heard the roar of fire; and it was not because he could not, that he did not save.

And if we leave the ruins of Jerusalem to seek the Jews, where are they? One of their old prophets, looking along the vista of time, exclaims, A nation scattered and peeled! And into what countries have they not been scattered, and what country has not scattered and peeled them in return? For eighteen hundred years have they been fugitives and vagabonds; nor have their weary feet ever found a resting place on earth. Strange fate! For this they have to thank their fathers. They drank the water in which Pilate washed his hands—taking the guilt of Christ's murder on themselves. His blood, they cried, be on us, and on our children; blood this, the only blood, whose stain years never have effaced; nor will, till the time to favour Zion, the set time is come, when God will bring back his banished ones, and make good the promise: "I will bring them again into the land that I gave unto their fathers. Behold, I will send for many fishers, saith the Lord, and they shall fish them; and after will I send for many hunters, and they shall hunt them from every mountain, and from every hill, and out of the holes of the rocks." Till then, a church without a temple, a people without a country, a race without a home, a nation meted out and trodden down, they shall be a proverb and a by-word and a perpetual hissing.

Strange fortunes these! yet, far from proving God's hand to be shortened, they prove the very reverse With the regularity of a law of nature, one of two fates has befallen all other conquered nations. Like the Indians of America, who have fallen before the white man, as their forests before his axe, they have been extirpated; or the conquered have intermarried with their conquerors to breed a race like ours, in whose veins flows the mingled tide of Roman, Celtic, Saxon, and Scandinavian blood. The fate of the Jews how different and how singular! They have been oppressed, persecuted, trodden under foot; and, like the grass which grows thickest when trodden on, they have thriven under oppression—bearing a charmed life—the true sons of their fathers in the land of Egypt; of whom it was said, the more they were afflicted, the more they multiplied and grew.

The Jews are everywhere—inhabiting every country, yet belonging to none; mixed with every people, but combining with none. By the thrones of kings, in the senate-house of nations, in the mart of business, in the ranks of armies, everywhere the same, the Jew preserves his nationality; his faith; his haughty pride, his blood so pure that, whether you encounter him in the streets of London, or Paris, or Rome, or Petersburg, or Pekin, you can tell at once by his features that he is a son of Abraham. They exist among others as no other race ever did—like oil in water; and like oil, too, where their talents and ambition have free play, they usually rise to the top. They are not a holy nation, nor are they zealous of good works; yet they are a peculiar people—a standing moral miracle; their history a mystery. Living, multiplying, flourishing amid circumstances that, by all the common laws of providence, should have been fatal to their existence, they illustrate my text—proving the unchanging and unchangeable power of God as plainly as Daniel safe among hungry lions, or the bush that burned, and, burning, was not consumed.

II. Consider the truths expressed by these words.

1. God's power to save is neither lost nor lessened.

Where there is a will there is a way. Applicable as that saying is to many cases where people could do what they pronounce impossible if they would only try, it is absolutely, universally true of none but God. What father and mother would not wish all their children to be saved, and that all should meet, none amissing, before the throne in glory? What pastor, worthy of a pulpit, does not wish all his people to be saved—every member of his flock gathered at last into the Good Shepherd's fold? But our power to help, to save, is not boundless. Limited by many circumstances, it often falls far short of our inclinations. So it was with that unhappy man whom the sinking wreck left in the roaring sea—with a child clinging to this arm, and its mother, his wife, to that. With his right hand free to buffet the billows, one he may bear to yon blessed shore, but not both. Encumbered, his strength fast failing, to save both is impossible; and now he must choose which to save. Dreadful alternative! He shakes off the child, and striking for the land, away from its dying cries, he leaves the creature that had clung to him to perish. It was for no such reason that Jesus bore to heaven one only of the thieves crucified by his side. True, but one was taken while the other was left; true, the wind bloweth where it listeth, and so is every one that is born of the Spirit; but that wretched man who perished by the cross, sinking into hell while he saw his fellow go soaring like a lark to heaven, was not lost because Christ's hand was shortened that it could not save; he was not, like that unhappy child, shaken off, though clinging to the Saviour and crying, Lord, save me, I perish. No, his loss finds its explanation in the key to the perdition of thousands who sit in churches and go to hell, in these sad, solemn, awful words, "Ye will not come to me, that ye might have life." Those only are excluded from heaven who exclude themselves.

Again, our power to help may not only fall short of our inclination, but, such as it is, may be lessened and impaired by years. What a striking illustration of this have we in David's history! He began and closed his battles by a personal encounter, a hand-to-hand fight, with the giant sons of Anak. But how great a change had the forty years of cares and griefs, of public toils and domestic trouble, that elapsed between these two battles, wrought on him who, lithe of limb, and fleet of foot, and quick of eye, and sure of aim, ran, sling in hand, to meet the boaster; and stopped his boasting, laying his head in the dust. At the last of his conflicts the old courage is there; the fire of youth blazes up from the ashes of age, but the strength is gone; gray locks fall from beneath his helmet; his eye, dim with years, has lost its eagle glance; no bursting away now like a deer-hound from the leash, to meet this other Philistine. They meet; and when sword strikes fire with sword, before the shower of blows that ring from the giant's arm on his casque, David is borne back; and but that Abishai threw himself before his king, one of Goliath's race had avenged Goliath's death, and plucked his greenest laurels from David's brow. His hand was shortened; and, more wise than he, the men of Israel, as they bore off their aged king and received on their shields the blows aimed at his old, gray head, said, Thou shalt go no more out with us to battle, that thou quench not the light of Israel.

Ah! the time comes when the actor must leave the public stage; when the reins drop from the leader's grasp; and the orator's tongue falters; and the workman's stout arm grows feeble; and the fire of wit is quenched; and the man of genius turns into a drivelling idiot; and men of understanding, without any second birth, pass into a second childhood. But the time shall never come when it can be said of Jesus, his hand is shortened, that it cannot save. No; "the same yesterday, and to-day, and for ever," there is nothing he ever did, in saving, blessing, sanctifying, that he cannot do again. This gives undying value to all the offers, invitations, and promises of the gospel. What he has done in other cases he can do in yours, closing wounds deep as Job's; healing backslidings bad as David's; receiving penitents vile as she who bathed his feet with tears; and saving sinners near to hell as he who found salvation on the very brink of death. I promise you the same pardon, grace, and mercy as that of which there is any record in the word of God. Christ's resources are inexhaustible; and here, therefore, one man's gain is no other man's loss. People fight for a place in the life-boat, because its accommodation is limited, but Christ has room for all. He is able to save to the uttermost. We cannot be too long or too great sinners to be saved; and my answer to any who, yielding to despair, say, Ah! it is impossible that we can be changed, is this, It is not impossible that you, but it is impossible that he can be changed. He cannot change or lie who said, " Him that cometh to me I will in no wise cast out."

2. The Lord's power to hear and answer prayer is neither lost nor lessened; his ear is not heavy, that it cannot hear.

On one occasion a party of our soldiers happened to enter a cottage that stood on ground which had been occupied by an enemy whom they were driving before them at the point of the bayonet An infant's cries attracted their attention, and they turned to look on a spectacle which, inured as they were to scenes of horror, woke their tenderest pity. A father's corpse lay stretched across the threshold where he had fallen, bravely fighting to protect those within ; on the floor, amid a pool of blood, lay the mother, dead ; and on her bosom an infant, all unconscious of its loss, wailed and cried as it sought to draw nourishment from her empty breast. Time was when its feeblest cry roused her from deepest slumbers ; but there it cried, and there she lay unmoved,—her ear was heavy, that it could not hear. And had not God directed thither the steps of those brave men, and had not they, touched with pity, and gilding with so bright an example of humanity war's lurid clouds, wrapped up the creature tenderly, and borne it away through the smoke and fire of battle to be the child and care of their regiment, it had perished in a mother's arms, on a mother's bosom ;—her hand was shortened, that it could not save. So perish none in Christ !

The saints of God are never in the circumstances of children on whose home death's darkest shadow lies, as, standing round his bed, they gaze with mingled grief, and fear, and awe, on a father's pallid face and lifeless form. The cause of their emotion, he lies himself unmoved ; their cries pierce other ears, not his ; their sorrows move others' pity, not his ; their tears wake others' sympathy, not his ; whatever betide them, now that the arm which won their bread has lost its power, they may starve, crying for food, and their mother has none to give them ;—but his ear is heavy, that it cannot hear ; his hand is shortened, that it cannot save. Our nearest and dearest earthly friends are but broken cisterns at the best. They are running low; day by day lower; and they one day shall be dry; but "the portion of Jacob is not like them." He hears the cries, the sighs, not the words only, but the wishes of his people; even the unuttered and unutterable sorrows of a broken heart.

This imparts undying value to all those instances of heard, accepted, answered, prayer of which the Bible is so full; answers common and miraculous, to prayers for blessings temporal and spiritual, in all variety of imaginable circumstances—prayer by saints and sinners; prayers offered with life's last breath and by childhood's lisping tongue; in royal palaces, and in loathsome dungeons; in a den of lions, and in the depths of ocean; for health in sickness, and for bread in famine; for patience under the sorest trials, and deliverance in the most hopeless circumstances; for pardon of the greatest sins, and mercy to the greatest sinners. Never was the Lord's hand shortened, that it could not save, nor his ear heavy, that it could not hear. Why, then, should you despond, far less despair? Did he save the thief when his own hands were nailed to the accursed tree? When dying himself, amid the agonies of the cross, with all God's billows and waves roaring over his own head, did he hear and heed the cry of that poor wretch sinking at his side?

> "'Tis finish'd—All his groans are past;
> His blood, his pain, and toils."

And now, exalted to the right hand of God, seated on

his Father's throne, with all power in earth and heaven, how confident may we be that he will hear the prayer of the destitute, and save them who are ready to perish! While the shadow of their crowns falls at our feet, the saints—among whom I see Job and Jonah, Moses and David, the man who was a thief, and the woman who was a sinner—bend from their celestial thrones to hold up the arms of prayer. Hear what they say: If we found mercy to pardon and grace to help us, if we washed away our sins in the fountain of Jesus' blood, if we were brought up from deep pit and miry clay, to sit on thrones and wear blood-bought crowns, why not you? Behold, the Lord's hand is not shortened, that it cannot save; neither his ear heavy, that it cannot hear.

III. This truth is full of comfort and encouragement—

1. To God's people.

One wonders in reading the early history of the Israelites how, after what they had seen of God's power, they could ever doubt or distrust it. We think, Had I stood beside Moses on the banks of the Nile, and seen her waters at a wave of his rod change to blood; or, girded for the journey, and listening, had I heard the cry which rose over the first-born at the midnight hour; or had I seen the gates of the sea thrown back and held open, till, walking its floor between two walls of water, I reached the other strand; or had I pitched my tent where the skies dropped not dews, nor rain, nor hoar-frost, but food on the wilderness, and made barren sands more fertile than fields of corn ;—recollecting how the waters had been turned into rock, would not I have waited to see the rock turned into water, nor joined the unbelieving crew in their cries to Moses, " Give us water that we may drink. Wherefore is this that thou hast brought us up out of Egypt, to kill us and our children and our cattle with thirst ?" So we judge. But may we not think more highly of ourselves than we ought to think ? for as the bravest troops have sometimes been seized with a panic, or as where an epidemic rages, killing thousands, the stout and healthy who survive may yet suffer some touch of the prevailing malady, even Moses himself on one occasion gave way to despondency,—in reply to God's promise, I will give them flesh, asking, The people, among whom I am, are six hundred thousand footmen ; shall the flocks and the herds be slain for them, to suffice them ? or shall all the fish of the sea be gathered together for them, to suffice them ?

Is the Lord's hand waxed short ? was God's answer to Moses : and it is mine to all the believer's doubts, and difficulties, and fears. Since you were called, converted, first visited with saving grace, is the Lord's hand waxed short ? No ; then let that thought inspire you, as it did David, with dauntless faith. As with a touch of gentle pity Saul looked on the stripling who offered to do battle with the Philistine, he said, Thou art not able to go against this Philistine to fight with him: for thou art but a youth, and he a man of war from his youth. "Thy servant," was the bold reply, "kept his father's sheep, and there came a lion, and a bear, and took a lamb out of the flock: and I went out after him, and smote him, and delivered it out of his mouth: and when he arose against me, I caught him by his beard, and smote him, and slew him. Thy servant slew both the lion and the bear: and this uncircumcised Philistine shall be as one of them, seeing he hath defied the armies of the living God. The Lord that hath delivered me out of the paw of the lion, and out of the paw of the bear, he will deliver me out of the hand of this Philistine." Sound logic, as well as sound theology! And if God has graciously delivered you from the curse, shall he not deliver you from the power of sin? if he has justified, shall he not also sanctify you? if he has brought you out of Egypt, shall he not guide your steps to Canaan? He did not pluck you from the burning to throw you again into the fire. Cast your burden on the Lord, and he will sustain you. Pray, and wait the answer. As Moses said to Israel, with Egypt's hosts pressing on their rear, and the Red Sea roaring on their front: Stand still and see the salvation of the Lord. His hand is not shortened, that it cannot save; neither his ear heavy, that it cannot hear.

2. This truth is full of hope and encouragement to sinners.

In the annual Reports of hospitals we read of a certain number sent away cured, a certain number remaining under cure, and, to say nothing of the dead, of a number who have been dismissed as incurable—their cases baffling the skill of man and the power of medicine. The Great Physician knows no such class; the gospel brings glad tidings to the chief of sinners. This is a faithful saying, and worthy of all acceptation, says St Paul, that Christ Jesus came into the world to save sinners; of whom I am chief. He is able also to save them to the uttermost that come unto God by him.

People sometimes say of the dying, they were too late in calling the doctor. With the cold sweat standing like beads on the brow, the features pinched, the countenance changed, the eye glazed, the death-rattle sounding in the throat, and the last struggle begun, the skill of man is hopeless. He cures disease, not death. Alas! 'tis true; too late, too late! It is never so for Christ. David had one in his flock that he had plucked out of the lion's very jaws; but Christ has many such—many saved who were as near destruction. Tell me not, then, that you have sinned too much or too long to be saved. Is his hand shortened since the day he saved the dying thief, and set his soul free to go up to heaven, like a bird out of the fowler's snare? Look what he has done for others, and learn what he can and will do for you. Too great sinners to be saved? Hast thou with Peter looked Jesus in the

face, and, cursing, said, "I know him not?" Hast
thou with Saul imbrued thy hands in holy martyrs'
blood? Hast thou with the thief joined thy fellows
in reviling a dying Lord? Hast thou stood on Calvary to shake the head and point the finger and cry,
in cruel mockery of him whom the nails fastened, and
his own blood glued to the tree, If thou be the Son
of God, come down! No? Then why should the
door be shut against you that opened to these? Who
gets to heaven will find seated on its thrones, in Abel,
Enoch, Abraham, Moses, greater saints than he has
been, and in others, perhaps, greater sinners. God
has done more marvellous works of power and mercy
than saving you. Though he had not, though you
were the vilest sinner that ever polluted his beautiful
earth with your feet, or profaned his holy sanctuary
with your presence, you have only now, and as you
are, to throw yourself at the feet of Jesus, crying, Save
me, I perish—and you are saved. Then in the words
of the poet—

> "Out of your last home dark and cold,
>   Thou shalt pass to a city whose streets are gold;
> From the silence that falls upon sin and pain,
> To the deathless joys of the angels' strain;
> Well shall be ended what ill began,
> Out of the shadow into the sun."

IV.

THE GRACE OF FAITH.

"Now abideth faith."—1 COR. xiii. 13.

HAST thou faith? To this, an apostle's question,
all men could, in a sense, return an answer in
the affirmative; for it is not more true that no man
liveth and sinneth not, than that no man liveth and
believeth not; or devil either, for "the devils also
believe and tremble." Suppose a man without faith
in any one, without faith in the honesty of his servants, faith in the integrity of his friends, faith in the
affections of his children, faith in the fidelity of his
wife, death would be to be preferred to a life like his.
Better that our eyes were closed in death than that
they should see every one with a mask on their face
and a dagger beneath their cloak; with such a jaun-
diced vision, we should be "of all men the most
miserable." On looking into the matter, you will find
that faith, instead of belonging only to the elect of
God, holy and chosen, is common to all, even the
worst of men. The backbone, indeed, of the social,
and the foundation of the commercial fabric, remove
faith between man and man, and society and com-

merce fall to pieces. There is not a happy home on earth but stands on faith ; our heads are pillowed on it ; we sleep at night in its arms with greater security for the safety of our lives, peace, and property, than bolts and bars can give.

I. In illustration of the universality of faith, observe—

1. Faith, which is the source of so much human happiness, is the mainspring of human activity. It moves more than half the machinery of life. What leads the husbandman, for example, to yoke his horses when, no bud bursting to clothe the naked trees, no bird singing in hedgerows or frosty skies, nature seems dead ? With faith in the regularity of her laws, in the ordinance of her God, he believes that she is not dead but sleepeth ; and so he ploughs and sows in the certain expectation that he shall reap, and that these bare fields shall be green in summer with waving corn, and be merry in autumn with sun-browned reapers. The farmer is a man of faith. So is the seaman. No braver man than he who goes down to see God's wonders in the deep. Venturing his frail bark on a sea ploughed by many keels, but wearing on its bosom the furrows of none, with neither path to follow nor star to guide, the master knows no fear. When the last blue hill has dipped beneath the wave, and he is alone on a shoreless sea, he is calm and confident—his faith in the compass-needle,

which, however his ship may turn, or roll, or plunge, ever points true to the north. An example his to be followed by the Christian with his Bible, on that faith venturing his all, life, crew, and cargo, he steers his way boldly through darkest nights and stormiest oceans, with nothing but a thin plank between him and the grave. And though metaphysicians and divines have involved this matter of faith in mystery, be assured that there is nothing more needed for your salvation or mine than that God would inspire us with a belief in the declarations of his word as real, heartfelt, and practical, as that which we put in the laws of providence—in the due return of day and night, summer and winter, seed-time and harvest.

2. The followers of the world have faith. For their salvation it only needs to be rightly and divinely directed. Where will you find it stronger than in those who, in spite not only of others' sad experience, but also of their own, seek true, lasting happiness in earthly pleasures. One gourd has perished after another; the ground beneath their feet is strewed ankle deep with their withered leaves; yet see how they train up another gourd in hope of better fortune. These men might have learned, one would think, that the happiness which they expect from the possession of any earthly object is a delusion. The phantom has ever eluded their grasp; yet, as it dances on before them, they persevere; nor cease the vain pursuit, till they stumble into the grave. There is a

faith in the world which no succession of disappointments seems able to destroy, or even to disturb.
It is very sad to see it! We have not to go to a
heathen hell to see the Tantalus, who, though he has
always found that so soon as the cup touches his
thirsty lips, the water vanishes, yet ever raises it
anew; or the Sisyphus, who, though the stone with
sore labour has no sooner been rolled to the brow of
the mountain than it has always slipped from his
hands and bounded back to the bottom, yet begins
again, and again, and again, the wretched task. This
world is the hell where such tasks are done, such disappointments are borne; and borne often with a
patience and an endurance of faith in the worldling
which almost tempts us to adopt the language of our
Lord, and say, We have not found so great faith, no,
not in Israel! If surpassed at all, their faith in the
world is only exceeded by that which Job expressed
in God, when, from the ashes where he sat over the
graves of his children, the patriarch lifted his eyes to
heaven, to cry, Though he slay me, yet will I trust
in him!

3. Unbelievers have faith, notwithstanding that that
appears a contradiction in terms.

They present a still more remarkable and melancholy illustration than the last, of the fact that faith,
though in one and the most important sense a special
gift of God, is natural to the human heart. Many
people, for instance, who do not believe in the

divinity of the Bible, will be found giving credit to
the ravings and wretched nonsense of *spiritualism*, as
it is called. The credulity of sceptics is quite remarkable; but this is still more remarkable, that thousands who are not sceptics, though they withhold their
faith from the truths of God's word, put it in these
old threadbare lies of the devil—"Thou shalt not
surely die;" you can sin to-day and repent to-morrow;
you may turn religious at a more convenient season;
it will be time enough to seek another world when
this has lost its enjoyments, and "the years draw nigh
when thou shalt say, I have no pleasure in them;"
the evening of life, like the last quiet hours of day,
is best adapted for prayer and meditation; farewell
to all enjoyments so soon as you allow your attention
to be occupied with such gloomy subjects as death,
the grave, judgment, and eternity; banish your idle
fears; God, unlike man dressed in a little brief
authority, is much too generous to be an exacting
judge, and too merciful to be a severe one; at any
rate, should the worst come to the worst, you can
reasonably calculate on a season for repentance; and
you will find it much easier to attend to these things
when your head is gray, and your passions are cooled,
and the night's falling shadows dispose you to solemn
thoughts, than it is now. By such lies as these, the
cunning fiend leads thousands on, step by step, to
everlasting ruin. And thus, strange as it may sound,
it is true that it is as much by faith—of a kind—that

some go to hell, as it is by faith that God's people go to heaven.

Therefore, as a man approaching a precipice does not need to get feet, but to get the feet he has turned round, so that every step becomes one from danger to safety, it is not so much faith we need, as that the faith we have be set on new and right objects, and turned in a new and right direction. What we need in order to be saved is the faith that, looking to Jesus, becomes saving faith—and saving because it embraces the Saviour ; which has God for its author, Christ for its object, these other graces for its fruits, and for its reward a kingdom and a crown in heaven. This is the faith of which Paul says, Now abideth faith, hope, charity.

II. Let us attend to the importance of sound scriptural views of this matter.

This was never more necessary than now. Liberty of thought, of private judgment, on which our Protestantism stands, is in danger ; and in danger from the conduct of rash and unwise men. Such a calamity threatens it as befell the cause of civil liberty, when the revolutionists of France, confounding licence with liberty, destroyed everything and built up nothing ; and, leaving their country without a government, and by their worship of the goddess of Reason, I may add, without a God, made the very name of liberty to stink in the nostrils of the world. We are invited now-a days, to lift those anchors of the faith by which our fathers rode out many a storm; yet it were well and wise, before doing so, to see into what position we are likely to drive. So far as concerns either the religious or civil condition of those communities from which these novelties in faith and practice have been imported, I see no reason to envy them; to copy them; or to turn a deaf ear to the prophet's warning, Stand ye in the ways, and see, and ask for the old paths, where is the good way, and walk therein, and ye shall find rest for your souls.

Men seek to soothe our very natural alarm by drawing a distinction between doctrines and duties, saying that if our life and practice are good, it is a small matter what we believe. True, and so if the stream is pure, it is a small matter that the fountain is polluted; if the fruit is good, that the tree is bad; if the vessel is rightly steered, that both compass and chart are wrong. But who ever heard of such things? Who has gathered grapes of thorns, or figs of thistles? How can a man's conduct be right if his creed be wrong—wrong, not in its accidents, but in its essence and substance? The Spartans thought theft no crime if secretly committed; and so, that being their belief, they stole. David Hume thought the same of adultery; and so, that being his belief, what hindered him, or now hinders his followers, from such a crime? The Hindu widow thinks it meritorious to give herself to the flames which consume the body of her husband;

and so, that being her belief, she mounts the pile and commits suicide. Simon Magus thought that the Holy Ghost might be bought and sold; and so, that being his belief, by the proffer of money he offered such an insult to God, that Peter indignantly exclaimed, Thy money perish with thee! Saul of Tarsus thought it was for God's glory that he should persecute the Christians; and so, that being his belief, he steeled a naturally tender heart to the claims of pity, and imbrued his hands in the blood of martyrs. It is no answer to this to tell us of men, of whom, alas! there are too many, who set much value on an orthodox creed, and little on a holy, or even moral life; who talk much of faith, but are not careful to maintain good works. What does their case prove against the importance of sound views on such high subjects as faith, salvation by grace, and redemption through the blood of Christ? It only shews that men may sin against light and conscience—no new thing, nor peculiar to Christian ages; since an old heathen has said, "I see the better, and approve; yet follow the worse."

Such importance did Martin Luther, no mean authority, attach to the doctrine of justification by faith in the blood of Christ, that he called it the article of a standing or falling Church. I subscribe to the sentiment: ceremonies, forms, and even some doctrines, are but the ornaments of the building or parts of its superstructure; but this, lying at the foundation, touches the security of all. Embodied in her creed and faithfully preached from her pulpits, this doctrine should protect any Church when assailed by the rude hand of violence. It consecrates, if I may say so, not its errors, but its life. Were we armed with power to remove such a Church, and bent on supplying its place with what might appear to be a better system, it says, as David said to Abishai, on turning aside his spear from Saul, "Destroy him not: for who can stretch forth his hand against the Lord's anointed, and be guilt-less?" Whether the candidate for baptism should be immersed or sprinkled; whether that ordinance should be administered to infants or only to adults ; whether, in commemorating the death of Jesus, we should sit or kneel; whether the Church should be ruled by deacons, presbyters, or bishops ; whether it should be maintained at the expense of the State, or depend only on voluntary liberality ; are questions on which no man will spend dying thoughts or waste dying hours. No. The nearer we approach to another world the less these questions will appear, but the greater this—Am I, being justified by faith, at peace with God through my Lord Jesus Christ? Other foundation than this can no man lay. Destroy it not! Destroy it; remove it, or rather me from my confidence in it, in Jesus Christ and him crucified as the only refuge of a sinner, and gone is my peace, my hopes in death, and my heaven in eternity,—I have suffered greater loss, I am a poorer man than he who pursued the plunderers of his shrine, crying, Ye have taken away my gods, and what have I more?

E

III. Salvation through faith, and not through works, is a feature peculiar to the gospel.

An atheist is a moral monster. Man has fallen, but not so low as to be satisfied with the atheist's cold, and dark, and dreary creed. Recoiling from that, he has erred on the side of a multiplicity of gods. The soul craves for a god as the body craves for food. It clings to the thought as a creeper to the pole it climbs; and, rather than his spirit should want such a support, man will catch at the wildest and most childish notion of beings above himself—just as ivy, when it has not a rock, will embrace a rotten tree, or as a drowning wretch, for lack of something better, clutches at a straw. So in the darkness amid which men were left to grope, may be found I know not how many false systems of religion. Some worship the serpent, others the crocodile; here the ox is adored, there the elephant. These Parsees, prostrating themselves before the rising sun, worship fire; while those Hindoos, believing its waters to possess a virtue capable of washing away sin, account the Ganges sacred, and regard it as divine. In yonder desert which he treads with naked foot the savage starts back, with a look and a cry of horror; he has trodden, not on a deadly serpent, but on a poor insect, which, wounded, dying, and all unconscious of the honours paid to it, he kneels to worship. Nor do the modes of heathen worship differ less than its objects. The blood of calves reeks on this altar; the blood of man on that. At the shrine of one divinity they present the golden fruits of earth, and at another the gory spoils of battle. Here, her abode beneath sunny skies, a benevolent deity is worshipped by boys and girls crowned with garlands of beautiful flowers, and dancing to the sounds of music. Another dwells in the recesses of the gloomy forest; his temple a circle of rude and roofless stones, and the offering for his worship a young and lovely maiden, who fills the woods with unavailing shrieks as cruel priests drag her to the altar which she is to dye with blood.

Yet, different as these religions are, they have one feature in common. In every case the worshipper expected, by his works, offerings, or sufferings, to be his own Saviour. Ask yon Hindoo, for instance, who has lain for long years on a bed of iron spikes, or held up his arm till it has become rigid and withered like the blasted branch of a living tree, or travels painfully on his knees to the distant shrine of a favourite god, why this pain, these horrid, self-inflicted tortures? They have one answer. Through these, reproaching our indolence, and apathy, and self-indulgence, and ready with the men of Tyre and Sidon to rise up to condemn many of us in the day of judgment, they expect to purchase pardon and to open the gates of Paradise. Since men never yet corrupted, as you see in Popery, the true religion, nor, as you see in Paganism, invented a false one, but the great, prominent doctrine of their creed was salvation through works the gospel in proclaiming salvation, not through merit, or by works, but by faith, stands out in a character all its own. It is thus as much distinguished from common creeds as was its author, a virgin's child, from common men; and we may apply to his gospel the very words spoken of himself — whether he spoke peace to a troubled bosom or to a stormy sea, bade the water turn into wine, or the dead corpse into life, it could be said of Jesus, Never man spake like this man. What other religion ever spake such words, offered salvation to the lost on such terms as these— sent forth a cry like that which is echoing from pole to pole and ringing round the world, Ho, every one that thirsteth, come ye to the waters, and he that hath no money; come ye, buy, and eat; yea, come, buy wine and milk without money and without price: Believe on the Lord Jesus Christ, and thou shalt be saved: Come unto me, all ye that labour and are heavy laden, and I will give you rest: Not by works of righteousness which we have done, but according to his mercy he saved us, by the washing of regeneration and renewing of the Holy Ghost. Blessed sayings! faithful as blessed, they are worthy of all acceptation!

IV. Salvation through faith dislodges and sweeps away all confidence in our own works. The gospel, as I could most clearly shew, while resting all on faith, recognises the importance of good works; insists on the performance of them ; and regards them, indeed, as the only trustworthy evidence of conversion—"the tree is known by his fruit." Still it does not recognise, but sweeps them away as grounds of a sinner's justification in the sight of God and acquittal at the bar of judgment. I know no more remarkable illustration of this than is found in the history of that eminent Reformer to whom I have already referred. One day, while he was reading the Bible, Luther's eye caught these words—The just shall live by faith ; and out of that sentence, as from a little seed, the Reformation sprang. It fell into his mind as an acorn drops into the soil beneath which it bursts its shell, and rising a tender shoot, grows up into an oak that flourishes in the sunshine of a thousand summers, and defies the storms of a thousand winters. By God's blessing on these few words, Luther broke loose from the trammels of Popery, a freeman whom the truth makes free. With these, as with a wedge, Heaven lending him strength and courage to drive it home, he split up and shivered into fragments the strong and hoary system of Romish superstition. "The just shall live by faith !" Shall he ? Then if eternal life is by faith and not by works, man is not saved by penance—and he swept that away ; nor by the merits of saints—and he swept those away ; nor by indulgences, nor by fasts and vigils, the voluntary poverty and the sackcloth, the pilgrimages and the prayers of the Church of Rome—and he swept all

away.   Thus working, as they say, with a will, with
stout heart and strong arm, Martin Luther cleared
away the rubbish which had been gathering for long
ages above the true foundation of a sinner's acceptance with a righteous God; and on, and deeper on,
he wrought, till he reached and laid bare the rock.
That Rock was Christ; and there a jubilant world
read these words, written by the finger of God, in
letters large and legible—Other foundation can no
man lay than that is laid, which is Jesus Christ.

V. The practical conclusion is, that while we are
to abound in the work of the Lord, and be careful to
maintain good works, we are to be no less careful not
to trust in them.   The two are quite compatible—incompatible as they seemed to one who, speaking of a
distinguished saint, said, I do not understand him; he
speaks of his good works as filthy rags, yet no man
takes such care to cover himself with such rags.   How
compatible they are, appeared also in that chamber
where, while the last hours of faith and piety were
offering the grandest spectacle beneath the sun, a by-
stander reminded the dying Christian of the good
that he had done, of his holy, useful, and illustrious
life.   He bade him cease—saying, I take my good
works and my bad works, and, casting them into one
heap, turn from both to Christ.   Faith in an unseen
Saviour is, I admit, not easy.   It is our nature to walk
by sight rather than by faith; and the gift of God,

faith, is acquired "not by might, nor by power, but by my Spirit, saith the Lord of hosts."

A boy once threw himself down from the upper window of a house on fire into his father's arms. He did not see him; from the ledge where, hesitating to leap, he stood till it burned beneath his feet, he saw only the smoke rolling between them, pierced with tongues of flame. But up through that suffocating, sulphurous cloud, high above the roar of the rising flames, he heard and recognised his father's voice—crying, in urgent, imploring tone, Leap for your life! I am below to receive you into my arms. And when, confident in his father's word, and love, and power, he sprang from the height, right into the lurid darkness, it was a brave leap—a grand act of faith. Still, he had the evidence of sound, he heard his father's voice. And yon old man had the evidence of sight, when, taking the babe from Mary's arms into his own, he bowed his head, and raising it to heaven, exclaimed, Lord, now lettest thou thy servant depart in peace, according to thy word: for mine eyes have seen thy salvation. Simeon saw the tree in the tender shoot; the day in the opening dawn; in the little cloud no bigger than a man's hand the whole heavens overspread by thickest vapours, and pouring down such rain on the thirsty ground that streams burst foaming from the hills, and deserts were pools of water. Not so our eyes and ears! We never saw our Saviour's face: we never heard our Father's voice.

Faith here achieves what in other things would be impossibilities, and what in earthly affairs would be regarded as the height of rashness. In Jesus Christ, whom having not seen we love, we believe in one we never saw ; and in our souls we commit the keeping of our most precious treasure to one who dwells in a remote and unknown land—a country from which no traveller has ever returned to assure us that his trust was not, and that ours will not, be misplaced.

Yet blessed are they that have not seen and yet have believed. The seen are shadows ; the substance is found in the unseen. These are the most real objects—God, whom no man ever saw and lived ; the soul, which does not grow infirm with time and defies the sharpest darts of death ; not this world of matter, which shall vanish in the smoke of its own funereal fires, but that world of spirits, where saints enjoy a glory that never fades and crowns that never fall, and sinners suffer the worm that never dies and the fire that is never quenched. No doubt, in Christ the foundation of our faith is unseen ; but so is that of yonder tower that lifts its tall erect form among the waves over which it throws a saving light. It appears to rest on the rolling billows ; but beneath these, invisible and immovable, lies the solid rock on which it stands secure ; and when the hurricane roars above, and breakers roar below, and ships are wrecking, and men are drowning, and women are weeping, I could go calmly to sleep in that lone sea-tower. Founded on a rock, and safer than the proudest palace that stands on the sandy, surf-beaten shore, it cannot be moved. Still less the Rock of Ages! Who trusts in that is fit for death, prepared for judgment, ready for the last day's sounding trumpet, since the Lord redeemeth the soul of his servants; and none of them that trust in him shall be desolate. Happy is that people that is in such a case: yea, happy is that people whose God is the Lord.

V.

THE GRACE OF FAITH.

"Now abideth faith."—1 COR. xiii. 13.

ON a Sabbath-day, years ago, a young minister appeared in a church of this city as a candidate for the vacant charge. He preached; the people were all attention. The discourse was worthy of one whose ministrations since then have been elsewhere much blessed to bring many souls to Christ. That did not save it, however, from the adverse judgment of a critic. So soon as the sermon was concluded, this modern Athenian turned round to him who related the circumstance, and said, with a shrug of his shoulders, and a tone bordering on contempt, Ha! there is nothing new there! Fancy a man to whom I offer a rose fresh plucked from the parterre, dyed in the richest hues, breathing the most fragrant odour, with the dew-drops still shining like diamonds on its pure bosom, tossing it from him with an air of contempt, to say, Ah! there is nothing new there! This were not more absurd than that. New? Anything in religion that professes to be new, beyond the light which modern researches into the geography and natural history, the manners, customs, and languages of the East, may throw on the contents of the Bible, is to be regarded with grave suspicion ; and, since the tendency of our times is to leave the old paths, and seek for something new—

I. Let me exhort those in whom faith abideth, to abide in the faith.

It is not much more than a century since Galvani, a native of Bologna, happened one day to bring two metals in contact with the limb of a dead frog. It quivered. The result was the discovery of a power whereby, making us able to annihilate space, rival the flight of time, and so flash our thoughts through the bosom of the ocean and the bowels of the earth, we can send a message and get an answer almost as soon from the capital of Russia as from the house of an acquaintance in the street next to our own. Modern facts are more wonderful than old fables. It is not even one century since Benjamin Franklin, by means of a child's plaything, entered, if I may say so, the bosom of the cloud, and, seizing the thunder-bolt, returned with it to the earth, like a magician who has thrown his spell on some mighty spirit, and bound it to his service. Every day almost presents us with some new invention, and science is ever and anon interesting its votaries by some new discovery, or startling the world by some strange one. We know what our forefathers never so much as dreamed of, —

that there are metals which swim on the top of water, and take fire at the touch of snow—that the diamond which flashes on a lady's finger is but a bit of coal—that the pearls which gem a royal crown are but the excrescences of disease—that the water which we employ to extinguish fire is composed of two elements which burn with the brightest light and fiercest heat—and that there is thus stored up in the sea itself a magazine of combustibles sufficient, when God shall kindle them, to wrap this world in flames, and turn it to a heap of ashes. In new planets and comets, new plants and animals, new metals and earths, science is adding page on page to the volume of nature's wonders, teaching the Christian to kneel before the Lord our Maker, and exclaim with deeper, devouter feelings, The earth is full of thy glory—the earth is full of thy riches. Such progress has the world made since the days of Solomon, that, were he to return to the scene of his former studies, he would no longer be a wonder queens might go to see, but, in point of knowledge, would stand below some whom we count little better than fools. Indeed, there is not a boy whom you meet in a morning, creeping with satchel on his back to school, but knows much that even Newton did not know, and is familiar with facts which would have excited the astonishment, perhaps the doubts, of that prince of philosophers.

How different the region of religion! and different because our faith has been revealed from heaven. In spired of God, it is intended not for the learned and wise only, but also for the humble and the poor ; complete—nothing can be added to it; perfect—nothing can be taken from it; plain—there is line upon line, precept upon precept, here a little and there a little ; intelligible to the humblest understanding, he who runs may read, and the wayfaring man, though a fool, shall not err therein. Since the days when heads now gray were black, since mothers were girls and men were boys, discoveries have been made in science which would have astonished Newton ; but during the last eighteen centuries has anything been discovered in the Bible that would have astonished Paul ? Since the beloved disciple closed this volume on the shores of Patmos, has one line been added to the Word of God, one doctrine or one duty been discovered there with which he was not acquainted? I know nothing in the writings of modern theologians that would have astonished the apostles but the audacity with which, not avowed infidels, but professed Christians, have treated their characters and their writings. We are to search the Scriptures with the eagerness of one who digs for hidden treasure. But this field is not like those gold regions on Californian coasts or the Australian continent which, left for long ages to the lowest savages, have been but recently explored. The road to heaven has been too long travelled by the feet of devout men, and too carefully surveyed and examined by them on their knees, for anything

of importance to have escaped their notice. **Long as**
familiar to the wise and good, as the path between
a cottage door and cottage well, there is nothing in
the world so improbable as that the gospel of Jesus
Christ will yield anything new in matters either of
doctrine or duty to the keenest or most curious eye ;
and therefore, though inapplicable to works on
science or art, to books of theology, to systems of
doctrine, or codes of duty that pretend to set forth
discoveries in the Word of God, we may safely apply
the adage, What is new in them is not true, and what
is true is not new.*

It is not the practice of Protestants blindly to follow
any leader, to pin their faith to church or churchmen.
Like the Bereans of old, who were therefore more
honourable than those of Thessalonica, we regard it
as a duty, and claim it also as a right, to bring everything to the test of God's Word ; and with all due respect to the creeds of Churches and the writings of the
Fathers, to search the Scriptures whether these things

* "I believe," said Webster, the great American statesman,
"that the Bible is to be understood and received in the plain and
obvious meaning of its passages ; since I cannot persuade myself
that a book intended for the instruction and conversion of the whole
world should cover its true meaning in such mystery and doubt
that none but critics and philosophers can discover it ; and believe that the experiments and subtleties of human wisdom are
more likely to obscure than to enlighten the revealed will of God,
and that he is the most accomplished Christian scholar who
hath been educated at the feet of Jesus, and in the College of
Fishermen."

are so. Still, he is a fool who, travelling over desert, moor, or mountain, allows himself to be easily persuaded to leave the beaten track for some new untrodden way. Depend on it that the old path which men with the Word of God in their hands and his grace in their hearts, took to serve him in this world, and to dwell with him in heaven in the next, is the right one. By abiding in their old path, we are most likely to abide in the true faith. Such is the very counsel which Christ himself gives to the Church, when, in the Song of Songs, she asks, Tell me, O thou whom my soul loveth, where thou feedest, where thou makest thy flock to rest at noon? If thou know not, he replies, O thou fairest among women, go thy way forth by the footsteps of the flock. God expresses himself to the very same effect by the prophet in a figure drawn from pastoral life, and intelligible to all who are in any measure familiar with the scenery of our glens and the habits of the sheep. Wherever they have to skirt a precipice, or wind through the black morass, they march in single file, and stick to the old, beaten path, trodden down and marked even on scattered stones and outlying rock by the feet of generations that have gone before ; and referring to this, God addresses his people thus—"Stand ye in the ways, and see, and ask for the old paths, where is the good way, and walk therein, and ye shall find rest for your souls." And so shall we, in the old ways of keeping the Sabbath, amid the quiet observ ances of that hallowed day; and so shall we likewise, in the old faith of "Jesus Christ and him crucified," safely and sweetly sheltered from every storm in the clefts of that Rock of Ages.

II. Salvation through faith in the righteousness of Jesus Christ does not supersede the use of means.

A heathen relates how he, when about to set sail on a dangerous voyage, selected the best ship, manned her with the stoutest crew, chose the most propitious season of the year for the enterprise; and that after having done this, all that man could do, he committed himself to the protection of the gods. Were it needful to learn from a heathen, this old worshipper of the false might teach us how to trust in the true God—both for the bounties of providence and the blessings of grace. Faith is undoubtedly the gift of God, the work of the Spirit, and the answer to prayer. But, if the necessity of looking above ourselves for ability to believe, be clear, and if it be plain from the Word of God, that we cannot depend too much on Divine strength, it is equally evident that we cannot be too diligent in using the means of Divine appointment. "I can do all things," says Paul, "through Christ which strengtheneth me,"—this his bold yet modest confidence, not that Christ would do the things, but would strengthen him to do them.

Therefore we ought to work at least as diligently for spiritual as for temporal mercies. But we do not.

Alas! Who does? In proportion to their importance, who gives as much time to prayer as to business; as much thought to their Bibles as merchants
to their ledgers; as much trouble to cultivate their
souls as husbandmen expend in ploughing and sowing and weeding the soil, and reaping the crop? No
wonder that many are lost; they take no trouble to
be saved. And no wonder that even those who are
saved make such slow progress in the divine life, that
they find self-examination to be such an unpleasant
task, and that their Christian course corresponds so
little to the beautiful and familiar image of the shining
light that shineth more and more unto the perfect day.
Making the doctrine of man's inability an excuse for
sloth and idleness, we seem to entertain the vague
and vain expectation that we shall be borne onwards to
heaven like a boat without sail or oar on the bosom of
a flowing tide; and that, instead of having laboriously
to climb the ladder, hand over hand, we shall some-
how or other rise to glory as in angels' arms and on
angels' wings. Is this to honour the grace of God?
Certainly not. The diligent and anxious use of
means casts no reflection or disparagement on the
doctrine of faith, of salvation not by the law, but by
grace. What madness is it for a man to rush naked
into a battle-field? It is he who arms himself for the
combat, and none else, that honours the Providence
without whose permission not a hair of his head shall
be touched, though he charge up to the cannon's

F

mouth, or throw himself headlong into the fiery
breach. It is the ship that has a steersman at her
wheel, and an outlook on the bows, that sails under
the flag of Providence—owning and honouring him
who doth fly upon the wings of the wind and hath
measured the waters in the hollow of his hand. That
is faith; anything else is presumption, and can only
end in a miserable shipwreck. Who, for instance,
considers himself guilty of mistrusting the promise,
Thy bread shall be given thee, and thy water shall be
sure, by toiling at his work? There is not more harmony between the divine perfections, between the Old
and New Testaments, between the songs of saints and
angels, than there is between the prayer for bread on
a good man's lips, and the sweat of honest labour on
his brow; between the hard toil of the field and the
hopeful trust of the closet. And, in calling on you,
in entreating and urging you to put on the whole
armour of God, to watch and pray, to guard against
temptation, to flee youthful lusts, to depart from all
iniquity, to give all diligence to make your calling
sure, to work out your salvation with fear and trembling, I am no more casting a doubt on salvation
by grace than I am denying a presiding Providence when I tell a youth about to go out into
the world that "the hand of the diligent maketh
rich," and that unless he work, "poverty" shall
"come as one that travelleth, and want as an armed
man."

III. Consider how faith is a saving grace.

Can faith save him? says St James, speaking of one who says he has faith, but not works. Certainly not; for I no more believe in the reality of a faith without works, than of a fire without heat. But assuming the faith to be genuine, Can faith save him? Well, it can, and it cannot. In explanation of this, I remark—

1. It is not by our faith, but by Christ's righteousness, that we are justified.

To illustrate this, let me recall two incidents in our Saviour's history. He is standing one day by the shore of Galilee, when the lake, dotted with the white sails of fishing-boats, spreads itself out at his feet, and over his head a sycamine throws its branches, yielding a grateful shade from the heat of the burning sun. To a prayer of his disciples, which we would all do well to offer—Increase our faith, he returned this remarkable reply, If ye had faith as a grain of mustard seed, ye might say unto this sycamine tree, Be thou plucked up by the root, and be thou planted in the sea; and it should obey you. Suppose that they, retreating to a safe distance, had tried the bold experiment, and with such success as Peter's, when, in the strength of faith, he leaped from the boat to stand erect on the rolling billow, and advanced, stepping from wave to wave, to meet his Master. Fancy this, and that the people, with wondering eyes, saw the sycamine, as by whirlwind power, torn up from the ground, rise like a balloon, sail through the air with leafy branches and naked roots, till, having been lowered slowly down, it buried its roots in the bosom of the waters, and stood there upright, firm, green as its neighbours on the shore. Might they not have pointed to the tree growing where never tree grew before, to say, See what faith has done! Yet faith had not done it. How could that which is but a feeling in the mind, reverse the laws of nature, and, plucking up a mighty tree, plant its roots as firmly in water as when they were anchored in the soil, or matted around a rock. Faith accomplishes the work only by bringing into play the power of God; as, to use a humble comparison, even a child can turn a gigantic wheel by opening the sluice, and letting the water on.

Or take, in illustration, a case that actually occurred. On another day our Lord is in a crowd. A woman, who has long suffered from an incurable disease, edges her way through the throng; and stooping down, unseen, reaches out her hand to touch the hem of his garment, and rises cured of the bloody issue. As she retreats, his voice arrests her. Trembling, she retraces her steps, and approaches him to hear these blessed words, Daughter, be of good comfort; thy faith hath made thee whole. Such is Matthew's account of the transaction. Mark throws further light on it, and on the point before us. According to his account, so soon as the woman touched our Lord, in an instant, suddenly as one who feels the stab of a knife, or the hand that steals his purse in a crowd, Jesus faces round on the throng, to demand, "Who touched my clothes?" The disciples were surprised; the woman was alarmed; and, knowing herself to be the culprit, if this was a crime, she came, in the words of the Evangelist, fearing and trembling, knowing what was done in her, and fell down before him, and told him all the truth. Now, what made Jesus ask a question, apparently so unreasonable that his own disciples remonstrated with him, saying, Thou seest the multitude thronging thee, and sayest thou, Who touched me? Mark tells us the why and wherefore. He states, that our Saviour knew that virtue, or, as we should now say, power, had gone out of him. This it was—not her touch, nor his garment, nor her faith, but the power that had gone out of him, that cured the woman; just as it is the water, not the cup, that quenches the thirst; the medicine, not the hand that takes it, nor the faith that swallows it, which arrests my malady, and saves my life; or, as when I place my finger on the ball of a Leyden jar, it is the subtle, invisible, electric fluid enclosed within its crystal walls, that, discharged by the touch, sends a shock thrilling through my frame. Even so, notwithstanding that it is said, Being justified by faith, we have peace with God, it is not faith, but the virtue which faith draws out of Christ, that justifies us; in other words, that righteousness which he wrought out when, taking our sins on himself, as man's substitute, he bore their punishment; and taking our obligations on himself, he performed our duty, and paid all our debt.

This righteousness is not imputed in any case because it is deserved; but imputed, thank God, in every case where it is sincerely desired. Whosoever, however unworthy he be, is willing to receive Christ as his Saviour, as well from the power as from the punishment of sin—whosoever, in other words, believeth in him shall not perish, but have everlasting life. Jesus stands in the presence of every congregation, willing and mighty to save, as on the day when he looked on the woman who lay trembling at his feet, to address her in the language of tender affection, and calm the tumult of her soul with these blessed words, Daughter, be of good comfort; thy faith hath made thee whole. Were we as prompt as she was to seize the opportunity, our humility would be crowned with still greater honours, and our faith with a more enduring reward.

2. While we are not saved by faith, it is through faith only that we receive the righteousness of Jesus Christ.

There are two arts, the one simple and very old, the other very complex, but modern, which are illustrative of important Bible truths. We have, like Jeremiah, in the words of Scripture, gone down to the potter's house, and, behold, he wrought a work on the wheels. Before him is a revolving horizontal disk; beside him a heap of clay. Seizing a handful of the clay, he throws it down, a rude, unformed, shapeless mass, on the flying wheel; and how curious it is to see that lump, as it spins round and round, begin at the touch of his skilful fingers to lose its shapelessness, assume a definite form, and by and by swell out and rise up into a vessel of perfect proportions. It is more than curious; it is instructive. One cannot watch the plastic clay growing to the workman's will and touch into a vessel of honour or dishonour, for common or sacred uses, for roughest hands or jewelled fingers, without seeing God in the potter, and man in the clay—feeling the beauty of Scripture figures, and how much ourselves and fortunes are in the hands of him who said, "O house of Israel, cannot I do with you as this potter? saith the Lord. Behold, as the clay is in the potter's hand, so are ye in mine hand, O house of Israel."—Shall the thing made say of him that made it, Why hast thou made me thus?

An art much more complex and modern than the potter's may supply us with an illustration of salvation through the transference of righteousness from the Saviour to the sinner. Before you stands a bath, as it is called, a large vessel full of acid liquor. At one end, immersed in the fluid, hangs a sheet of silver; while above, and passing from side to side, is extended a thread of metal, ready to be connected with a powerful battery, which, when I saw the process, was concealed in a room below. A vessel of common metal being produced, was hung on the wire and plunged into the bath, in which, I may remark, the fluid was so clear, that you could see to the bottom. The wire on which it was suspended was then connected with the electric battery; and what happened! A very remarkable result. By means of the mighty though unseen agent that was thus brought into action, the particles of silver were taken from the sheet of it, and, passing invisibly through the translucent fluid, were transferred to the vessel that had been immersed in the bath. No sound accompanied the mysterious process, no violent action, no sign of motion; the eye saw nothing but the dull metal beginning to assume a brilliant appearance, and in time, through what looked more like magic than common art, this base vessel shone in a coating of the purest silver. Such change, but far greater and more thorough, is wrought on the soul through the unseen and almighty influences of the Holy Spirit, so soon as faith has established a connexion between the Saviour and the sinner. Righteousness is withdrawn from the former and transferred to the latter. In the words of an inspired apostle, the believer puts on Christ—to stand before God covered with those merits, and justified by that righteousness which makes a sinner just.

If this process of art suggested that resemblance, it presented under one aspect a mighty difference. Robbed of its precious metal, what was once a sheet of silver became in time a dull, attenuated, worthless thing. Its treasures were exhausted; Christ's never are. It could coat and cover a certain number;

no more. But in him there is righteousness sufficient for all the world ; and, with enough of mercy in the Father, of merit in the Son, and of grace in the Spirit, oh ! why should there be one of us, one child of guilt and sin, of whom it cannot, as it might, be said, Blessed is he whose transgression is forgiven, whose sin is covered ? It were easier to empty the sun of his light, or the ocean of her waters, than Jesus of merits which are as free to all as is that sun and sea. In him dwelleth all the fulness of the Godhead bodily.

May that encourage you to go to Jesus. When ?— —now. Where ?—here. How ?—just as you are. Pharaoh's message found Joseph in prison, and in a prison dress ; nor did the black, begrimed, bearded tenant of a dungeon, venture to present himself before the impatient king till he had "shaved himself and changed his raiment." Must we likewise wait till our habits are changed ere, responding to his call, we go to Jesus ? By no means. Go as you are, just as you are. There is no need for good works at this stage, nor may there be time for them—little more time for you than for the dying thief who threw himself on bleeding mercy, and, clasped in Jesus' arms, was borne on his bosom to the gates of Paradise. May God help you to adopt the sentiments of this precious hymn :—

> " Just as I am, without one plea,
> But that thy blood was shed for me,
> And that thou bidst me come to thee ;
> O Lamb of God, I come !

" Just as I am, and waiting not
To rid my soul of one dark blot,
To thee, whose blood can cleanse **each spot**;
   O Lamb of God, I come!

" Just as I am, though toss'd about
With many a conflict, many a doubt,
Fightings and fears within, without;
   O Lamb of God, I come!

" Just as I am, poor, wretched, blind,
Sight, riches, healing of the mind,
Yea, all I need, in thee to find;
   O Lamb of God, I come!

³ Just as I am, thou wilt receive,
Wilt welcome, pardon, cleanse, **relieve**;
Because thy promise I believe,
   O Lamb of God, I come! ²⁰

VI.

THE GRACE OF HOPE.

"Now abideth hope."—1 Cor. xiii. 13.

IT is related of Lord Nelson when a child that, on his mother telling him not to expose himself to some danger, but to fear it, he turned round to her saying, Mother, what is fear?—there the boy was indeed father to the man, who, brave even to rashness, stept on the quarter-deck of the *Victory* for his last battle wearing all his orders; a glittering mark for the bullets of the enemy. But strangers as some may be to fear, who ever asked, What is Hope? Kings and beggars, saints and sinners, childhood, youth, manhood, and old age, all have tasted her pleasures; and the motto on the crest of one of our old families, *Dum spiro spero*, While I breathe I hope, is one that may be adopted by the whole human race. To expect when circumstances are at the worst that they will become better, ay, and better when at the best, is as natural to us as it is to breathe.

Hope presided at all our births; and in yonder mother whose busy fancy is weaving a bright future for her child, she rocks the infant's cradle. Other pleasures, like streams which summer dries or winter freezes, fail us; hers never—like the waters of the smitten rock, they follow us to the close of life. Constant as the emblem of God's presence to the wandering host, the pillar that was a cloud by day and a fire by night, she accompanies us to the end of our pilgrimage. Hovering like an angel over the bed of death, she often stays when physicians leave; and lingering in the bosoms of beloved ones while there is breath to move a feather, only departs with the sigh with which as if unwilling to part, the body yields up its soul into the hands of God. God be thanked for Hope!

Often, it is true, but a fair enchantress, still she has been the parent of noble deeds; of patriots' and martyrs' heroic struggles; of the Church's and the world's greatest and boldest enterprises. Lighting up the dark future, and supporting thousands of afflicted and tried ones, of poor, hard-working, heavily-burdened men and women, who were ready to sink beneath their load, to her the world owes a large, perhaps the largest, measure of its happiness. She throws her bow on the stormiest cloud, and kindles her star in the darkest sky; for the deadliest malady she has a medicine, and for the deepest wound a balm. It is under her flag the exile sails; and beneath her banner that the soldier fights. By her lamp the pale student pursues his midnight toils. In husbandmen it is she who ploughs the wintry fields, and in seamen the watery deep. Hers is the brightest beam that

shines into the captive's dungeon ; and hers the hand
that smooths life's thorniest pillow. She brings the
wanderer home ; she gives back the fallen one to a
mother's arms, and to the eyes of a father mourning
a long-lost son, she presents a vision of the wreck,
though broken and shattered, steering to its haven—
the returned prodigal weeps on his father's bosom, the
fatted calf smokes on the board, music wakes up that
long-silent house, and floors shake to the dancers'
feet. This world's good Samaritan, Hope pours her
wine and oil into the wounds of humanity ; and,
approaching the miserable in the mercy and might of
him who came to Jericho, she casts a healing virtue
into misfortune's bitterest springs. This world without Hope would be a world without a sun.

The darkest hour is that before the dawn ; when
things are at the worst they mend ; the longest road
has a turning—so Hope bravely speaks to all. And
some there are whom no misfortunes seem able to
overwhelm ; blessed with a happy, hopeful, tempera-
ment, they ride the waves of adverse fortune like a
sea-buoy, which, though submerged one moment, is
up the next, mounted on the back of the billow that
broke over it. No doubt, a large proportion of our
hopes suffer the fate of these billows, so soon as,
rolling landward, they meet the shore, and breaking,
are dashed into froth and foam. But thanks be to
God, that never hinders us from forming new hopes
as yonder sea new waves, that, rising from its bosom,

succeed each other so rapidly that one is no sooner broken than another comes rolling joyously in.

Now, if the hopes that are followed by disappointment are better than gloomy despair, if skies lighted only by dying meteors are better than utter darkness, if nights of happy dreams are better than days of dull despondency, how much better, and how blessed the hope of my text. She springs from faith, and aspires to heaven. Born of the promises of a faithful God, and never doomed to disappointment, she finds in her dying grasp no fleeting shadow, but an immortal crown.

Let us consider—

I. The object of this hope—immortality; which is,
I. The hope of nature.

All nations, whether barbarous or civilised, have cherished this hope ; and, even when they shrank from the grave, have regarded it as but a gloomy passage to another and an eternal world. It was left to the infidels of Paris, amidst the ungodliness of their bloody Revolution, to inscribe over the gate of their cemetery the sentiment, Death is an eternal sleep. Among the rudest pagans death never quenched the hope of immortality. That hope rose over the grave, shining to weeping eyes, like the evening star above the place where the sun had gone down. They saw the body turned into cold, unconscious clay; they saw it wither into a whitened skeleton ; they saw it moulder into a heap of dust ; yet, despite these changes, the power of death, and the foul ravages of the tomb, hope, tenacious of her hold, clung to immortality. This hope was not shaken by the convulsions of dissolution ; it did not expire with the passing breath ; it was not buried in the dead man's tomb. If buried, it sprang like the flowers that bloomed above the sod ; but not to wither and die with them.

There is no nation that does not shew some evidence of such a hope. It breathes in the prayers and flowers which are offered by the Chinese to the manes of their departed ancestors. It is painted in those pictures of a final judgment that are found on Egypt's oldest tombs. It shone in the lamps that lighted the sepulchres of Greece and Rome. It triumphed over death in the evergreen wreaths which they hung on their tombs. And nowhere is this blessed hope more distinctly expressed than at yon forest grave, where plumed and painted and silent warriors bury with his body the bow and arrows of the Indian, that his spirit might follow the chase in the land of spirits. The conclusion I draw from these things is, that hopes of immortality are as natural to the human heart as are those seeds to the soil which spring up so soon as it is stirred, and quickened into activity by the influences of light and air. Like these, they were planted by no human hand ; they are the gift of God.

This belief, that in its universality presents the character of an instinct or intuition, found in remarkable analogies what nursed its hopes, and were their props, though not their parents.   Men saw an image of death in sleep—the closed eyes, the dull ears, the speechless lips, the unimpassioned countenance, the prone form, the profound unconsciousness of all life's griefs, or joys, or cares ; and to some happy genius, might not sleep's awakening suggest another ?—the thought that as sleep is a short death, so death may be a long sleep.   Might not this truth burst on a thoughtful savage at the moment of sunrise ?   Standing on the shore, yesterday at even, he saw the declining sun sink, full-orbed, in the western waves, and expire amid a flood of glory, unshorn of a beam ; and to-day, after a period of darkness, he hails his rise, as, with ever-fresh light and splendour, he climbs the eastern heavens, to bathe hill and dale, shore and waves, with gold.   And why, might he not ask, may it not be so with the spirit that, retaining its faculties to the last, and strong amid the body's decay, sank, full-orbed also, into the darkness and night of death ? May it not have gone, like that sun, to shine in other lands—perhaps, after long years of absence, to return and shine once more in this ?

The wish might have been father to the thought ; but might not the yearly revival of nature have suggested to some the hope of a resurrection, though, when proclaimed by Paul, that doctrine startled all, and shocked some of, the men of Athens ?   Winter surrounded them with the emblems of death ; trees turned into naked skeletons; the sweet flowers all gone; unbroken silence in groves and skies; every stream glazed like a dead man's eye, and motionless in the frost's embrace; and the earth lying stiff and cold beneath its shroud of snow. And when spring returns to clothe the trees anew, and the flowers spring up to bloom upon their graves, and songs, breaking the long silence, burst forth afresh from skies and woodlands, might not a mother, hanging over her dead, fancy that her flower also would bloom again, and some future day restore the lost one, breaking the seal of death and silence of the tomb? These things they might see through a glass darkly.

2. The object of hope is immortality as clearly revealed in the Word of God.

What was once probable, is now certain. The heathens had immortality in its shadow; we have the substance. It is not a fancy now, but a certainty. Life and immortality, the objects of a believer's hope, are clearly brought to light by the gospel; and that grand old prophecy is fulfilled, was fulfilled on the cross by its expiring, yet rejoicing and conquering victim, "O death, I will be thy plagues; O grave, I will be thy destruction." The object of this hope, the grandest man can cherish, or mind aspire to, allies us to him who is the same yesterday, to-day, for ever; whose life knows no end and his happiness no change. It is not that life which, brief as it is, men

dread to lose, and the dying would buy at the price
of a fortune; which the woman in the gospel spent
all she had to preserve; which kings account of
greater value than their crowns; nobles, than their
titles; a miser, than his glittering heaps of gold. The
hope of the Christian is immortal life—the purchase
of a Saviour's blood,—the boon which God that cannot lie promised before the world began. It is begun
on earth, for in the germs and seeds of it, he that
believeth, as the Bible says, hath eternal life—much
as the tree has the leaves and flowers of next year
wrapped up in the buds of this. Commenced at the
new birth, and consummated in the hour of death, it
is enjoyed in that world where there is neither woe,
nor want; nor griefs, nor graves; nor sickness of
body, nor sorrow of heart; nor cares, nor sighs, nor
sin; where the crown hides no thorn, and the heart
bleeds from no secret wound; the sky wears no cloud,
and day never darkens into night. Into such blessedness believers enter at death. Such blessedness has
their God and Saviour laid up for all those that love
him. Instead of being reluctant, the wonder is that
we are not impatient to depart, saying, as we raise our
eyes to those realms of bliss from this chequered and
sinful world, Oh that I had wings like a dove! for
then would I fly away, and be at rest.

II. Consider the source of this hope.

On opening an Etruscan tomb they found it occupied by the skeleton of a king. After thousands of years of sepulture, he still wore, amid the gloom of the grave, a memorial of his former state. The skull was bound round with a fillet of gold, a remnant of his past greatness, and a bitter mockery of his present condition. Such a crown man wears in his hopes of eternal life ; these, like the indestructible gold of the royal tomb, have survived his fall, and are little else now than the vestiges of departed glory. Then, bereft of power to be or to do good, of the purity of his nature, and his peace with God, man lost all true life, and became " dead in trespasses and sins." Those hopes of happiness beyond the grave, in which, whether Pagan, or careless, unconverted Christian, he now indulges, delights, wraps himself up, are but the ivy that, clothing, conceals a ruin ; or, by folding a green mantle around its trunk, gives the appearance of life to a dead and withered tree.

I believe that no man lives in utter, blank, black despair. Voyaging to hell or heaven, to the haven of rest or to a fearful wrecking, every one carries hope in his heart, as all our ships do her symbol—the anchor hung at their bows. Who believe that they shall be lost when they die ? None. Who lives a life of sin in this world without some expectation of escaping its punishment in the next ? None ; not the lowest, basest, vilest slave of vice. If men believed that death was the end of their existence, that there was no here after, they might toss the reins on the neck of passion

—this their motto, " A short life and a merry one !" or, as they raised the foaming cup, this, " Let us eat and drink ; for to-morrow we shall die." But no man says, or could say, Let us eat and drink, for to-morrow we shall be in hell. It is no more in human nature to quaff the cup and toy with pleasure under such dread feelings, than it was in Damocles to linger at the banquet when he discovered a sword above his head, hung from the roof by a single hair. The worst have hope. Tenacious of life, she can live in an atmosphere that is fatal to every human virtue. She blooms on the grave, where all innocence, and beauty, and grace lie buried ; a phenomenon more wonderful to behold than the rose of the Alps, with its roots planted on the edge of the glacier, and its arms, thickly covered with blushing flowers, thrown on a wreath of snow.

And what is the source, what are the foundations of hopes by which many are deceived till, like the rich man, they lift up their eyes in torment? Here they are ; judge ye what they are worth, and see that they are not yours—God, they say, is merciful ; we have been guilty, no doubt, of many bad actions, but we have done some good ones ; if we are not what we should be, we are not so bad as we might have been, or as some others are ; if God did not mean us to indulge our appetites, why did he give them ? he does not, cannot expect perfection from those in whom he has planted passions more powerful than reason, and whom he has placed in circumstances of all but irresistible temptation ; youth must sow its wild oats ; we will grow better as we grow older, and find leisure to repent before we die ! Thus, fed by the devil's hand, that of others, or their own, the lamp of hope burns on in this city's darkest haunts of vice.

More specious, yet not more solid, are the foundations on which a different class rest their hopes of eternal life. With a sort of general and indefinite trust in Christ, but without any humble, real, appropriating faith in his finished work and all-sufficient merits, your hopes, in the main, rest on what your-selves have done, or have not done, or intend to do. You are sober and chaste, — which many are not ; you are honest men, or virtuous women ; you bear an unblemished reputation ; you have won the respect of the world ; you maintain a reputable Christian profession ; you are known by your charities ; you say your prayers ; you read your Bibles ; you go to church ; you attend the communion table. "These be thy gods, O Israel ;" but, oh ! wait till death comes, and if God have mercy on you at last, perhaps whether or no, you will turn to them to say, as said Job to his friends, Miserable comforters are ye all !

I do not deny that these hopes look bright ; but so does the *ignis fatuus* that plays in the quagmire, luring the steps of the belated traveller to death. I grant that they yield bright visions ; but so does the opiate which, while it pleases, poisons. Borne on their bosom your course is pleasant ; but so is that of the boat which, with blue skies overhead, and beauty on either bank, is gliding on to the fatal cataract. From these hopes, if yours, I beseech you to turn to Christ,—" Turn you to the stronghold, ye prisoners of hope."

The hope of my text rests, not on the sinner's work, but on the Saviour's ; on works, certainly, but not our own. God justifies none but those who condemn themselves, and loves none but those who, hating the works of the flesh, abhor themselves. Those only who have felt themselves lost, are found ; nor are any pardoned but those who, putting in no plea but guilty, have cast themselves on the mercy of God through Jesus Christ our Lord. As the apostle says, it is " Christ in you, the hope of glory ;" Christ on us in his righteousness, and in us in his image ; enthroned in love on our hearts, and dwelling there by the indwelling of his Holy Spirit. Have you found him ? Often offered, have you accepted him ? Is it he whom your soul loveth ? Have you laid the burden of your sins on his back, and your sick head on his bosom ? Have you felt the beating of a new heart ? and in new desires, new loves and hatreds, new aims and objects, can you say, Old things are passed away ; behold, all things are become new ? I congratulate you ; the greatest kings might envy your condition. What though you are tossing on a sea of troubles, your anchor holds fast, having entered into that within the vail ; and, to borrow an illustration which that well-known symbol suggests, some of you, old men if not old Christians, have not long now to lie off the harbour, exposed to the temptations and tossed on the storms of life—the hour comes when, having heaved your anchor and spread out your sails, you shall be borne safely over the swell that breaks on death's moaning bar, and pass into the haven of eternal rest.

> " Such are the hopes that cheer the just ;
> These hopes their God hath given ;
> His Spirit is the earnest now,
> And seals their souls for heaven."

III. Consider the certainty of this hope.

In that how different it is—

1. From such hopes of happiness as the world offers.

A fruit-tree in early summer, covered with a sheet of flowers, sounding with the hum of bees, topped by a thrush that pours forth a flood of song, standing on a sward enamelled with flowers and under calm blue skies that ring with music, offers a striking contrast to the same tree as it appears in autumn, with the ground around it strewed with withered leaves, and only a few fruits of all those rich blossoms hanging on its half-naked branches.   Still greater the contrast between this world, as it presents itself to the eyes of youth, and as it appears to those of age.   How rarely are its expectations of happiness fulfilled ! of its blossoms how few ever ripen into fruit !   It is common here for speakers and authors to summon two famous kings,—

the Jew, laying down the cup of all earthly pleasures to seize the pen, and write, Vanity of vanities, all is vanity; and the Greek, laying down the sword to weep, that having conquered one world he had not a second to conquer. Those crowned heads may be left undisturbed in their graves. Every man with gray hairs can tell as well as they, that this world, in whatever of its pleasures he has sought for happiness, is full of disappointment. How many parents, lovers, friends, have met bitter misery where they looked for joy! They indeed may be accounted fortunate who, merely disappointed, have not had their experience of the world foreshadowed by what befell St Paul, when from the fire at which he expected to warm his shivering limbs, a viper sprung to sting him. Without the hopes of my text, this world were vanity at its best; and how often also vexation of spirit?

2. From the hopes of the ungodly and unbelieving.

Who among us, asks Isaiah, shall dwell with the devouring fire? who among us shall dwell with everlasting burnings? Change the *shall* there into *will*, and I answer, None. As we have often seen and sought to prevent, the poor moth, allured by its glare, may, narrowing its circles, dash at length into the flame, and drop dead on our book; but such a fate, every sinner, however near to hell he ventures, intends and hopes to escape. He resolves on amendment, but not now—at some future date. Buoyed up with such hopes, and grown bold, he ventures further and deeper into sin, till he is lost, like the heedless boy who, borne up on his airy float, pushes out from the calm waters of the bank, further and deeper into the body of the current, and caught at length in its resistless sweep, is hurried down helpless and powerless into the fatal pool. They hope to amend, and never do ; growing worse instead of better, dying as they lived. Be assured that, if it be true that as the tree falls so it lies, it is about as true that as the tree leans so it falls. A solemn fact! On you who are hesitating, hanging, halting between the two opinions— God or the world, Christ or pleasure, the indulgence of the flesh or the hopes of heaven—how should it enforce this saying, "Behold, now is the accepted time ; behold, now is the day of salvation."

I am not charging you with hypocrisy. No. You do not profess to be religious, though you intend one day to be so ; yet Job's description of the hopes of the hypocrite applies equally to yours—they are a spider's web. What more beautiful than those threads thrown from branch to branch of the golden gorse— an aerial bridge—all gemmed with diamonds of morning dew? But would any man in his senses trust his weight to it? And while, most false security, it snaps at an infant's touch, see how, crouching in the centre of her web, a cruel, cunning, bloody, venomous, ugly murderer sits, watching for her prey ; and how over those silken strands lie scattered the wings, and limbs, and disembowelled carcasses of once happy creatures, that shone in the gayest colours, and danced, all day long, in sunbeams. Equally ensnaring and insecure are the hopes of the unbelieving and ungodly, "whose hope," to use the words of Job, "shall be cut off, and whose trust shall be a spider's web. He shall lean upon his house, but it shall not stand; he shall hold it fast, but it shall not endure."

3. Now look at the certainty of the hope of my text.

I have a good security in the word of an honest man, still better in his bond, and, best of all, in his oath. On such an oath I will embark my fortune; I will believe the most extraordinary statements; sitting on a jury, I will hang a man—set him free, or send him to the gallows. If such certainty is afforded by the word of an honest, though fallen and sinful, man, what security is that which lies in the oath of God? So anxious is he, our heavenly Father, that poor sinners should believe that he will save them, is anxious to save them, has no more pleasure in your death and damnation than I would have in seeing my son die or damned, has given his own Son to save you, and will save you now if you will only come to him, that he has sworn it, passed his great oath for it—"Wherein God," says the apostle, "willing more abundantly to shew unto the heirs of promise the immutability of his counsel, confirmed it by an oath: that by two immutable things, in which it was impos-

sible for God to lie, we might have a strong consolation, who have fled for refuge to lay hold upon the
hope set before us : which hope we have as an anchor
of the soul, both sure and steadfast." I can add
nothing to that. To paint a rose, or gild the bur-
nished gold, would be a less waste of time and labour
than any attempt to augment the force of that.
Heaven has no further security to offer ; and if
people will not believe the oath of God, I have
nothing more to say.

As to those who rest on his word and oath, what
hopes, what happiness like theirs ! Now, said one, I
can shake hands with death—Save Christ's, said another, no countenance to me so beautiful as death's !
Enjoying this hope the believer may walk in perpetual sunlight, and go singing on his way to heaven.
Under her eye how do all things change—sick-beds,
losses, disappointments, bereavements ? They throw
their furnace-light on the face of Jesus, as sitting by the
fire, a refiner, he purifies, not destroys his gold; and
the death-struggle itself, with its tossings, and groans,
and pains, appears as the effort of a bird to burst its
shell, of the insect to shatter its case and enter on a
new and bright existence. Looking on the grave as
a bed for the weary, and as one from whose long and
quiet sleep we shall rise, not as we do now, with the
infirmities and weaknesses under which we lay down,
but in the beauty of perfect holiness and the bloom
of everlasting youth, there are times when Christian

hope can use the words of Brainerd, My heart turns longing to the burying-place. Yes; we shall be happiest when our heads lie beneath the sod—we shall then be with the Lord ; and, as surely as faith falls short of sight, we shall find that our brightest, dearest, loftiest hopes never rose to the height of our enjoyments— "Eye hath not seen, nor ear heard, neither have entered into the heart of man, the things which God hath prepared for them that love him." May these hopes draw us more and more heavenward ; purify our hearts ; wean our affections from earth, and wed them to the skies ! May they help us to live above this world, and to look beyond it ; and, as sailors, homeward bound, crowd every sail on the mast where the watch sits aloft looking out for land, may we, guided by the Spirit of God, inspired with the hopes of the gospel, and enabled to welcome such failings of nature as prognosticate the change at hand, haste, to use the words of Peter, be "hasting unto the coming of the day of God !" Then what ?

> "The pains of death are past ;
>   Labour and sorrow cease ;
> And, life's long warfare closed at last,
>   The soul is found in peace.
> Soldier of Christ, well done ;
>   Praise is thy new employ ;
> And while eternal ages run,
>   Rest in thy Saviour's joy."

VII

THE GRACE OF CHARITY

"Now abideth charity ;
The greatest of these is charity."—1 Cor. xiii. 13.

OUR version of the Bible, like the men who made
it and those also who use it, is not faultless. It
cannot be so, for "who can bring a clean thing out of
an unclean ?" The web must ever, more or less, partake of the imperfection of the loom. Still, the good
and learned men to whom King James committed the
work of translation, take it altogether, have done it
well; so well, that all succeeding attempts to produce a
better have failed. And perhaps the time and labour
which some authors have spent in detecting and ex-
posing the small faults of our version, would have
been as well employed in correcting the large faults
of their own creeds and conduct. Could I form a
better wish than that the errors of our heart and life
were as insignificant as those that have been detected
in our English Bible ; and that Christians, in their
spirit and life, were as faithful copies of Jesus Christ,
as it is of the divine original !

Beside those mistranslations which make our version somewhat erroneous, but which are hardly in

any case of the smallest practical importance, a few passages of Scripture are liable to misunderstanding, in consequence of the change of meaning which some English words have undergone in the course of time. We have an example of this in the first chapter of St Paul's Epistle to the Romans. He says, " I would not have you ignorant, brethren, that oftentimes I purposed to come unto you, but was let hitherto." Now, *let*, in modern language, means permitted ; but there, with its old meaning, it expresses the very opposite, *hindered*. And of such change, my text also affords a very striking example. Charity is a term now limited almost entirely to mean kindness bestowed on the poor. So by a charitable man, we understand one whose name is a household word in their homes ; and who of his substance, be it great or small, gives liberally to feed the hungry, to clothe the naked, to instruct the ignorant, to house the homeless, and to supply the need of widows and orphans. This chapter itself proves that that application of the term does not exhaust, or at all come up to the meaning of the word as employed by Paul ; for he supposes, as quite a possible case, a man who, though very charitable in the common sense of the term, is yet destitute of charity—declaring, " Though I bestow all my goods to feed the poor, and though I give my body to be burned, and have not charity, it profiteth me nothing." Before, therefore, setting forth some of those features of charity which led Paul to exalt her over all the other graces, awarding her the palm and crown, let us consider—

I. What we are to understand by charity.

It is an old word for love, that inner fountain of which kindness to the poor is but one of many streams; and where, when neither ruffled by passion nor polluted by sin, God, who is love, sees his own face, the reflection of his features, as we see ours on looking into a draw-well. I need not tell you who have been familiar with love from your earliest days what it is. At our birth she received us into her arms and welcomed us into the world. Love is associated with the first face our opening faculties recognised, with the first name our infant lips ever lisped, and with the pure, deep affection of one who pressed us, new born, to her happy bosom; and nursing us from the fountains of her breast, forgat all the world in the helpless creature cast upon her care. Flowing through the earth like streams amid desert sands, shining in life's darkest nights like stars in a wintry sky, throwing a bright bow over every cloud of fortune, to love, more than to anything else, this world owes what blessedness it enjoys. Life without it would not be worth the having; and without it, though we had a house, and that house a palace, we could not have a home.

Of this tenderest and strongest passion, what beautiful illustrations lie, shining like diamonds, in Bible story! In Rizpah, lone woman, who by seven gibbets guards the bodies of her sons, nor rises by night or day for weeks but to scare away the vulture or front the hungry wolf, love forgets herself—her only care the rotting dead.   In Judah, yonder, she pleads for Benjamin, and offers, so he be set at liberty, to wear a brother's bonds.   In that wronged though guilty mother, who, on seeing her babe in the hands of the executioner, raises a piercing shriek, and, casting herself at the king's feet, cries, O my lord, give her the living child, and in no wise slay it, love consents to part with her dearest object to save its life.   Nay: in David, who, forgetting all Absalom's crimes at the news of his death, bursts into this cry of wildest, deepest grief, O my son Absalom! my son, my son Absalom! would God I had died for thee, O Absalom, my son, my son! love would buy another's life at the expense of her own.   In the graves of the dead she buries all their crimes, and waters with her tears the memory of their virtues.   In the garden where Peter sees his Lord betrayed, beset, and ready to be bound, she takes no count of numbers; but, casting prudence to the wind, rushes on the foremost foe, striking for her master.   In Paul her hand trembles while she writes the doom of the ungodly, her eyes blot the page with tears, and she is willing to be herself accursed from Christ, so that countrymen and kindred are saved.   One example more! You have anticipated it, and your thoughts, outrunning my words, have fixed on that amid whose transcendent glory these all are lost—like stars swallowed up in the blaze of day. Love, perfect, divine, hangs on the Cross of Calvary; and speaks in him who, turning an eye of pity on his bloody murderers, cries, Father, forgive them; for they know not what they do. Well may Paul say, Now abideth faith, hope, charity, these three; but the greatest of these is charity.

This love embraces not itself, but others—God, and all down from the throne of his majesty, to the lowest creatures of his hand. I have seen a plant with tendrils fitted to seize on any object within its reach, that, lying prostrate on the ground, had its leaves and flowers all soiled with mud, and its arms twined, and twisted, and tangled into each other—like a rope of many strands; and near by was another of the same species, with its arms flung lovingly around a tall and friendly tree, whose stem they held in close embrace, while they lent it, in return for its support, a robe of green leaves spangled all with flowers. Lying basely in its own embraces, the first was an image of selfishness; but in that which clothed and adorned the object to which it fondly clung, and from which no storm could tear its arms, I saw the love which, Queen of the Graces, "suffereth long, and is kind; seeketh not her own; beareth all things, believeth all things, hopeth all things, endureth all things."

H

II. Let us look at some of the features of this grace.

1. It is a power of universal influence. Many powers of nature are not always or everywhere in action. There are lands where rain, and others where snow never falls ; rivers of water which no winter freezes, of ice which no summer melts. There is a metal which fire cannot burn ; there is life which water cannot drown ; and the lightning that flashes along a thousand miles of iron is stopped by a film of glass. Happily for the world, the destructive powers of nature are not always active. Etna and Heckla exhaust their forces, and long ages may pass ere they recover them for a new eruption. It is at rare intervals that earthquakes shake our globe, or the skies flash with lightnings, or hurricanes sweep through the troubled air, and lashing the sea into mountain billows, strew its shore with wrecks. Day leaves our world, and that light which paints its colours on every flower, and touches the clouds with gold, and wakes each morning the song of birds and hum of busy cities, departs with the setting sun. Winter ascends her throne, and waving an icy sceptre over fields and forests, stops all growth ; once clothed in green, the trees are leafless ; once enamelled with flowers, the meadows are bare. But the powers of winter in their turn cease ; nature bursts her icy tomb ; rising, she throws off her shroud of snow, while, their chains melted by the breath of spring, the streams, like

happy children set loose from the constraint of school, rush off, laughing, dancing, singing on their way to their home and parent in the deep.

But while substances, and places, and seasons limit the action of many material agencies, there is a power— that which England's greatest philosopher discovered— which neither substance, nor place, nor season limits. Universal in its action, it is everywhere, affecting everything. It determines the movements of the motes in a sunbeam, and of the planets in the firmament; it shapes the tear on your infant's cheek, and has given its rounded form to the sun; it makes the rain-drops fall to the earth, and prevents the stars from dropping out of the sky. Most powerfully affecting every atom of matter on earth, and every planet and sun in heaven, amid all the agencies which science studies, art employs, and God has established, gravitation alone extends its empire from the centre to the circumference of creation. In a subordinate sense, indeed, we may say of it what is said of God, It reigneth over all.

Now, such place Love holds in the kingdom of grace. In representing it as the ruling principle which should shape and influence all our conduct to God, in our families, to our friends, ay, and also to our foes, for, followers of him who died for his enemies, we are to love ours—blessing them which curse us, and praying for them which despitefully use us—I do not exaggerate its importance. Love was the dominant power in St Paul, and the principle of his whole obedience; "The love of Christ," he says, "constraineth us." And did not our Lord himself assign it such an imperial place? Those ten commandments from which all duties branch, like the boughs of a tree from the parent stem, he brings into the compass of a word, a single, simple word; that word—Love. Thou shalt love thy God, and Thou shalt love thy neighbour, are the whole duty of man. It is this that makes a religious, a happy life. With love, a dinner of herbs is better than a stalled ox; obedience is liberty with it; and without it slavery, call it by what name you may. And as it is earthly love, not its walls, however lofty, nor its furniture, however costly, nor its inmates, however great or beautiful, that makes a home below; so it is holy love that makes a heaven above, not its crowns, or palms, or harps, or robes; no, with reverence be it spoken, not God, or Christ, or saints, or angels, but love—their love. And as if by some strange power we could leave this nether world, and, winging our way upward, alight on a distant, starry sphere, we should find that we had not left that gravitation behind us, which binds all things and holds this world together; so saints shall find, on rising from the bed of death, and entering heaven, that they have but ascended into a region of purer and more perfect love.

> "Faith, Hope, and Love now dwell on earth,
>   And earth by them is blest;
> But Faith and Hope must yield to Love,
>   Of all the graces best.

" Hope shall to full fruition rise,
    And Faith be sight above ;
These are the means, but this the **end,**
    For saints for ever love."

2. Love is a mighty power. Take Paul's description of it.

First, It "beareth all things." So I thought, on seeing a woman who presented a blessed and, though clad in rags, a beautiful contrast to those mothers who, committing most revolting murder, lay bloody hands on their new-born babes. To appearance she was one of those homeless creatures who are tossed about our city like the sea wrack that, torn by the rude storm from its native rocks, goes floating about the shore, washed in and washed out with each flowing tide. A threadbare shawl fell in scanty folds from her shoulders, and covered something held on her left arm. As, struck by her forlorn aspect, I was watching her movements, she suddenly stopped and raised the shawl. Then, as when a flood of golden sunlight, bursting through a rift in the clouds, and suddenly falling on some field, or hillside, or lake, or village, lightens up the scene, such change came over her face when she turned its earnest gaze on an infant that lay asleep, nestling in her bosom. You never saw a smile of more ineffable delight than this poor, perhaps guilty creature threw on her helpless charge. It was plain that she would have died for it—true to nature as the bear, who protects her young by offering her shaggy breast to the hunter's spear; and there, where love was turning what others might deem a burden into the one joy and blessing of the outcast's life, I thought of the words, it "beareth all things."

Second, It "believeth all things, hopeth all things." What will not parents bear from their children, and believe and hope of them? Did not Augustine's mother pray twenty long years for his conversion? And what is it but the hope that love breeds which still sustains the arms of praying fathers and mothers? You may quench the hopes of reason, but not those of love. It hopes against hope, and will soar like an eagle, which, rising with the rising tempest, mounts highest in stormy skies. Such hope sustained the mother, whom I saw intently gazing on the stone walls that immured her boy. Opposite the prison gate, raised on the steps whence she could see the windows of the upper cells, her tall form clad in the attire of humble but honest life, and stooping under the burdens of grief and age, she stood, oblivious of all around, while her body went rocking to and fro with that swaying motion which bespeaks the deepest grief. An hour thereafter, rooted to the spot, there still she stood; her eyes, that swam in tears, and were fixed on an iron-barred window, telling as plainly as if her choking words had told it, that within those gloomy walls lay one that had once been cradled in her happy arms, and to whom, hoping all things, believing all things, her love yet clung, like ivy to a crumbling ruin.

Third, It "endureth all things." Take this example of that the last of those things which, according to Paul, love has the mind and also the might to do.

A ship, named the *Golden Gate*, takes fire some fifteen miles off the shores of America. Then rises a scene of the wildest and most terrible confusion. It is a battle now for life. Between the flames and the sea, it is every man for himself. While the roar of the fire, which rapidly gains on the fatal bark, is mingling with the prayers of some and the imprecations of others, a lady, with one child in her arms and another three years old at her knee, approaches the narrator of the story. I believe, she said, addressing him by name, that you are Mr Holloday? On being told that he was, she cried, Can you save my children? Madam, he replied, I do not know that I shall be able to save myself. Whereupon, pointing with a solemn air to the flames as they raged furiously in the centre of the ship, she exclaimed, Oh! if my children can be saved, I will consent to be burned in that fire!—they were saved, and she perished, an example of the might of love. It "endureth all things."

How should such cases of natural affection confirm God's people in their trust that he will not forget or forsake them; and others in their hopes that he will not refuse to forgive, but open wide his loving arms to every penitent, returning sinner! "Thus saith the Lord," speaking of his Church, "Behold, I will extend peace to her like a river, and the glory of the Gentiles like a flowing stream : then shall ye suck, ye shall be borne upon her sides, and be dandled upon her knees. As one whom his mother comforteth, so will I comfort you." What a depth is there in that love which God chooses as an image of his own ! and yet the love of a mother's heart is but a drop from that illimitable ocean into which our sins, though great as mountains, once cast are lost for ever—buried out of sight. I believe that his love as far exceeds a mother's, when it is deepest and strongest, as does the strength of his almighty arm that of the infant which hangs helpless on her breast. She may forget—a fact which the blood of murdered infants proclaims, as, unheeded by a justice that wears her sword in vain in this guilty land, it cries aloud to heaven for vengeance : "yet," he says, "will I not forget thee. Behold, I have graven thee upon the palms of my hands."

Now, as it is by his love, seen in the face and form of a dying Saviour, that God melts the stony heart and subdues sinners to himself, so to this power also, under God, we must trust if we would bend stubborn wills, reclaim the vicious, and save the lost. The voice that grates harshly on the ear, the eye that does not glisten with tears but glares with anger, never made the bad good, or the good better. Men are not to be scolded into the love of God ; nor can the terrors of hell frighten any into the love of heaven. Who would revive dead souls, let him learn his lesson in the chamber where the prophet, to restore the Shunamite's son, rose from his knees, and took the boy into such loving, close embraces, that the heart of the living beat against the heart of the dead. Deal not with ungodly children, or careless and irreligious friends, without taking care to shew that you love the sinners as much at least as you hate their sins. Cultivate true, gentle, Christ-like love. What good may you not do, what stubborn hearts may you not melt, what hatred and hardness may you not subdue by the out-goings and expression of that love which is averse from censure but prone to praise ; which pities while it blames ; which, unselfish, "seeketh not her own ;" which touches wounds with a tender hand ; and which, ready to cover a multitude of sins, spake through him who, purest of the pure, and holiest of the holy, said, as he looked with pity on the guilty woman, Neither do I condemn thee : go, and sin no more ?

3. Love is the grand principle of the gospel.

A child had strayed from its mother's side, and, gathering buttercups and daisies, had approached the edge of a precipice. On raising her head, what was the mother's horror to see her darling tottering on the dreadful brink ! If she cries, alarmed or in gleesome play, he takes another backward step, and perishes. With prompt, instinctive wisdom, though with trembling hands, she bares her bosom ; and caught, to use St Paul's words, by guile, the infant, seeking its accustomed pleasure, runs into her arms. She saved her child by addressing its self-love. And so also was one saved who, where a bridge thrown from rock to rock spans a yawning chasm, was wont to lie over watching the waters that, ground into snowy foam, rushed, and whirled, and roared below. A servant found the urchin on his way from school hanging over the dizzy ledge, and so absorbed in the strange pleasure as not to notice the other's approach. Clutching him, as the hawk her prey, he seized the boy, and raising, held him out for a moment at arm's length over the brink of death. The dreadful experiment had the desired effect. The fright cured him; and, indeed, when that boy had grown into a man he used to tell that he never passed the place without recollections that made him shudder.

Now, dealing with us not as angels, which we are not, not as unfallen, but as sinful, disobedient, head-strong, and foolish children, God does employ means like these. He addresses himself to our self-love—to our taste for pleasure, and our dread of pain. Unwilling that any should perish, like a father or mother in such circumstances, he loves us too well to leave any argument untried; therefore heaven has been revealed, that its palms, and crowns, and thrones, might draw us to God; and the pit also has opened, that the worm that never dieth, and the flames that are never quenched, and poor wretches gnawing their tongues and gnashing their teeth might scare away the thoughtless and turn them from the paths of sin. Therefore Jesus also, lover of our souls, presents salvation in the form of a matter of profit and loss. Making such an appeal as does a father who implores his son, if he will not regard his father's and mother's feelings, to look to his own interests, and think of the misery and ruin which his sins and follies will bring on himself, Jesus asks, and I would urge you all to consider and answer the question, "What shall it profit a man, if he shall gain the whole world, and lose his own soul?" Therefore God also puts these solemn, awful questions, "Who among us shall dwell with the devouring fire? who among us shall dwell with everlasting burnings?" Would God men would look these questions in the face, and flee to Christ's open arms, hasting from the wrath to come—nor long, perhaps, to come! There is but a step between us and the grave.

There is a fable of a tree, which, as it fell groaning to the earth, discovered that out of its own timber the woodman had hafted the axe which entered its heart and felled it to the ground; and there is another of an eagle that, pierced by an arrow as it soared in the skies, discerned, while it lay dying on the ground, that its own wing had furnished a feather to the shaft that drank up its blood. Well, sceptics, abandoning the weapons with which Hume, Gibbon, Tom Paine, and Voltaire vainly attempted to overthrow our faith, have thought to find in the Bible itself that which would feather their arrow or haft their axe. Because the Bible, in addressing itself to our self-love, appeals t the lowest principle of our nature, it cannot, they say, be divine. An objection this that only proves the darkness of their understandings, or the malignity of their hearts! Restrained within proper bounds, self-love is a right feeling; one that, divinely implanted, is not a vice but a virtue which—winning the drunkard, for example, to practise sobriety and respect himself— would gladden many a wretched home.

Nor is it to this only, or chiefly, that our heavenly Father appeals. Take the apostle Paul as a type of the Christian! His strongest passion was the love of Christ. Gratitude for his salvation, affection for his person, admiration of his character, regard to his will and honour, his crown and kingdom, these constrained him to love, not himself, but him who died for him and rose again. And what motive nobler, tenderer, than that love to God, to Christ, to saints, to sinners, to friends, to foes, under the influence of which all come on entering into a state of grace. In leaving sin we leave selfishness; the less sinful we become, in that very proportion we become the less selfish. The whole case is related in the story of the prodigal. The pangs of hunger, his shame, his ragged misery, death in prospect, with no gentle forms by his side, or kind hands to wipe his brow, and close his eyes, and give his poor body decent burial, these troubles, no doubt, turned his thoughts homeward, and, blessed of God, led to the reflection, "How many hired servants of my father's have bread enough and to spare, and I perish with hunger! I will arise and go to my father, and will say unto him, Father, I have sinned against heaven, and before thee, and am no more worthy to be called thy son: make me as one of thy hired servants." As ships run before the storm to anchor-ground and sheltering bay, he made for home, if I may say so, through stress of weather; and, as when the tempest-tossed have reached the desired haven, how sweet the change—fatted calf for swinish husks, that goodly robe for rags, the flowing bowl, and merry music, and gay dancers for the neglect and wretchedness to which his harlots and boon companions had left him —first their slave, and then their victim! Yet it was not these home-pleasures that kept him there; but love for that loving father, who, forgiving all, had folded him to his bosom, and bathed his face with tears of overflowing joy, and, glad to have a long-lost son restored, had assembled the neighbours to share his happiness; for the grave had given up its prey—he that was dead was alive again, he that had been lost was found.

Love is the chain that binds us to the throne of God, each to all and all to each. May its golden links be strengthened! Gift to be coveted above all others, rather than eloquence lofty as angels' speech, than power to pluck mountains from their roots and cast them into the boiling sea, than knowledge that penetrates into the deepest mysteries and climbs to the heights of heaven, than the courage that wins the martyr's crown at a burning stake, than the faith that tramples death beneath its feet, than the hope that, stretched on a dying bed lays a mortal hand on an immortal crown, rather far than these, give me the love that dwells, dove-like, in many a lowly bosom, and turns the rudest cabin into a little heaven. "Now abideth faith, hope, charity, these three; but the greatest of these is charity." St Paul crowns her queen; and so I say, with this apostle elsewhere, Put on therefore, as the elect of God, holy and beloved, bowels of mercies, kindness, humbleness of mind, meekness, long-suffering; forbearing one another, and forgiving one another. . . . . And above all these things, put on charity, which is the bond of perfectness.

VIII.

THE GOOD FIGHT.

"I have fought a good fight."—2 TIM. iv. 7.

"THE gods do so unto me, and more also, if the dust of Samaria shall suffice for handfuls for all the people that follow me." Such insolent message did Ben-hadad send to the king of Israel. Ahab's reply was as spirited as it was wise, and one that, from such a man as the husband of Jezebel, and the cowardly murderer of Naboth, was like the fire that flashes, when it is struck, from a cold, black flint ; "Tell him," said the king, roused by the insult, and perhaps inspired for the occasion, "Let not him that girdeth on his harness boast himself as he that putteth it off." Prophetic words ! Ere four-and-twenty hours the Syrian host was scattered by the arms, or, rather, by the God of Israel, like autumn leaves before the wind ; and this proud boaster, foremost of a band of horsemen, was galloping away for life.

When the apostle, the humblest as well as the holiest of men, used the words from which I intend to speak, he did not lie open to any such taunt as Ahab's. He was no young disciple on his way to battle with armour unsoiled and arm unwearied. Nor, like many a Christian man, was he in the thick of it, now giving and now receiving blows; now with sword flashing and voice shouting, pressing forward, and now, alas! borne back; now brought to his knees, and again, rescued by his captain and revived by prayer, rising to his feet to rush on his foes and renew the combat. Paul was in none of these circumstances. He had reached the close of a long warfare. In him we behold a veteran great in fight and gray in years. On his arm a battered shield; his hand returning to its scabbard a sword that had been often buried in the body of his sins; on his head the helmet of salvation, dinted with the blows of many a hard-fought fight; he stands before us—covered, if I may say so, with the scars of a hundred battles, and crowned with the laurels of a hundred victories. His sufferings, toils, trials, travels, preachings, prayings over, with foot planted on the threshold of glory, he is about to enter on his reward. The battle fought, the victory won, nothing remains but to die—and that he accounted nothing. The dark valley, in fear of which so many are all their lifetime subject to bondage, dreading it as the hardest part of the course, he does not reckon as else than the goal by which the racer stands, panting, to receive the crown; he says, "I have finished my course." Nor does he regard death as his enemy; not he. He has no quarrel with death; no fear of it; no battle to fight with it; "I have fought a good fight," he says—fought it out. It is done and over, and never were silent night and soft couch more welcome at the close of a long day's journey or of a hard day's fighting, than death and the grave to him who exclaimed, "I am now ready to be offered, and the time of my departure is at hand. I have fought a good fight, I have finished my course, I have kept the faith: henceforth there is laid up for me a crown of righteousness, which the Lord, the righteous judge, shall give me at that day: and not to me only, but unto all them also who love his appearing."

I. Look at the Christian life under the aspect of a fight.

In a sense, this aspect of life is not peculiar to that of the Christian's. Look at the world! What a scene of disquiet and disorder! what a succession of struggles, which many begin at the cradle and leave not but at the grave! With poverty, or hard toil, or disease, or domestic trials, or unavoidable misfortunes, or, in some cases, all of these together, many have to battle their whole way through life—they rise up early, and lie down late, and eat the bread of sorrow. How does ambition, not confined to any class, spur on the eager competitors in the race for honours or riches! What a struggle there is amongst the different members of society to get uppermost! and while some are straining every nerve to improve their position, it needs the utmost endeavours of others to keep theirs.

How like this world often seems to a rock at sea, on which, eager to escape the jaws of death, more drowning men seek standing-room than it offers; and when they whose gain has been others' loss, when the few that have risen on the shoulders of the many that sink, have possessed themselves in wealth, or power, or pleasure, of the objects of their ambition, they have only reached a bare, black, unsheltered rock, on which, at some future day, a giant wave rises roaring to sweep them from their slippery footing. Let no man deceive himself. Even this world is not to be got without fighting; and, compared with the nobler struggles and prizes of the faith, though its rewards be laurel or even golden crowns, it presents a scene of no more real dignity than a nursery quarrel—children fighting for some gilded toy—the street where ragged boys struggle, and tear, and roll over each other for a few copper coins. I admit that it has pleasures; but its sweetest enjoyments perish in the using. I admit that it has roses; but they are beset with thorns, and the hand that plucks them bleeds. Nor are any of these to be obtained without a struggle. The few prizes which, among many blanks, the world offers to a host of competitors are won only by the hard work, hard struggling, hard fighting, without which you gain no topmost place in any profession, no heaps of money, no niche in the temple of fame. Its pearls are not to be picked up among the pebbles of the shore; he who would possess, must seek them in a sea where sharks are swimming and storms rage. Indeed, I dare to say that, so far from the followers of the world being exempt from toil and hardship, it would not take a man half the care and time and trouble to get to heaven, which it takes any man to get rich, and many a man to get to hell. The question, therefore, is not whether we shall fight, but what for, and on whose side?—on that of Jesus, whose award is life, or on that of sin, whose wages is death?

Now, with regard to the Christian's fight, I remark,

1. He has to fight against the world.

It hated me, says our Lord, before it hated you. It had no crown for his brow but one of thorns; it found no way to exalt him but on a bloody cross; and when he, at whose approach happy angels threw open the gates of heaven, appeared at its door, it refused him a night's lodging. The foxes have holes, was his complaint, and the birds of the air have nests; but the Son of man hath not where to lay his head. And if there was a time when Jerusalem poured forth her exultant thousands to escort her king to his capital, this popularity was but such a fitful gleam as I have seen light up a cold and stormy day. The servant is no better than his master; and I do believe, were we more true to God, more faithful and honest in opposing the world for its good, we should get less smoothly along the path of life, and have less reason to read with apprehension these words of Jesus, Woe unto you, when all men shall speak well of you. Not less true than shrewd was the remark of a Scotchwoman respecting one who, just settled in the ministry, had been borne to his pulpit amid the plaudits of all the people,—If he is a faithful servant of the Lord Jesus Christ, he will have all the blackguards in the parish on his head before a month is gone.

I am not saying that the world is always wrong in its judgments, or that it is always right to go against its customs. Alas! the children of this world are sometimes wiser in their generation than the children of light. But, as a living fish is often found cleaving its way against the stream, and that fish is certainly dead which, floating on the top, is always moving with it, so he is no living Christian whom you ever find walking according to the course of this world. They who would wear a crown in heaven must be ready to oppose its maxims, to encounter its offence, to brave its opposition, to scorn its contempt, and to sacrifice to its friendships as well as to resist its allurements. "Be not conformed to this world : but be ye transformed by the renewing of your mind," says this same apostle. Nor is that easy. Alas! how often do Christians follow a multitude to do evil ; yield to the customs of the world because they are afraid of being thought singular ; and fail in their duty because they are afraid of giving others offence! Few are bold for Christ, and dare avow themselves before the worldly, not ashamed of his cause, and cross, and crown. Bad men glory in their shame, and it would seem as if good men were ashamed of their glory. It ought not so to be. In the strength of God, then, stand up for the good, the holy, and the true; seeking men's profit, not their praise; pitying the world, though your reward here should be none else than his, who, finding a serpent frozen, warmed it in his bosom, to have it sting him for his pains. Be not discouraged by this, as if some strange thing had happened unto you. The servant is no better than his master, nor the disciple than his Lord.

2. He has to fight against Satan.

When Napoleon Buonaparte, watching the fortunes of the battle, saw the charge of our Scots Greys at Waterloo, as, launched on his columns, they dashed like a thunderbolt into the thick of them, crushing and bearing down all before them, he exclaimed, How terrible are these Greys! But what mortal foe so terrible as him we have to fight ? — so relentless, so malignant, ever walking about seeking whom he may devour. No serpent so cunning, no roaring lion so savage! From other enemies escape may be found, from him none. Neither the world, nor the Church itself, offers any asylum, nor the universe, other than the hollow of God's hand, the shadow of his wings. Flying from the world, the hermit has courted solitude among the heights of the mountain, or in the depths of the gloomy forest; but, tracking his steps far from the haunts of men, in the desert region, where he was conquered by the Master, the Devil has often tempted and triumphed over the servant.

The Sabbath proclaims its weekly and welcome truce, a breathing time to such as have the temptations of the world's gaiety and the cares of its business to contend with; but Satan keeps no Sabbath,—he takes no rest, and gives none. More persuasive than the most eloquent preachers, and more wakeful than the most anxious hearers, if on holy Sabbaths, in sinners converted, in careless ones roused, in the perishing plucked from destruction, he sustains his greatest defeats, on those days he wins his most signal triumphs. Pardon is freely offered to the guilty, salvation to the lost, but, listening to him, they refuse to be saved; as never happened on the stormy ocean, they see the lifeboat leave them, straightway to resume their dance on the sinking wreck—Christ is rejected, warnings are despised. And, hardening the heart, not against the pleadings of a man, but the tears of divine pity and the very blood of Christ, Satan marches off thousands from the doors of the house of God, unconverted, unsaved, harder than they came in, to resume their way on the broad path that leadeth down to destruction.

Men have taken up arms against the greatest odds; and fighting on their own thresholds, with wives and children at their back, bleeding patriots have wrung victory from superior numbers. But, suppose a foe able to make themselves invisible; able to pass in a moment over leagues of country; able to live without sleep, to march without wearying, to work without food; who seldom fought but to conquer, and though repulsed often, were never destroyed; who pitied none, spared none; and regarding neither sex, nor innocence, nor age, dragged off their unhappy captives to horrible and nameless tortures—who would take the field against these? Such an enemy has no place in the pages and horrid annals of war; nor did man ever find such a foe in man. True, but he has such a foe in Satan. That you do not see him is nothing; you never saw the pestilence which it is death to breathe. That you do not see him makes him not the less, but all the more formidable. Victory over a foe like this I could neither expect nor dream of, but for such promises as these: "Fear not, thou worm Jacob, and ye men of Israel; I will help thee, saith the Lord, and thy Redeemer, the Holy One of Israel:" "How should one chase a thousand, and two put ten thousand to flight, except their Rock had sold them, and the Lord had shut them up?" "Thou shalt tread upon the lion and adder: the young lion and the dragon shalt thou trample under feet:" "Fear thou not, for I am with thee: be not dismayed, for I am thy God: I will strengthen thee; yea, I will help thee; yea, I will uphold thee with the right hand of my righteousness." Courage! A little child with God at his back, is mightier than the devil and all his angels. He that is with us is greater than all that be against us.

3. He has to fight against the flesh.

"The prince of this world cometh," said our Lord, "and hath nothing in me." Can we say so? Assuredly not. Hence the disadvantages under which we carry on the combat. He hath much in us, having in our natural depravity a traitor inside the gates, an ally to open the door and admit the enemy. Called, with such a nature, to contend both against the influences of a world that lieth in wickedness and the temptations of the Evil One, we sail, as it were, in a poor, crazy, damaged, leaking bark which has both wind and tide against her; nor is it any wonder that in circumstances so untoward multitudes make shipwreck of the faith. The wonder is, not that many never reach the harbour, but that any do—entering heaven as once I saw a vessel gain yonder port, bows crushed, masts sprung, and bulwarks gone; saved, but almost lost. And if the righteous scarcely be saved, where shall the ungodly and the sinner appear?

The prince of this world cometh, says our Saviour, and hath nothing in me; and so his temptations fell into Christ's bosom like flaming darts into the sea—hissing, but instantly quenched. It is otherwise, alas! with us. Our corrupt nature is food for temptation, as flax is food for flame; we are ready "to be set on fire of hell." And with such natural dispositions, the marvel is, not that we sometimes fall into sin, but that we ever withstand. Satan had no corruption to work upon in his fellow-angels, yet he triumphed over their loyalty; and with one sweep of his dragon tail cast down perhaps a third part of the stars of heaven. He had no innate depravity to work upon in our first parents, yet again he triumphed, seducing the innocence of Eden. And to whom but God shall we ascribe the glory of this, that in yon Christian resisting the devil till he flee, earth stands fast, where heaven fell; and faith conquers, where innocence was defeated, — in the words of Scripture, and the spiritual history of many, " the lame take the prey." Like Samson, who made a greater slaughter of the Philistines after his locks were shorn, than he had ever done when they fell flowing over his ample shoulders, man achieves a greater triumph after his fall than he did before it. Such is the power of imparted and omnipotent grace! He giveth power to the faint; and to them that have no might he increaseth strength; and thus God makes all things work for his glory—the wrath of devils, as well as of men, to praise him.

II. The character of the Christian's fight; it is " a good fight."

1. Because it is in a good cause.

With the justice and reason of any war, our soldiers are supposed to have nothing to do; these are to be discussed in Parliament, but not in barrack-rooms. The theory of a standing army is such, that from the

commander-in-chief down to the drummer-boy, the
soldier is considered as much a mere machine as the
musket in his hands. This presents to many, one of
the most serious and difficult questions as to the law-
fulness of his profession. While we may feel no such
scruples, it ought to make us, as far as possible, live
peaceably with all men, and never but as a last resort
appeal to the arbitrament of arms. How often have
good men been found fighting on the bad side ! and
how often has the trumpet summoned from their distant
homes and peaceful occupations, those who had no
quarrels to settle, nor wrongs to complain of, to the
bloody work of slaughter ; to destroy each other's
lives and to mangle each other's bodies, till, in that
poor, mutilated humanity, a mother would not know
her own son ! In war both sides cannot be right ;
and the death of every man, therefore, who falls on
the side that stands up for the right against the wrong
is a murder, on which the Almighty Judge will hold
severe and solemn inquest—laying the guilt at the right
door. But, however soldiers may come to regard
themselves, or be regarded by others, as machines
who are to obey orders without inquiring into the
merits of the war, still a man is a man—he has what
his arms have not, reason and conscience ; nor can
he, though he would, suppress their voice within
him. I can fancy cases where he has little heart to
fight. He is not sure that it is " a good fight."
Ordered to cut down one, who, though a naked

savage, stands on the shore of his country to defend it
from aggressors, or on the threshold of his door to
protect his wife and daughters from the hands of a
brutal soldiery, the sympathies of a generous man
cannot be on the same side as his sword.

Now, if, soldiers of the Cross, you have formidable
enemies to contend with, you have an immense advantage in this—that your cause is just, and noble, and
holy, and good. It is "a good fight." Your enemies
are not your kindred, bone of your bone, flesh of your
flesh; they are the enemies of God and Christ; of virtue and liberty: of light and peace; of your children
and of your race; of your bodies and of your souls—
tyrants that would bind you in chains worse than iron,
and burn, not your house above your head, but your
self in hell for ever. I am not saying that the sword
has not often flashed on the side of right and been
bathed in tyrants' blood; but men never drew sword
in a cause like this; nor to any battle so much as
that to which I summon you with the world, the devil,
and the flesh, are the few pithy words of a brave old
general so appropriate. His men were waiting to be
addressed ere the fight began. Erect in his saddle,
with his gray hairs streaming in the wind, he stretched
out his arm, and pointing to the foe in front said, ere
he rang out the word Fire! There are the enemy; if
you do not kill them, they will kill you. So with us.
We must destroy sin, or be destroyed by it. Be assured
that unless your prayers stop your sins, your sins will

stop **your** prayers; and that by God's **help you must** kill sin, or sin will kill you.

2. Because here victory is unmingled **joy.**

It is not so in other fights. The laurels that are won where groans of suffering mingle with the shouts of battle, are steeped in tears; and when cannon roar and bells ring out a victory, and shouting crowds throng the streets, and illuminations turn night into day, dark is many a home, where fathers and mothers, brothers and sisters, widows and orphans, weep for the brave who shall never return. It is said of God, that, in sweet flowers, and singing birds, and painted shells, and shining stars, in all the beautiful and happy works of his hands, he takes delight; but the best and bravest soldiers have sickened at the sight of the work of their hands in that field of carnage where, locked like brothers in each other's arms, friend and foe lie quietly together in one gory bed. There are thorns in victory's proudest crown. He whom men called the Iron Duke, is reported to have said that there was nothing so dreadful as a battle won, but a battle lost.

Thank God, our joy over sins slain, bad passions subdued, Satan defeated, has to suffer no such abatements. Heaven, that I can fancy hiding its eyes from other battles, watches the fortunes of this with keennest, and kindest interest; angels rejoice in your success; nor are any tears shed here but such as poured from the father's eye, when, kissing the returned prodigal and folding him in his happy embraces, he cried, Let us eat, and be merry: for this my son was dead, and is alive again; he was lost, and is found.

I wish to enlist you as soldiers of the Cross. This is a good fight in other than these, in all its aspects: what a captain in Jesus; what arms in the whole armour of God—the very ring and sight of which, as they shine in the beams of the Sun of righteousness, make Satan tremble; what a helmet for the head in salvation; what a shield in faith; what a breastplate in the righteousness that protects the believer's heart; what a sword in that of the Spirit, the word of God; what a girdle for the body in truth; in peace what shoes for the feet; and last of all, in a crown immortal, what a prize to reward your watchings and prayers, your tears and toils, the blows you strike and wounds you suffer! I can understand men in that terrible war which is now raging beyond the Atlantic, flying, as they are said to do, not through cowardice, but to escape military service. So long as the battle-cry is the Union *with* slavery, not *without* it, to me the ground of battle is not clear; I cannot feel, to use the words of my text, that it is "a good fight." But who can doubt that here? It is a fight for your soul; it is a battle for heaven; it is bleeding slaves up in arms against their old masters; doomed prisoners fighting their way to the open door, and dashing themselves on those who would bar their escape to life and liberty. Break away from your sins; and, taking unto you the whole

armour of God, throw yourselves into this battle. By
that I cannot say you will win heaven, but you will
win to it; and thus possess the prize which your
Saviour purchased.

No doubt it is a hard fight; I do not conceal or dis-
guise that.   How can it be easy for a man to overcome
the world and crucify his own flesh? But if that is
hard, it is harder far to suffer the pains of a lost soul,
to lie down in everlasting burnings.   Oh! surely better
lose a hand, than have the whole body burn; better
part with some darling sin than part with Jesus.   You
have no choice; they only that carry swords on earth
shall wave palms in heaven; nor shall any but they
who walk here in armour, walk there in brightness.
The crown is for saints, not for sinners; not for
cowards, but for conquerors.   And how can you con
quer unless you fight?   The promises are to him that
conquers, to him that overcometh, — not, indeed,
by might, nor by power, but by my spirit, saith the
Lord of hosts,—" To him that overcometh will I
give to eat of the tree of life, which is in the midst
of the paradise of God;" "He that overcometh shall
not be hurt of the second death;" "He that overcometh, the same shall be clothed in white raiment;
and I will not blot out his name out of the book of
life, but I will confess his name before my Father,
and before his angels;" and still higher honour, "To
him that overcometh will I grant to sit with me in my
throne."

IX

THE TRIAL AND TRIUMPH OF FAITH.

"Arise, get thee to Zarephath, which belongeth to Zidon, and dwell there : behold, I have commanded a widow woman there to sustain thee."—1 KINGS xvii. 9.

THE plough is fatal to the picturesque. A country under husbandry, with its farms and formal divisions, each field throughout its whole extent of the same crop and colour, with all God's beautiful flowers cut down and cast out under the name of weeds, is as inferior in point of beauty as it is superior in point of profit to moor or mountain. How tame your levelled fields of wheat or barley compared with the rudest hill-side, where green bracken, and the plumes of the fern, and the bells of the foxglove, and brown heath with its purple blossoms, and the hoar, gray, rugged stones that lie scattered in wild confusion, unite to form a mantle, in richness and variety of hues, such as loom never wove and queen never wore. This variety should minister to more than taste. A pious mind, extracting food for devotion from the flowers which supply honey to the bee, finds profit where others find only pleasure, and, rising from nature up to nature's God, exclaims with David, O Lord, how manifold are thy works! in wisdom hast thou made them all!

Without this variety, how tame our gardens with every flower in form and colour the counterpart of another; and how monotonous the music of early morn did every lark in the sky, linnet in the bush, rook and ringdove in the woods, all utter the same notes! But variety characterises every department of nature. Each lamb of the flock has a bleat known to its own mother; each rose on the bush has its own shape and shade of colour; and there is not a lark that hangs carolling in the clouds but has a voice recognised by the brood above whose grassy nest she sings her morning hymn, calling the drowsy world to rise for worship and for work. Nor is this variety anywhere more remarkable than in mankind. It is calculated that there are ten hundred millions of our race scattered over the five continents and countless islands of the globe. Now, while in their grand characteristics, in their features, organs, voices, limbs, and general form these all resemble each other, yet there are not two faces, for instance, out of these ten hundred millions, which are exactly alike. Nor does a rich, boundless, divine variety characterise and adorn only this world of ours in the living creatures of its lands and seas, the shells which strew its shores, the flowers and fruits of its fertile plains, its shaggy mountains, up to their snowy crests. It shines above us—in stars fixed or moving, stars single, stars in pairs, stars in clusters, some sparkling with borrowed, others with native light: in the sun that runs his daily round, and comets, that with fiery locks streaming out behind them rush away into darkness, nor return for a hundred, perhaps for a thousand years. And high above that starry firmament, amid the splendours of the upper sanctuary, in angels and archangels, in cherubim and seraphim, in saints on higher thrones and crowns of brighter glory, in the various orders of unfallen and the various honours of ransomed spirits, we see a manifold and magnificent diversity in the works of God.

From this we might conclude that the kingdom of grace would present something of the same variety as that which distinguishes all his other works; and that as neither all angels nor all insects are formed alike, no more would all Christians be so. And thus it is; for variety is one of the many points at which the kingdoms of grace and nature touch. Christians have individual peculiarities which, as much as their faces, distinguish them from each other; and this is rather a beauty than a blemish—a charm rather than a fault. Some have one grace and some another, in such prominence, that John's love, and Peter's ardour, and Paul's zeal, and Job's patience, and Moses' meekness, and Jeremiah's tenderness, and Abraham's faith, have become proverbial. Nor is this variety, as among the flowers of moor and meadow, an element merely of beauty. It is a power; an element of the highest utility in the Church. Hence the mistake of those who would have all Christians modelled on their own pattern, as, for example, of some modest, retiring, gentle spirits, who cannot appreciate the worth and usefulness of those whom God has cast in a rough mould and made of stern stuff.

In the early ages of the Church, when she is endowed with supernatural powers, and some have the gift of wisdom, others of knowledge, others of faith, others of healing, others of miracles, others of prophecy, others of tongues, others of interpretation, Paul by a beautiful analogy recommends mutual respect—illustrating the advantages of variety, and shewing how people with very different gifts may nevertheless be true members of Christ's true Church. "If the foot," he says, "shall say, Because I am not the hand, I am not of the body ; is it therefore not of the body? And if the ear shall say, Because I am not the eye, I am not of the body ; is it therefore not of the body? If the whole body were an eye, where were the hearing? If the whole were hearing, where were the smelling? But now God hath set the members every one of them in the body, as it hath pleased him. And if they were all one member, where were the body? But now are they many members, yet but one body. And the eye cannot say unto the hand, I have no need of thee : nor again, the head to the feet, I have no need of you." We live in an age of ordinary gifts ; but it is as true of these ordinary as of those extraordinary gifts of the

Spirit, that there is as much utility as beauty in the diverse temperaments and endowments of Christian men. What is diverse is not of necessity adverse. God has different kinds of work to do; and since he chooses to employ men, he has need of different kinds of instruments.

I. In what is recorded of Elijah, he appears as one specially fitted for his work.

Go into the workshop of a mechanic; what a variety of tools is there! Some are straight, others crooked; some are blunt, others sharp as a razor; some are rough, others have the polish of a mirror; some are soft as silk, others hard as steel; some are light enough to be the playthings of his children, while it needs his own brawny arm to swing the ponderous weight of others. He finds a use for them all; nor can he dispense with any. Now, to compare great things with small, God's work to ours, it is by a corresponding diversity of accomplishments, and gifts, and dispositions in her members and ministers that the Church is thoroughly furnished for every good work. It had fared ill, for instance, with the cause of truth at the Reformation, if the gentleness of Philip Melancthon, however much we may admire it and love him, had not been associated with the rough and ready energy of Martin Luther. Knox, our own great Reformer, has been severely handled for his lack of courtly urbanity to Mary, and called rude, a brute, a rugged savage. But, as he himself said, when, having thwarted the Queen in her attempt to reimpose the hateful yoke of Popery on our land, he left her in tears, and was reproached, as he passed from the council chamber. for his rudeness, Better that women weep than bearded men! Of this heroic man we say what the Irish Presbyterian said, when asked beside the ruins of an old castle which the Protector had assailed with fire and sword, what he thought of Oliver Cromwell, he replied, God gave him stern work to do, and he did it! Knox was not more stern or rugged than the time required. Rugged? Who quarrels with the ruggedness of the rock that presents a bold front to the roaring sea, and, withstanding their shock, flings back the proud waves into their bed; defending the land from deluge, and its inhabitants from death? The times, it is said, make men. True; but it is as true that men are made for the times—raised up by God with gifts and graces suited to the work they have to do.

Of these remarks the illustrious man whose life supplies the incident recorded in my text, is a remarkable illustration. Elijah's lot was cast in evil and stormy days; and with his bold and dauntless spirit, how well was he fitted to face the dangers, and conquer the difficulties he had to encounter? The times called for a Boanerges, a son of Thunder; and, raised up by God, Elijah, stern in aspect and wild in dress, appears on the scene—rushing on the stage with a curse on his lips, and leaving it for heaven in a whirlwind and chariot of fire. He pronounced a doom of drought on the guilty land,—skies that should shut up their treasures, and yield neither dew nor rain ; and it was in consequence of this, that he was placed in the circumstances which the text brings before us. Directed by God, he fled for protection from the vengeance of Ahab to the lonely banks of Cherith, where the brook gave him drink, and the ravens brought him meat, as day by day, he whiled away the time, and woke the echoes of the rocks with the songs of David, singing,

> "The Lord 's my shepherd, I 'll not want.
> He makes me down to lie
> In pastures green : he leadeth me
> The quiet waters by."

Steering on black wing through the hot and stagnant air, the ravens supply his morning and evening meals ; and laying them at his feet, those caterers go to croak and whet their beaks on the overhanging trees—like servants who wait to satisfy their own wants with the fragments of their master's feast. Thus, by a singular miracle, did God answer his prayers, and give him day by day his daily bread. But at length, no dew falling from clear nor rain from cloudy skies, Cherith's stream begins to fail ; each day its gurgling sound grows more and more faint ; betimes it contracts to a tiny rill ; at length it vanishes, leaving nothing in its bed but a course of dry, white stones Now it is that God, who watched over his servant, says, Arise, get thee to Zarephath, which belongeth to Zidon, and dwell there: behold, I have commanded a widow woman there to sustain thee.

II. Consider the trial to which this put the prophet's faith.

1. He is sent for safety to a heathen city.

Unlike Moses, Samuel, David, for whose future greatness their previous history prepares us, as does the gray dawn for the full blaze of day, Elijah bursts on our notice. His appearance as a prophet of the most high God startles us not less by its suddenness than by its terror ; how much more the weak and wicked Ahab that day, when, stalking into the palace in uncourtly robes, his shaggy raiment bound by a leathern belt, his aspect severe and stern, he walks up boldly to the king, and fixing his eye on him, says, " As the Lord God of Israel liveth, before whom I stand, there shall not be dew nor rain these years, but according to my word"—and so saying, vanishes. As the words of Christ which blasted the fig-tree—that emblem of formal Christians, these went forth like a poisonous breath, withering all vegetation in the guilty land. Gaunt famine came, but no repentance with it ; only death, and deeper exasperation against the servant of God. No wonder, therefore, when the brook fails, that Elijah is not sent back to Ahab and the land of Israel. But God might have sent him to

Judah? True; and I can fancy the welcome and ovation he would have received from those who, unlike their kindred in Israel, clung to the temple and worship of their fathers' God. It does seem strange that, for protection from the dangers to which his opposition to idolatry had exposed him, he is sent, not to Judah, but to Zidon and Zarephath; to a land and city of idolaters. Like a man who has got out of his depth, and, drowning, turns his back on the shore and his face to the sea, was not this but making bad worse? It was as if one flying in terror from a lion, was directed to seek refuge in the lion's den.

I conferred not, says St Paul, with flesh and blood. Had he done so, he had never, counting all things loss for Christ, become the great apostle of the Gentiles; had Moses done so, he had never, esteeming the reproach of Christ greater riches than the treasures in Egypt, become the lawgiver and founder of the Jewish nation; had David done so, going back to his flock, he had never plucked the laurels from the giant's brow, or worn royal crown upon his own; and had Elijah conferred with flesh and blood, then worldly wisdom, cautious prudence, everything but the faith that trusts in God, and laughs at impossibilities, had pronounced his going to Zidon and Zarephath to be an act of downright madness—rushing, not blindfold, but with open eyes on ruin. Surely in vain, says the proverb, the net is spread in the sight of any bird. But from Israel to Zidon, from a land

where idolatry was but of recent growth and thousands beside Elijah remained true to their God, to
one where all were old, bigoted idolaters, was from
bad to worse. If he had run with the footmen and
they had wearied him, how was he to contend with
horsemen? If they had wearied him in, compara-
tively speaking, a land of peace, what was he to do in
the swellings of Jordan? If his life was in danger in
Samaria, how was he to be safe in Zidon? This was
a perplexing question. He walked, perhaps, in darkness, and had no light; but he walked boldly on.
He stayed himself on God. It was enough that He
bade him go there; and there he went as bravely as
he strode into Ahab's palace, and bearded that lion in
his own den. What a pattern to us, when, though the
way be dark, the duty is clear! A most noble example of what a man can dare and a man can do,
whose faith is fixed on God!

2. He is sent for sustenance to a widow woman.

Who that has read the story has not admired the
tender and touching delicacy of the couriers who,
stained with the blood of battle and flushed with
victory, communicated to his father the dark tidings
of Absalom's death? One messenger has already
come; and deeply touched by the anxiety visible
in David's countenance, he drops but a hint of evil;
announces the victory, but, having no heart to lift
the veil and quench at once the hope that breathes in
the eager question, Is the young man Absalom safe?

evades it, saying, I saw a great tumult, but I knew not what it was. It falls to Cushi, the second messenger to deal the blow that reaches the father's heart. But, how delicately done! "Tidings, my lord the king; for the Lord hath avenged thee this day of all them that rose up against thee," are the words with which he bursts, panting, into the king's presence. Not thirsting for vengeance, but thinking only of his misguided son, the father's heart, true as needle to its pole, turns to Absalom. These words, "avenged thee of all them that rose up against thee," have an ominous sound; still he clings to hope, again eagerly inquiring, Is the young man Absalom safe? Cushi's hand is red with blood, yet, though more familiar with inflicting wounds than with healing them, how gently he unveils the dreadful truth! Taking care, by not even pronouncing Absalom's name, or making any allusion to the fact that he was David's son, his first-born, a son of much anxiety and many prayers, to avoid everything that might aggravate the blow and increase the burst of grief which he saw would come, he, as I can fancy, bowing his head and dropping his voice, just says, or, addressing David's God rather than himself, prays, The enemies of my lord the king, and all that rise against thee to do thee hurt, be as that young man is!

What a contrast did this exquisite tenderness on the part of man present to the tone and whole style of God's address to Abraham, when he demanded the sacrifice of his only son! How much in that case did the manner aggravate the matter? With, as we would say, all the skill of oratory, everything is planned to magnify the difficulty of the dreadful task, and, by awaking a father's tenderest emotions, to harrow his feelings and open up the deepest springs of grief. "Take now thy son;" and as if God had a pleasure in wringing the old man's heart, he goes on, "thine only son," reminding Abraham that he is childless when Isaac dies; still more, he names the lad "Isaac," child of promises that nature fears may henceforth lie like withered leaves beneath a father's feet; and still more, as if it needed to be told, or that was a time to tell it, God adds, "whom thou lovest;" and so, by this most tender introduction, prefaces this most dreadful conclusion—"and offer him for a burnt-offering upon one of the mountains which I will tell thee off." Fancy how Abraham started as these words fell like a thunder-peal on his ear, or, rather, struck like a knife through his heart! Had the earth opened at his feet, he could not have been more astonished. And what horror succeeded astonishment! Yet God's purpose was to try, and by trying to strengthen his servant's faith; not to extinguish it, but by this rude wind to blow it up into a brighter flame, that it might shed its light adown the course of time, and make him an example to God's people in all future generations, to be "not faithless, but believing."

And as there, so here every circumstance tends to

increase the difficulty of the prophet's duty. It was not enough that he must seek protection from persecution in a city of idolaters, but, worse and more trying still, he is thrown for bread in famine on a poor widow. Strange! he is not only to expect safety in a land of persecutors, but also plenty in a house of poverty. Our faith, alas! is weak at the strongest. With fightings without and fears within, how ready is it to fail? how often has it failed—overcome by the trials and temptations of life? But when or where was it ever put to a trial like that? A widow woman! "Let thy widows trust in me," "A father of the fatherless, and a judge of the widows, is God in his holy habitation," are words which prove how helpless widows were in those lands where violence so often usurped the place of law. A widow woman! the least likely person in Zarephath to be able to feed this hungry man. The head that had counselled her in difficulties, the arm that had defended her from wrong, the hand that had provided for her wants, laid in the cold grave, mouldering in the dust, in her the prophet seemed to have a forlorn hope indeed. Famine had roused the fiercest passions of our nature : might was right, men fought with men in the streets for bread ; and, within-doors, mothers driven mad did worse. If at such a time there were an empty cup and cold hearth in Zarephath, these would be the widow's; one poorer than another, it would be she. Would it have been wonderful had Elijah said, If God is to preserve me, why throw me into the lion's jaws? if he means to support me, why send me to take the bread out of a widow's mouth? why not send me to board with those that have bags of gold and barrels of meal? To cast me for support on a widow, is to lay the burden on a broken back—to bid me turn for help to the hand of the drowning. The ravens are gone, the brook is failed, and I may as well wait death where my unburied bones shall whiten my native soil, as go to seek him in a land of foreigners and a house of famine. What a trial had faith here? and what a triumph? He cast himself on one whom we shall see, gaunt with famine, coming from a house where she has left her dying boy, to gather a few sticks for their last earthly meal; and so doing, Elijah, acting by faith and not by sight, laid the burden on Him who says, Cast thy burden upon the Lord, and he shall sustain thee.

III. Let us learn faith and confidence from the prophet's example—following "them who through faith and patience inherit the promises."

The distant ranges of the Alps or the Andes, on first coming into view, appear but snow-wreaths left by departing winter. The nearer we approach them, they rise higher, and higher, and still higher against the sky, till, resting on stupendous precipices, those snow-crowned summits seem to support the vault of heaven. This effect is often reversed in the case of the believer's trials. Formidable at a distance, dreaded when remote, the nearer his approach to them, not the greater, but the less they grow. The cloudiest day has more gleams, the barest rocks more flowers, the bitterest cup more sweetness, the darkest night more stars, than his fears allowed him to expect; the work is more easily done, the burden more easily borne, than he anticipated; he survives trials that he once thought would have crushed and killed him; and to the last and greatest trial, how applicable often are those words, "Who art thou, O great mountain? before Zerubbabel thou shalt become a plain." He has dreaded death; and death is swallowed up in victory. His latter end is peace. As I have seen the sun as he declined in the west scatter the clouds that hung over the place of his setting, and in his last hour light up heaven and earth in a blaze of glory, so faith, growing stronger as flesh grew weaker, has dissipated all the fears of the dying Christian—leaving his sun to set in a cloudless sky, and weeping friends to exclaim amid their tears, Let me die the death of the righteous, and let my last end be like his!

It happened quite otherwise, however, in the case of the prophet. Bad as it appeared to be cast for maintenance at a time of famine on a widow's help, the trial was worse than his worst fears, perhaps, anticipated — it was like going into a cavern, the further in the darker; into the sea, the further in the deeper. As has befallen others of God's people, the hour of deliverance was preceded by that of greatest trial; just as the pain of an abscess is severest before it bursts, as the darkest hour is before the dawn, and the coldest before sunrise. When the prophet left the banks of Cherith for Zarephath, hope, which often tells a flattering tale, may have suggested that the widow's circumstances might not be so poor as he had at first feared. No doubt famine raged throughout the land, but Zarephath might be an oasis in the desert, supplied with corn through the foresight of a second Joseph; what had occurred before might occur again; and, since the world is preserved for the sake of the saints, as had already happened in Egypt, the fields of the idolater might be made to feed the servants of God. Or this widow might have been left to the comforts of an ample fortune; with gold to buy bread enough even in a famine. Besides, she might have stout, and kind, and gallant sons to sustain her in her widowhood and old age; as I have seen a tree support a wall that had fallen into decay—screening with its leaves, and with its strong, tough arms holding up the stones that had lent it in former days both shelter and support.

Alas! for Elijah, as his weary steps bring him to the gate of Zarephath, if he had no better trust than that. A sight met him there to dash such hopes in the dust, shivering them like a potter's vessel. The widow is at the gate to receive her guest. It is not politeness, or kindness, or, as people meet a great visitor, respect for the man of God that brings her there; no, nor anticipation of the blessing this new burden is to bring. A spectral form, with head bent to the ground, creeps slowly along, ever and anon stretching out from beneath her cloak a skeleton arm to pick up some withered sticks. We have stood in cold and empty room to hear children cry for bread when the mother had none to give them; we have seen hunger looking out from hollow eyes and wasted cheeks, but, never perhaps, such an object as this. The skin like yellow parchment; the bony hand; the eyes sunk in their sockets, whence they emit an unearthly glare; the hollow cheeks; the sepulchral voice; the wasted form, seen sharp through scanty rags; the slow, tottering gait—these bespoke a victim of the famine. And while Elijah gazes on her with mingled emotions of pity and horror, the voice of God is in his ear, saying, Behold the widow woman whom I have commanded to sustain thee!

Was God mocking him when, with finger pointing to this bruised reed, he said, Lean your weight on that? Was it for this he had brought him, buoyed him up with hope, to Zarephath? How did it look as if God were saying to him, as he shall say to his enemies on that day when, having rejected Christ, they find no refuge from impending wrath, I "will laugh at your calamity; I will mock when your fear cometh." What a trial was here! Elijah asks a morsel of bread. Bread? God help her! She ha none; her haggard aspect and hollow tones correspond too well with her terrible apology, for him to doubt its truth, " As the Lord thy God liveth, I have not a cake, but an handful of meal in a barrel, and a little oil in a cruse ; and, behold, I am gathering two sticks, that I may go in and dress it for me and my son, that we may eat it, and die." How great the faith that staggered not under this blow, but strengthening with the trial, and believing impossibilities, in tones of cheerfulness to which she had been long a stranger, replied, Fear not ; go and do as thou hast said ; but make me thereof a little cake first, and bring it unto me, and after make for thee and for thy son. For thus saith the Lord God of Israel, The barrel of meal shall not waste, neither shall the cruse of oil fail, until the day that the Lord sendeth rain upon the earth.

And why should not we face our trials and difficulties, whatever they may be, with Elijah's faith? These things were written not for our entertainment, but for our instruction ; not so much for our admiration as for our admonition. Let them teach us, saints and sinners both, to place unbounded trust in every passage and promise of God's word that suits our circumstances —to venture our souls upon them. No doubt Elijah, having much in God's past dealings to sustain his faith, could say with David, I will remember the years of the right hand of the most High. He who made the wild ravens serve him could make poverty sustain him. The man who had seen these shy birds sweeping past their nests and clamorous young to lay their plunder at his feet, and wait at his table as dutiful and familiar servants, might look on this gaunt and ghastly widow to trust her for bread—leaning his whole weight on a support frail as the thread of a spider's web. But have we not grounds of trust in God as good and strong as he had? He has given his Son for us—his own beloved Son to die for us. The eye that saw the ravens desert their brood to cater for a hungry prophet, saw no proof of kindness and power and love to compare with Calvary's bloody cross. Miracles we do not look for: but that God, if you will truly and earnestly seek him, will forgive your sins for Jesus' sake; that whosoever believeth in his Son shall never perish; that he will cast out none that come to him; that he will save you now, and just as you are; that he will shut the door in no man's face; that he will make his grace sufficient for you, and perfect his strength in your weakness; that with or without miracles he will make good every promise in his word —these are truths I cannot doubt. All blessings which the Father has promised, and the Son has purchased, the Spirit is ready to bestow. He who spared not his own Son, shall he not with him freely give you all things? Now then, "Arise, be up and doing;" and whether your sins call you to the fountain of blood, or your sorrows to the fountain of consolation, or your weakness to the fountain of strength, "arise," as I can fancy Elijah rose, and, leaving Cherith's dry bed

L

behind, took his way to Zarephath; and as he went beguiled the road and woke the echoes of the lonely valleys with such songs as these—

> "The lions young may hungry be,
>   And they may lack their food;
> But they that truly seek the Lord
>   Shall not lack any good.

> "Oh! taste and see that God is good;
>   Who trusts in him is bless'd.
> Fear God his saints; none that him fear
>   Shall be with want oppress'd."

X.

THE TRUE TEST.

"The tree is known by its fruit."—MATT. xii. 33.

THERE are various kinds of knowledge; nor, not
withstanding the adage, "A little knowledge is
a dangerous thing," is there any kind or measure of
it without its value. I would sit at the feet of the
humblest man to learn what he knew and I did not.
The most important thing, however, to know, is one's
self, although, I may remark, no man can know his
own character aright, without first making himself acquainted with that of God. It is in his light that we
see light clearly. Hence it was not till Job had obtained full and clear views of the holiness, purity, and
providence of God, that he formed a just estimate of
himself—exclaiming, I had heard of thee with the
hearing of the ear, but now mine eye seeth thee:
wherefore I abhor myself, and repent in dust and
ashes.

To an ingenuous youth who sought his advice as
to the course of study he should pursue, and what
knowledge he should seek first to obtain, an old
Greek sage replied, Know thyself! No Christian

could have given a better answer. What a miserable thing it is for a man to know how to make money, and make it too—to know science so well that he is familiar with the secrets of nature, can measure the distance of a star, and follow a wandering comet on its fiery track—to know statesmanship so well that his country, in a crisis of her affairs, might call him to the helm, as before all others the pilot that could weather the storm,—and yet not to know whether he is at peace with God; whether, should he die to-night, he is saved or lost; is going to heaven or to hell! I undervalue no knowledge; but were I lying in jail under sentence of death, and, having got no answer to my application for mercy, did not know whether I was to be spared or to be hanged to-morrow, what would I care about the discovery of a new planet or new metal, a change of ministry, the rise or fall of prices, the rise or fall of kingdoms? The one question which would interest me, now awakening my hopes and now my gloomiest apprehensions, would be this: Am I saved? or, What shall I do to be saved? But we all lie under sentence of condemnation—death has passed on all men, because all have sinned. And so, though through a Christian profession we have a name to live, yet we may in fact be dead—dead in the eye of the law; and in such circumstances, I say with the Greek, that, to know ourselves, to know what we are and where we are, is of all knowledge the most important. If there shall be no more salvation out

of Christ on a day of judgment than there was found
out of the ark on that day when the avenging waters
pursued the shrieking crowd to the tops of the highest
hills, and washed off the last living man from the last
dry spot of land, how important for us to know
whether we are in Christ—united to him, not in name
and by profession only, but by faith, in deed, and in
truth! To try this, we have a plain and infallible test
in these words of our Lord, The tree is known by its
fruit. On this subject I remark—

I. It is possible to ascertain our real state and
character.

In the Southern Hemisphere, where the plants and
animals present some remarkable resemblances to
those which lived and died and were entombed in the
rocks before man's appearance on the earth, a strange
creature lives, that seems half bird, half quadruped ;
and, rooted to the rocks of our own shores, in the
briny pools that are left by each receding tide, we
find objects, in point of colour and form, beautiful as
any of the ornaments of our gardens—of such a character, that many would be puzzled to settle whether
they are most nearly, as flowers of the deep, allied to
the sea-weeds which wave over them, or to those
animals which, in every shape and size, from shrimps
to whales, have their home in the ocean. In the fields
of nature are birds that always walk and never fly, and
quadrupeds that always fly and never walk; plants

that, sensitive like animals, shrink from the touch, and animals that, fixed like a tree to the rock, live, die, and decay on the spot of their birth ; flowers that might be readily mistaken for butterflies, with painted, fluttering wings, just alighted on the plant, and insects which it is impossible at first sight to distinguish, some from green, and others from withered leaves. He who, though a God, not of confusion, but of order, delights in variety, has so linked together the vegetable and animal kingdoms, and also their various departments, that many objects might be placed in the hands of a peasant, nor could he tell whether they were plants or animals, or to what section of these two great kingdoms they belonged. There is no such difficulty when we attempt to settle the question whether we belong to the one or the other of those two grand classes into which all mankind, kings and beggars, men and women, white skins and dark skins, may be divided. A broad line, like the gulf that separates heaven from hell, divides saints and sinners. Addressing the latter, a saint of God may say, as Abraham did to the rich man in torment, "Between us and you there is a great gulf fixed, so that they which would pass from hence to you cannot ;" yet, thank God, he can add, Unlike yon gulf which no bridge of mercy spans, you can pass to us that would come from thence.

Unless Scripture is a mockery and its figures have no meaning whatever, it is not impossible, nor should it even be difficult, to determine our spiritual state, now and at once. Who has any difficulty in settling whether it is day or night: whether he enjoys sound health or pines on a bed of sickness: whether he is a free man or a slave? No man could mistake a Briton, sitting under the tree of liberty which was planted by the hands of our fathers and watered with their blood, for the negro who stands up weeping in the auction mart, to be sold with his master's cattle, or crouches in the rice swamp, bleeding under his master's lash. Degraded by a system that curses both man and master, the black man may be content to eat the bread and wear the brand of bondage. Still he, as much as we do, knows the difference between fetters and freedom; he feels that he is a slave, and I feel that I am free: even so may we know whether we belong to the class of saints or to that of sinners— for sin is darkness, sickness, bondage. What plainer evidence of this could be desired than these words, "The tree is known by his fruit." That is a fact with which we are all familiar. To stock the garden with fruit-trees, I repair to the nursery, but not in spring when all are robed alike in green; nor in summer when the bad equally with the best are covered with a flush of blossoms: it is when the corn turns yellow, and sheaves stand in the stubble fields, and fair blossoms are gone, and withered leaves sail through the air and strew the ground—it is in autumn I go to select the trees, judging them by their fruit. **And** as certainly—may I not say as easily?—as the tree is known by his fruit, may we know our spiritual state and character, if we will only be honest, nor act like the merchant who, suspecting his affairs to be verging on bankruptcy, shuts his eyes to the danger; takes no stock, and strikes no balance.

How otherwise could any man lay his head in peace on his pillow: go to sleep when he did not know but that the next time he opened his eyes it should be in hell? This would be a dreadful state in which to pass our life. In such circumstances, where were the pleasures of piety, the peace of God that passeth understanding, the triumphs of a Christian's dying hours? If death be, as some say, and as it must be if it is impossible to know our state, "a leap in the dark," what madness his who stands on the brink of another world, not shrinking, trembling, hesitating, but singing, O death, where is thy sting? O grave, where is thy victory? I do not aver that all God's people enjoy a full assurance of salvation. Still, unless a man can, by the witness of God's Spirit with his own, attain to some good hope that he has passed through grace from death to life, that the sentence of condemnation has been annulled, that his sins have been forgiven, that he has been reconciled to God through the blood of Jesus Christ, that a crown and mansion are waiting for him above the skies, how, in the name of reason, could he rejoice and be exceeding glad? The thing is impossible. He could not; any more than the

seaman can when his ship is driving on a lee shore
and he has dropped his last anchor, until, brought up,
she swings round on the very edge of foaming breakers,
rides on the top of the billows, and with her bow to
the storm. His anchor holds, and he knows that he
is safe: and, blessed be God, we also have hope as
an anchor of the soul both sure and steadfast, which
entereth into that which is within the veil.

II. Our religious profession is not always a test of
our state.

1. It may be a test in certain circumstances.

Look, for example, at two men on parade! They
wear the same dress and arms: and both, the result
of drill and discipline, have acquired such a martial
air that you cannot tell which is the hero and which
the coward. But change the scene! Leave the parade
ground for the field of battle! and when, as bugles
sound the charge, I see, through clouds of smoke
and amid the clash of arms, the sword of one flashing,
and his plume dancing in the very front of the fight,
while his comrade, pale and paralysed with fear, is
only borne forward in the tumult like a sea-weed on
the rushing billow,—how easy now to tell beneath
whose martial dress there beats a soldier's heart?
Or take, for another example, two houses that stand
on the banks of the same stream. Under a cloudless
sky, amid the calm of the glen in a summer day, with
no sound falling on the ear but the bleatings of the

flock, the baying of a sheep-dog, the muffled sound of a distant waterfall, the gentle murmur of the shallow waters over their pebbly bed, each house in its smiling garden offers, to one weary of the din and dust of cities, an equally pleasant and, to appearance, an equally secure retreat. But let the weather change : and after brewing for hours, from out the darkness that has deepened into an ominous and frightful gloom, let the storm burst ! Suddenly, followed by a crash like that of falling skies, a stream of lightning, dazzling the eye, glares out : and now the war of elements begins. Peal rolls on peal : flash follows flash : and to the roar of incessant thunders is added the rush of a deluge, and the hoarse voices of a hundred streams that leap foaming from hill and rock down into the bed of the river. Red, rolling, swelling, it bursts its dykes, overflows all its banks, and, attacking the foundations of both houses, breaches the walls of one, and at length tumbles the whole fabric, all of a heap, into the roaring flood : and while the houseless family that had fled from its rocking walls gather, shivering, on a neighbouring height to see where once stood their pleasant home only the rush and hear only the roar of waters,—how easy, as we look on the other, erect, and defiant in this wide-spread sea, to know that the one had been built on sand, but the other founded on a rock.

So, though the profession does not prove the possession of religion in a time of peace, shew me a man, like the house standing its ground against the sweep of floods, or the soldier following his colours into the thick of battle, who holds fast the profession of his faith in the face of obloquy, of persecution, of death itself, and there is little room to doubt that his piety is genuine—that he has the root of the matter in him. I care nothing for Hosannas when accompanied by crowds who cast their clothes on the dusty road and rend the air with acclamations—Jesus, enjoying a gleam of popularity, seems marching to a crown—the tongues that cry, Hosanna! to-day, changing their note, may cry, Crucify him! to-morrow. But who, not turning with the turning tide, like the blessed women that lamented and bewailed him, follows our Lord to the cross, goes without the camp bearing his reproach, is tested in a fire which only gold can stand. What are these which are arrayed in white robes? and whence came they? These are they, is the reply, which came out of great tribulation, and have washed their robes, and made them white in the blood of the Lamb. Therefore are they before the throne of God, and serve him night and day in the temple: and he that sitteth on the throne shall dwell among them. They shall hunger no more, neither thirst any more: neither shall the sun light on them, nor any heat. For the Lamb which is in the midst of the throne shall feed them, and shall lead them unto living fountains of waters: and God shall wipe away all tears from their eyes.

2. The profession of religion is not a test of the reality of religion in our times.

I should be sorry to believe that no man could be a lover of Jesus Christ who did not go to the table of communion to commemorate his death. Some go there who should not : and some, restrained from the enjoyment of that blessed ordinance by unsound views of its nature, or of their own qualifications, do not go who should. I would be sorry also to believe that a man cannot be a true, unless he is also a bold Christian, and makes a fearless profession of piety. Elijah did indeed buckle on his armour and stand forth alone —openly confronting the vengeance of the crown and hatred of the people. Yet, concealed from the public eye, and unknown even to this brave defender of the faith, God had seven thousand men in Israel with knees that had never bowed to Baal, and mouths that had never kissed him. In later times Nicodemus sought an interview with our Lord under the cloud of night, and Joseph of Arimathea was a believer some time before he openly avowed it. Like flowers which close their leaves whenever it rains, or birds that seek shelter and their nests when storms rise, there are Christians so timid by natural constitution, that they shrink from scorn, and could as soon face a battery of cannon as the jeers and laughter of the ungodly.

Granting this, still it is true, that where there is no profession of serious religion, we have little reason to expect its reality. We may say of it what Solomon said of the contentious woman who proclaims her presence in house or hamlet by her loud, sharp tongue, Whosoever hideth her hideth the wind, and hideth the ointment of his right hand, which bewrayeth itself. Out of the abundance of the heart, as our Lord says, the mouth speaketh. What is in will be out; there being always some seam through which the water will leak, some chink through which the light will shine. A look, a word, will disclose the secret; and sometimes a devout man by his silence more even than by his words will proclaim himself. So that, as no man could enter a company with ointment in his hand, but, however close he held his fist, the fragrance would oose through his fingers, a true, hearty, genuine piety will reveal itself notwithstanding that an attempt may be made to conceal it, and that the humble saint has none of that courage which won for Knox, from the lips of an enemy, this brave eulogium, There lies one who never feared the face of man.

But if a man can have no piety who makes no profession of it, it is still more plain that the scoffers have none, who ridicule zealous Christians, as hypocrites or fanatics, Pharisees or fools. Such profane scoffers have no more love to Christ than had the iron-hearted and iron-handed men who pressed the thorns into his bleeding brow, and casting over his mangled form an old purple robe, made a mock of the Lord of glory. Whether it has been a cup of water, held to the dying lips **of a poor** saint, **or a** sneer flung **at a** disciple's head, Jesus shall say, Inasmuch as ye have done it unto one of the least of these, my brethren, ye have done it unto me.

Perhaps there never was a time when the mere profession of religion was a less satisfactory test of its reality than at present. There have been dark and evil days, and these not long gone, when religion was, if I may so express myself, at a discount : piety was not fashionable : profane swearing and deep drinking were the accomplishments of a gentleman ; the man who assembled his household for prayer was accounted a hypocrite, the woman who did so a fool : missionary societies were repudiated by the courts of the Church, and eyed with suspicion by the officers of the Crown ; Robert Haldane was denied an opportunity of consecrating his fortune to the cause of Christ in India ; Carey and Marshman, while seeking to convert the Hindoos, were driven from the British territories, and had to seek protection from a foreign Power ; and such as formed missionary associations launched them on society with the anxieties and prayers of her who, cradling her infant in an ark of bulrushes, committed him to the waters of the Nile and the providence of her God. Power, rank, fashion, science, literature, and mammon were all arrayed in arms against everything that appeared in the form, and breathed the spirit of a devoted piety.

Thank God, it is not so now ! He has touched the

heart of the Egyptian, and she has adopted the outcast as her son. From holes and caves of the earth,
religion has found her way into palaces and the mansions of the great and noble. Science has become a
priestess at her altar. Literature has courted her
alliance. Infidelity assumes even a Christian-like dis-
guise. Iniquity, as ashamed, is made to hide her face.
The tide has turned ; and those who now make a profession of zealous and active piety, find themselves no
longer opposed to the stream and spirit of the age.
This is a subject of gratitude. Yet it suggests caution
in judging of ourselves ; and warns us to take care,
since a profession of religion is rather fashionable
than otherwise, that in making it we are not the creatures of fashion, but new creatures in Jesus Christ.
When the crown sat on the head of Mordecai, and he
himself sat on the royal steed, and Haman walked at
his bridle rein as he rode the streets of Shushan in royal
state—heralds proclaiming, " Thus it shall be done to
the man whom the king delighteth to honour," the
Jew knew right well to what he owed the reverence
paid him by many a supple Persian. And when religion rides through the land in triumph, many will
bend the knee, shew her respect, and do her reverence,
who would pass her in haughty scorn were she sitting
at the porter's gate. Hence the necessity for trying
ourselves by such a test as my text suggests. The
tree is known, not by its leaves, nor we by our pro-
fessions ; not by its blossoms, nor we by the promises

of which they are lovely images ; but by its fruit, and we by those things which the fruit represents—our hearts and habits, our true life and character. The tree is known by his fruit : moreover every tree that bringeth not forth good fruit is hewn down and cast into the fire.

III. The true evidence of our state is to be found in our heart and habits. The tree is known by his fruit,—by their fruits ye shall know them.

We have often sat in judgment on others. It is of more consequence that we form a right estimate of ourselves—leaving others to God; for in the words of an apostle, Who art thou that judgeth another man's servant ? to his own master he standeth or falleth. In attempting to form a correct estimate of our own state and character, in the words of the Greek sage, to know ourselves, let us bring to this solemn task all the care and the conscientiousness with which a jury weigh the evidence in a case of life and death. They return from their room to the court to give in a verdict, amid breathless silence, which sends him whom they left pale and trembling at the bar to liberty, or to the gallows ; yet, sacred as human life is, on our judgment here hangs a more momentous issue. A mistake there may send a man to the scaffold, but one here to perdition,—that involves the life of the body, this of the immortal soul. Judges sometimes find it difficult to know how to shape their charge, and juries how to shape their verdicts—the evidence is conflicting—not clear either way. The case is obscure, perplexing; perhaps a bloody mystery, from which no hand but God's can raise the veil. But light and darkness, life and death, are not more unlike than the heart and habits of believers, on the one hand, and those of unbelievers, on the other; and with such a catalogue of the works of the flesh and the fruits of the Spirit as Paul has given us, how can it be difficult for a man to settle under which of these two classes his are to be ranked—with which they most closely correspond? The works of the flesh, says the apostle, are manifest, Adultery, fornication, uncleanness, lasciviousness, idolatry, witchcraft, hatred, variance, emulations, wrath, strife, seditions, heresies, envyings: murders, drunkenness, revellings, and such like. But the fruit of the Spirit is love, joy, peace: long-suffering, gentleness: goodness, faith, meekness, temperance. A man may fancy himself possessed of talents which he has not, and a woman of beauty which she has not. But with all our strong bias to form a favourable and flattering opinion of ourselves, each "to think more highly of himself than he ought to think," it seems as impossible for a man who is an adulterer, a fornicator, unclean, a drunkard, whose bosom burns with unholy and hateful passions, to imagine himself virtuous, as to mistake night for day, a bloated, fetid corpse, for one in the bloom and rosy beauty of her youth. In regard to these tests, let me

M

also remark, we are to look for a correspondence be tween them and our hearts and habits : for no more Few have plunged into such excess of wickedness as to have their lives characterised by all these works of the flesh ; for there is a moderation in vice as well as in virtue ; and some vices, as one class of weeds eradi- cates another, unfit a man for indulging in other vices. Nor, on the other hand, are you to expect to find in any one all these fruits of the Spirit in luxuriant and equal abundance ; still as he who is but a child in sin is still a child of the devil, he is a son of God who is but a babe in grace.

It is only often by a careful application of delicate tests that the chemist discovers a deadly poison or a precious metal ; but how easy is it by a few simple questions to bring out our real character ! Have you suffered a heavy wrong, for example, at the hands of another ? You remember it. But where ? Is it at the throne of grace ; and to pray with him whose blood fell alike on the head of foe and friend, Father forgive them, they know not what they do ? Again, are you asked to contribute money to the cause of Christ ? while some calculate how little they can give to satisfy their conscience and meet the expectations of society, do you calculate how much you can spare for that blessed Saviour who did not spare himself for you ? Again, when tempted to sin, while some wish there were no hell to deter them from the un bridled enjoyment of its pleasures, do you rather long for that pure, blessed heaven, where there entereth nothing to hurt or to defile? Again, when you see transgressors, is it with indifference, or with somewhat of the feelings of him who said, I saw transgressors and was grieved—rivers of waters ran down mine eyes, because they keep not thy law, O Lord? Again, when you think of perishing souls, is yours the spirit of Cain, or of Christ? can you no more stand by with folded hands to see sinners perishing than men drowning? are you moved by such generous impulse as draws the hurrying crowd to the pool where one is sinking, and moves some brave man, at the jeopardy of life, to leap in and pluck him from the jaws of death? There is no better evidence that we have received the nature as well as the name of Christ, than an anxious wish to save lost souls, and a sympathy with the joy of angels over every sinner that is converted. Let me illustrate this by two examples — pictures drawn from life.

Years ago, and in a parish which I knew, there lived a woman notorious in the neighbourhood for profane swearing, habits of drunkenness, and manners rude; coarse as well as irreligious. She feared not God, neither regarded man; and trained up her children for the devil. One evening she happened to be within ear-shot of a preacher; and as he was emptying his quiver among the crowd, an arrow from the bow drawn at a venture was lodged in her heart. Remarkable example of free, sovereign, subduing grace! she was converted. Her case, as much as that of the thief on the cross, of the jailor at Philippi, o. Saul on his way to Damascus, was one of instant conversion—day burst on her soul without a dawn. She hastened home. She found her family asleep, and saw in each child a never-dying soul, that her own hand had rocked into deeper, fatal slumbers. Seized with an intense desire to have them saved, she could not delay the matter till to-morrow; and so, rushing on the sleepers as if the bed beneath them had been in flames, she shook them, woke them, crying, Arise, call upon thy God! And there at the midnight hour, with her children kneeling round her, her eyes streaming with tears, her voice trembling with emotion, did that poor mother cry to God, that he would have mercy also on them, and pluck these brands from the burning.

Near by the dwelling where a mother roused her children from their beds to flee, not from a house on fire, but from the fire that is never quenched, stood the cottage of one whose joy over a converted sinner carried us away to the heavens, where angels rejoice over one sinner that repenteth. He had long been a Christian; not so his wife, from whose side he had often stolen in the dead of night to pray for her salvation. He continued instant in prayer. Mothers, sisters, all who carry others in their prayers to the throne of grace, Pray on! God's time to answer—the time to favour her at length came. She was smitten; seized with anxiety; pierced with convictions; but she could find no peace. She walked in darkness and had no light; and giving herself up for lost, once said, for instance, when her husband and she had lain down for sleep, If you should die before to-morrow, it will be happy for you; if I should, farewell, an everlasting farewell—I shall open my eyes in torment! But the time of her redemption drew nigh. She had sown in tears, and was to reap in joy. A minister hearing of her distress, went to visit her. She was in the garden. Her husband left the house to call her. Who seeks me? she asked. Without forethought, as if the words had fallen from heaven on his lips, he replied, Jesus Christ seeks you! She started: an ashy paleness overspread her face: and, deeply affected, she followed him in silence to the house. There the man of God held up before her a bleeding, dying, loving, Saviour. Prayer followed, and praise followed prayer; for while they entreated God with strong crying and tears, the grave opened, and she that was dead came forth—to say, I confess that Jesus is the Lord, and to sing with Mary, My soul doth magnify the Lord; and my spirit hath rejoiced in God my Saviour; for he hath regarded the low estate of his handmaiden—he that is mighty hath done to me great things, and holy is his name. And what did you do? I asked the husband. Do, sir? he replied; I sprang to my feet; I clasped her in my arms; I exclaimed, This is our marriage day; and unable to restrain my joy, I cried

Hosanna to the Son of David! Praise him, all ye his angels; praise him, sun, moon, and stars; praise him, all ye orbs of light!

By their fruits ye shall know them. Grapes do not grow on thorns, nor figs on thistles—nor such fruits in any but renewed hearts. So to feel proves what no profession can, that the same mind is in us that was in Jesus Christ: nor is there room to doubt that if you bear such saintly and heavenly fruit, you are one with him who, communicating the influences of the Spirit to his people, as the tree does its sap to the boughs, hath said, I am the Vine; ye are the branches. Abide in me, and I in you.

XI.

SPIRITUAL VISION.

"Open thou mine eyes, that I may behold wondrous things
out of thy law."—PSALM cxix. 18.

THERE is a baronial castle in our country lost in
the bosom of a hoary wood, that stands, in its
lonely desertion, a picture of the family whose arms
are still seen on its mouldering walls, and whose
fortunes have fallen into a like decay. Many a wild
legend is told about this old pile by the country people
around their hearths on the long nights of winter.
They say that strange sounds, now cries of violence,
and now peals of laughter, are still heard in these
dismantled halls, and that belated travellers have seen
a female form, in antique attire, walking in the moon-
light on the mossy lawn, or gazing out of these empty
windows—one whose crimes deny her poor bones the
rest of the grave.

Among other strange things, they tell an incident
which is not only credible, but true. It befell one
generation of the family that, to the inexpressible
disappointment and grief of his parents, the eldest
child, their son and heir, was born deaf; sadder still,

so was the next; the third, also—one deaf mute succeeding another, till the cradle, where no lullaby was sung, and the nursery, where no merry laughter mingled with the pattering of little feet, were like the hand of an avenging Providence. The story goes that, after this, at the birth of each succeeding child, the father, devoured by anxiety, and impatient to know the best or worst, was wont to enter the natal chamber, and, while he turned a look of dread on his infant, to discharge fire-arms close by its ear. He sought to know, by its stillness or sudden start, whether the curse still hung over his house. Unhappy man! Yet still more unhappy father, all whose children are born blind! Unless to see them all lying around in their shrouds, a more touching sight you cannot fancy than a whole family stone-blind, from the eldest to the infant that sits prattling on a mother's knee—as unconscious of its misfortune as one that, brought to receive a mother's last embrace, smiles in her face, or one that laughs as she presses it to her bosom when their ship, taking the last lurch, is going down into the deep. Keenly alive as we are to the evils of a bodily infirmity, and ready, like the woman in the Gospel, who spent all that she had to be healed, to pay any money to cure a child's blindness, or to suffer any operation to remove our own—such a sight would sadden us. And it is sad to think, leaving the regions of fancy for facts, that there are a million of our fellow creatures blind, many of whom never saw the sun, nor saw a father's face, nor were ever cheered by a mother's smile. Yet, were we as sensible to spiritual as to natural evils, we should feel that a far greater calamity lies on us, and on our children. It may give us no trouble. Blind ourselves, we may be as insensible to their wants as to our own. Still, there is no parent who may not say of his child what they said to whose son our Saviour had imparted sight—"We know that he was born blind." Blindness to the things of the spiritual world lies by nature on us all. Having eyes, we see not, and ears, we hear not ; therefore, unless we would miss the way to heaven, and go stumbling over into hell, what need have we to go to Jesus with this prayer, Open thou mine eyes, that I may behold wondrous things out of thy law.

I. We are all born spiritually blind.

When Samson, too confident in himself, ventured on temptation, he fell into the snare of the Philistines. As if ignorant, that, to use the words of Solomon, "A whore is a deep ditch, and a strange woman is a narrow pit," he trusted his paramour ; and disclosing the secret of his mighty strength, was shorn of his locks. She sold him ; and he had nothing else to expect at such hands. The loss of vigour follows loss of virtue ; and he, like others from whom the Lord has departed, became an easy prey to his enemies. With no pity for fallen greatness, they triumphed over their once dreaded foe, heaping insults on his head. But his

locks might grow again, and strength return to the
broad shoulders over which they fell like a lion's
mane? In that case he may escape; and once free,
burning with rage and breathing vengeance, woe to
Delilah, to her house and people! They took effectual means to prevent this. They put out his eyes—
with these quenching their own fears and their
prisoner's hopes. And see the strong man now! poor,
blind, helpless; once the terror of men, and now the
laughing-stock of women; as a drudge, a slave, sunk
to the meanest condition; bound in fetters, he grinds
his masters' corn—his associates the lowest felons, his
home a common prison, and his lot made more bitter
by self-reproach, by remorse, by the memory of former
greatness, of happiness and honour exchanged for exile
and captivity.

What a picture of misery! and further, what a
picture of man! a mirror where unconverted men,
had they eyes to see, might behold, not Samson, but
themselves in Samson. Was he taken captive of
the Philistines?—so are they of their vices. Did he
pass his days in the service of his enemies?— slaves of
Satan, they serve one who, in the words of David,
hates them with cruel hatred. Was he bound in
fetters of brass?—what are fetters of brass or iron to
the chains of the drunkard, of the licentious, of the
miser, of the lover of this world? Was he blinded as
well as bound?—so are they. "Eyes have they, but
they see not;" "the god of this world," as St Paul

says, "hath blinded the minds of them which believe not ;" they are insensible to their state. But here fails the parallel. Samson felt his degradation keenly ; longed for liberty ; poured many a tear from those sightless eyes ; strained at his chain ; groped about to find a door of escape ; cursed his folly ; hated the thought of Delilah, and would, I believe, have struck her down had she come within his reach. How different the poor sinner ! He hugs his chain, and delights in the vices that enslave him ; to Christ's cry, Behold, I have set before thee an open door, he does not leap up, but turns away his ear ; and, as if he had lost his sense as well as his sight, in prison, in captivity, in misery, awaiting a dreadful doom, he says, " I am rich, and increased with goods, and have need of nothing," at the very time God is saying, " Thou art wretched, and miserable, and poor, and blind, and naked."

When man lost his innocence, he lost also his sight. Blindness is the effect of sin. Hence the appropriate-ness of the figure, so common in Scripture, which compares sin to leprosy—that foulest and deadliest of diseases. At its first appearance but a small spot on the brow, it spreads betimes over all the body ; covering its victim with a universal sore, and eating its way at length into the very seat of life. Isaiah's picture of a man or nation sunk in sin was no fancy sketch. A leper stood for this portrait ; " the whole head is sick, and the whole heart faint. From the sole of the foot even unto the head there is no soundness in it; but wounds, and bruises, and putrefying sores." As this hideous malady extends its ravages, the fingers and toes and limbs rot off, till little else remains but a mutilated trunk; within which, the eyes also eaten out, the miserable victim drags on a wretched existence in total, hopeless blindness. Even so sin affects the whole man, and destroys the image of God, as a cancer does the beauty of the sweetest face and finest form—making us as loathsome as once we were lovely in the sight of God and holy angels. Proud man may revolt from the portrait; but that does not prove it to be exaggerated. It is not untrue, because it is abhorrent. Abhorrent? who ever got their eyes opened to see themselves but they abhorred themselves—saying, with one who was no profligate or prodigal, but the best and most upright of men, even Job himself: "I have heard of thee by the hearing of the ear; but now mine eye seeth thee: wherefore I abhor myself, and repent in dust and ashes."

II. Leaving now the cause, let us consider some of the characteristics of this blindness.

Blindness deprives its subjects of many pleasures which God's goodness lavishes on us, and, through our eyes, pours into our hearts. To them the sun has no brightness; the meadow no gay flowers; the great vault of heaven no stars; and, worst of all, the faces that are beaming love on them are blank, without expression. In heaven the saints have no night, but on earth the blind have no day; only darkness; night unchanging, endless night.

Blindness makes the condition of its subjects one of painful dependence. Without his eyes, Samson was more helpless than the child who, holding his big hand, led him forward to make sport in the crowded theatre. We cannot but pity the helpless blind; yet how often is our pity misplaced? Touched by his sorrows, the women of Jerusalem wept for Jesus; yet had more cause to weep for themselves. Our blood boiling with indignation at the story of his cruel wrongs, we demand freedom for the slave; and yet may be greater slaves ourselves than one whose limbs are manacled, but whose soul is free. And on some who regard them with gentle pity, the blind, enjoying heaven's light within, might turn their sightless balls to say with Jesus, Weep not for me, but weep for yourselves. Oh, what blindness so deep, so dark, so incurable, so miserable, so fatal, as that of sin? as yours, unless you have been brought from death to life—out of darkness into marvellous light? And yet so general is spiritual blindness, that "darkness covereth the earth, and gross darkness the people."

Blindness exposes its subjects to deception. Look into that tent where, with head silvered and eyes dimmed through age, an old man sits, as with trembling hands he bestows the blessing on a son who eyes him with cunning look, and to his suspicious touch offers neck and arms masked with a borrowed skin.

The voice is Jacob's, but the hands are Esau's; and so, lulling Isaac's suspicions, and passing for the elder brother, the younger takes cruel advantage of the old man's blindness, to steal a brother's birthright and a father's blessing. A case of theft, the basest, and most cruel, that crime dogged the good man's heels through life, onward to his grave! Yet, in its direful consequences this foul trick is not to be men-tioned with the deceptions which the devil practises on men. Taking advantage of their blindness, their cruel enemy passes himself off as a friend—forsooth the friend of sinners. Believe the smiling fiend, and he would not hurt you, but rather minister to your happiness; you shall not surely die; life has time to sin now and repent afterwards; nor is God the just, righteous, and exacting judge your fears and your ministers repre-sent. And thus Satan makes thousands believe that all is right, that the path they tread is one of safety, when all the while, step by step, down, but gently down, he conducts his blind, deluded, singing, dancing, joyous victims on to the brink of ruin, and to that last, fatal step which plunges them into hell.

Again, blindness exposes us to danger. Provided the monster does not growl, a blind man will walk right into a lion's den. Though scared by the flood whose hoarse and angry roar warns him back, he will step into a dark and silent pool. He will linger on the sands around which the tide is stealing, till the waters wash his feet; and, all retreat cut off by deep lagoons, he has no answer to the friendly voices of the shore but the words of one who died in despair, Too late, too late! Shew a child a flower of brightest hues, heedless as childhood is, he plucks it not, but starts back in horror—his eyes have met those of a serpent, gleaming from out its painted leaves. But, tempted by its fragrance, the blind man stoops to pluck, and stung, he dies—he scented the odour, but saw not the serpent. A blind man will starve with bread within his reach; parched and perishing with thirst, he will pass the well that invites his lips to drink; drowning, with a rope thrown within his grasp, and the cries of eager voices in his ear, Lay hold of life! he will sink into a watery grave—lost, when he might have been saved. Such is the case of the unconverted! Who so blind as sinners? May God open their eyes! Oh, if they saw the hatefulness of sin and the beauty of Jesus, the danger of their souls and their great need of salvation, if they were other than blind, stone-blind, how would they pause in their career; and like one who, the mist suddenly opening to reveal his true position, starts with horror to see his feet on the dreadful brink, the very edge of a precipice, how would sinners, with eyes open to the greatness of their jeopardy, turn at the cry God is now sounding in all our ears, Turn ye, turn ye from your evil ways; for why will ye die, O house of Israel.

III. The eyes of the blind being opened, they behold wondrous things out of the law of God.

There was an eminent philosopher who had devoted a lifetime to the pursuits of science, and not, as he thought, in vain. She had crowned his brow with laurels, and inscribed his name in the temple of fame. In the evening of his days, at the eleventh hour, God was pleased to call him, open his eyes, convert him; and now, he who was deeply read in science and conversant with its loftiest speculations, as he bent his gray head over the Bible, (the law spoken of in the text,) declared that, if he had his life to live over again, he would spend it in the study of the Word of God. He felt like a miner, who, after toiling long and to little purpose in search of gold, with one stroke of his pick-axe lays open a vein of the precious metal and becomes rich at once—the owner of a vein that grows the richer the deeper the mine is driven. Such a treasure the Bible offers to those whose eyes God has opened to its wonders of grace and glory. It is inexhaustible. The further, leaving the shore with its sounding beach and shallow waters, you go out to sea, the deeper it grows; the higher you climb a hill, the wider grows the prospect of rolling land, and liquid plain; the deeper, at least in some instances, the shaft is sunk into the bowels of the earth, richer minerals reward your labour. Even so, the further and the longer we pursue our investigations into divine truth, and study the Bible, the more it grows in interest and in value. The devout Christian discovers new beauties every

day. We never tire of its pages; at every new reading we make new discoveries, and its truths are
always as fresh as new-blown roses which nobody
ever tires smelling, as each morning brings them
out blushing red and bathed in dew. Only let a
man's eyes be opened, and such wondrous things
will be seen in the Bible that he would part with
all his books rather than with that, esteeming it better
not only than any, but than all of them, and deeming those his best hours of study which were spent in
exploring the mysteries and mercies of redeeming love.

Some may regard this as little better than raving.
With Bibles, to use Whitfield's words, on whose dust
you might write damnation, put aside for the newspaper or the novel, they have no sympathy with this.
How can they have? In the words of the prophet,
They seeing, see not; and hearing, they hear not;
neither do they understand. The ancients tell of one
who played such exquisite music, that his skill drew
the birds from the sky, even serpents from their holes;
and gathered round him in strange companionship
and silent wonder the wild beasts of the field and
forest. Suppose this were no fable, and that, lyre in
hand, Orpheus were to walk our streets; stopping
the rushing tide of men and business, as the waters
were stayed in Jordan's bed. These notes fall on the
ears of the deaf as on those of the dead , the mute
passes by, let the charmer charm never so wisely—his
only wonder what arrests the gaping crowd, or what
they see to admire in these fingers that run up and

down the strings.   He thinks, as people with no musical ear are inclined to do, on seeing an assembly thrown into raptures by some grand melody, that, as Felix said of Paul, and the world is apt to say of sincere and ardent Christians, they are mad—beside themselves.

Now, as the deaf have no sympathy with those that hear, the blind have none with those that see.   On the wall of a church, for example, in a foreign town, there hangs a wonderful painting of Christ's last hours on the cross; with a countenance full of love, of the deepest awe, and greatest sorrow, John is gazing on the spectacle, while our Lord's mother, supported by Mary Magdalene, lies fainting at his feet.   On the curtain being rolled up that covers it, you cannot speak; you cannot take off your eyes; you forget the painter in the painting; and some such emotions of awe, pity, and wonder take possession of you as seized on the centurion, who feeling the earth quake, and hearing the cry of Calvary, declared as he left the scene, Truly this was the Son of God.   Yet take one of the blind mendicants who, cap in hand, beg by that old cathedral door, and set him before the pic ture; unveil its wonders before his sightless eyeballs, and he stands as unmoved as the cold, hard, stony pillar on which the canvas hangs.   Or, from the works of man, take the blind out to those of God. Guide him by the shore when the ocean shines like a silver mirror, or long white lines of breakers curl and foam on the sands, or the billows, swelling as they roll and bursting with the roar of thunder, fling themselves in sheets of snow on the rugged cliffs; or lead him forth on a winter night, when a thousand stars are sparkling in the frosty sky; or take him on a summer day to the meadow carpeted with flowers of every form and the richest hues: he sees no wonders; not he! He only marvels at your admiration, and is disposed, as the world deals with those whose delight is in the word and service of God, to set you down for a hypocrite or a fanatic, a liar or a fool. You are neither. There are stars in heaven and flowers on earth. The man does not see them, because he is blind; and so are we, if we have no relish for the Word of God, nor see any gracious and glorious wonders there.

Open a blind man's eyes. With what amazement, admiration, happiness, overflowing joy will he gaze, nor tire gazing, on all above and around him, from the sun blazing in heaven to the tiniest flower that springs in beauty at his feet! And let God open a sinner's eyes, the Bible will seem to him a new book, and he seem to himself a new creature. Wonders! He will see his heart, and wonder at its wickedness. He will see the Saviour, and wonder at his love. He will see how God has spared him, and wonder at his long-suffering. He will see sin in its true colours, and wonder he could love a thing so vile and so detestable. He will see his own righteousness as treacherous sand, and wonder that he could have trusted to anything so bad. He will see salvation as the one thing needful, and wonder he could have taken a night's rest, ventured to close his eyes in sleep, till he had found peace with God. He will see the King in his transcendent beauty, and wonder, as he throws himself at Jesus's feet, that all the world does not do so—that all men do not go after him, saying, as he does, Jesus, thou art all my desire. Whom have I in heaven but thee? and there is none upon earth that I desire beside thee. Thou art chiefest among ten thousand, and altogether lovely!

IV. God only can open our eyes.

We need sight as well as light. Unless our eyes are opened, the Bible is of no more use to us than a lantern to a blind man in a dark night, and on a dangerous road—of no more use to us than a guide-book in Russian, Chinese, Arabic, or any other to us incomprehensible tongue—of no more use to us than the way-post, with painted finger pointing out the path to that blind beggar, who, with head erect and careful steps, comes on in the leading of a dog. To shew the pass, we raise *cairns* of weathered stones on our Highland hills, and when the way was lost, and hope with strength was sinking, as they caught sight of the rude pile looming through the mist, or rising black above the levelled snows, many have blessed the hands that raised the cairn; they owe their life to it. Abroad, among the Alps, Christianity there, modifying a custom older than itself, they substitute crosses for cairns; and where the road, leaving the gay and smiling valley, climbs into the realms of eternal winter, or is cut out of the face of precipices, down which one false step hurls the traveller into a gorge where the foaming torrent seems but a silver thread, tall crosses stand. And so, when the path is buried in the drift that spreads a treacherous crust over yawning crevice and deadly crag, he, by keeping the line of crosses, braves the tempest, and walks safely where otherwise it were death to venture. But set a blind man on such a road, and he never reaches home; the earth his bed and the snow his shroud, he sleeps the sleep that knows no waking. Now, there is a cross that points out man's way to heaven. But unless the eyes that sin sealed are open—have been opened by God to see it, and all the way-marks that mercy has set up to that happy home—our feet shall "stumble upon the dark mountains," and we shall perish for ever.

God only can do this. Hence to him David directs the prayer of my text; and also this—Lighten mine eyes, lest I sleep the sleep of death. Men use instruments to restore sight, and nowhere does surgery achieve a nobler triumph, or bestow greater blessings on mankind, than in yonder theatre, where skill and a steady hand, cut into the sightless balls; and man, opening a way for the light of heaven, imitates Christ in his divine works of might and mercy—pouring light into the blind man's eyes, and joy into the blind man's heart. God also uses instruments—his instru ment the word, his agent the Holy Spirit. By these, working faith in men, and renewing them in the spirit of their minds, he has often answered, and is now ready to answer the prayer, Open thou mine eyes.

Let me illustrate the effect of this by three examples—

First, Look at Balaam. He is urging forward a restive and unwilling steed, as unconscious of danger as many who, in the pursuit of money or pleasure, are driving headlong on ruin. Wincing under its rider's blows, why will the beast not go forward? Why does she back and plunge? Balaam sees no danger ahead, nothing on the dusty path, but the flickering sunbeams, or the shadows of the vines that trail along the walls. What makes the obstinate, unruly brute run his limb against the wall, and bring down on its own head a shower of angry blows? Nothing that Balaam sees, till the Lord, as the Bible says, opened his eyes; and then and there, right in front of him, bestriding the narrow path, stands an angel, a sword glittering in his hand. And let God open a sinner's eyes, and how he would stare and tremble to see a sight more terrible—Justice, armed with the terrors of the law, barring his way to heaven. Learning, then, that by the deeds of the law no man living shall be justified, the poor soul gladly welcomes a despised, rejected Saviour, and falls at his feet, to cry, Lord, save me, I perish.

Secondly, Take a second case of divine illumina-
tion. A poor outcast, a wanderer in the thirsty desert,
Hagar, whose sins have brought this misery on her
head, has laid Ishmael down behind a bush to die.
She can submit to her own death, but not see his;
nor hear the cry, Water, mother, water! that comes
faintly from his blackened lips. With nothing over
her but a burning sun, nothing around her but glowing sands, and with the wind of that desert on her
cheek like the breath of a fiery furnace, she retires
out of earshot of Ishmael's moans, and sits down to
die. In that hour of her extremity, of dark and deep
despair, there comes a voice. She lifts her head, and,
listening, hears it say, "What aileth thee, Hagar?
fear not; for God hath heard the voice of the lad
where he is. Arise, lift up the lad!"—and at the same
moment there falls on her ear the blessed sound of
bubbling water. God opens her eyes; and there a
spring, inviting her to drink, is welling up from the
burning sands. And let God open the eyes of any one
who, amid terrors of conscience, feels ready to perish,
and in the gospel, which before seemed so barren of
pleasures, at the foot of the cross, and within his own
soul, he will find " a well of water springing up into
everlasting life."

Take another example. Alas, my master! how
shall we do? is the cry of Elisha's servant, as he
rushes into the house with pale terror in his face.
The Syrian host, by a forced night-march, has reached

their city, encompassing it like a wall; and he has seen the morning sun glitter on swords, and spears, and the terrible array of war. Calm and self-possessed, his master answers, Fear not: for they that be with us are more than they that be with them. With us! the servant might ask,—who are with us Where are they? The prophet prays, and in answer to his prayer, the Lord opens his servant's eyes. Now, as if they had started from the bowels of the earth, or every bush and every tree had suddenly changed into a flaming, celestial form, Behold, the mountain was full of horses and chariots of fire round about Elisha! And when memory has called up a believer's sins, and a sense of guilt has been darkening into despair, and Satan and his hosts, issuing from the pit, and drawn out in battle array, seem to have cut him off from escape, and he has been ready to cry, with Elisha's servant, Alas, my master, how shall I do? how has the Spirit of God flown to his help; and with eyes opened on the fulness, grace, mercy, pardon, and power we have in Jesus, how has he felt that, with God the Father, and God the Son, and God the Holy Spirit on his side, They that are with him are greater than all that can be against him.

XII.

THE APOSTATE.

"Demas hath forsaken me, having loved this present world."—
2 TIM. iv. 10.

IN old times our Nether Bow port and the gate of old
London Bridge were often garnished with human
heads ; and on these, in days of tyranny and wrong,
many a good, praying, and patriot head was spiked,
alongside those of notorious criminals, to bake and
wither in the sun. This, which we now consider a
barbarous and offensive custom, was continued, after a
fashion, down to our own age. Years ago, yet in our
time, you could see, in sailing on the Thames, certain
strange and fearful objects, close by the shore and
standing up within tide-mark between you and the
sky. They were gibbets, with dead men hung in
chains. This spectacle, though repugnant to modern
tastes and notions, had a good object in view ; it
accomplished something other and better than merely
frightening those who, passing there by night, might
hear the wind whistle through the holes of the empty
skull, and the rusty chains creak as the body swayed
round and round. Piracy, with its horrible atrocities
on men and women, was then much more commonly

practised by seamen than it is now, and as their ships dropped down the river, past these monuments of that crime and its punishment, the sailors carried away with them a salutary warning. They saw the abhorrence with which society regarded, and the vengeance with which justice pursued the perpetrators of so great a crime. Paul says, "Them that sin, rebuke before all, that others also may fear;" and these pirates were hung up before all for that good end. But the lesson, though striking, and well adapted, perhaps, to the rough men of rude times, was not perpetual. The work of decay went on, till bone dropping away from bone left only empty chains; and thus, mother earth hiding in her bosom the last relics of a guilty child, the criminal and his crime were both forgotten.

More enduring monuments than these of sin and of its punishment have perished amid the wrecks of time. For long ages, the stony form of a woman, dug from no quarry and cut by no sculptor's chisel, stood with its cold gray eyes turned on the sea that entombed the sinners but not the sin of Sodom. Lonely and awful figure, on her the traveller who skirted the shores of the Dead Sea, and shepherds tending their flocks on the neighbouring mountains, gazed with wonder and terror; and never did living preacher deliver such a sermon on the words, No man, having put his hand to the plough, and looking back, is fit for the kingdom of God, as that dumb statue. But time, the destroyer of all earthly things, has not spared even it; travellers have searched in vain for a relic more valuable and impressive far than the finest marbles of Greece and Rome. There is not a vestige of it to be found. She who, loving the present world too well, looked back on Sodom, has ceased to exist in stone, but she still lives in sacred story; and amid this world's temptations we would do well to think of and often to recall the words, "Remember Lot's wife."

The purpose which our ancestors had in view when they hung men in chains, and which God himself had in view when he turned Lot's wife into a pillar of salt, was St Paul's in his treatment of him whom he holds forth in this passage as a beacon to all future ages. He did not write these words to revenge himself on Demas, or to indulge any angry feeling against this poor and pitiable apostate. Nor was Demas the only man who had forsaken this champion of the truth. Stricken by such panic as has seized and scattered the bravest in battle, all Paul's companions deserted him at an awful crisis of affairs; and, referring to the scene where, with form bent beneath the weight of years and cares and labours, but spirit elastic and erect as ever, he stood alone at Nero's bar, he says, "At my first answer no man stood with me, but all men forsook me: I pray God that it may not be laid to their charge." But between these and Demas there was an essential difference, and now, they in heaven and he in hell, there is an eternal one. Recovering their courage, they rallied; and washed out in their own blood the stain of this disgrace. They fled the field for a time, he for ever; they abandoned the fight, he the faith; their conduct was a weakness, his was apostasy; theirs the failing of the disciples, for whom their Master offered the kind apology, "The spirit indeed is willing, but the flesh is weak," but his the crime and guilt of Judas. So, singling him out from the crowd, Paul, if I may so say, hangs the apostate up in chains. Recording the man's name and crime in these imperishable pages, he sets him before us to warn professing Christians against the love of the world; and teach all who, exposed to its influence and current, think they stand, to take heed lest they fall.

I. Let us consider the history and fall of Demas.

Men live after they are dead—some in their good deeds, others in their bad. Many a man would have been unheard of, but for his crimes; living but for these in happy obscurity, and going down to his grave unnoticed and unknown. But the case of Demas is not that of one who owes the world's only knowledge of him to his crimes, like a felon whom a scaffold raises above the heads of the vulgar crowd who have come to see him die. This is not the first time we hear of Demas; and, indeed, had St Paul written no second letter to Timothy, or had God in his providence been pleased to allow this epistle to perish with other writings of the apostles, Demas might have given a name to Protestant churches ; he might have been sainted in the Romish calendar, and had devotees soliciting his prayers, while they burned candles and offered gifts at his shrine.

In falling, this man fell from a height which few have reached, and that makes his fall the more impressive—he was a fallen star. If to be praised, not by the common crowd, but by those who themselves are praised, is fame, if to be held up by those who stand on others' shoulders, is admitted to be the highest honour, such honour Demas had. Paul himself, the greatest of the apostles, once regarded him with warm affection, and awarded him the honour due to a fellow-labourer in the Lord. No common man at arms, he had stood in the front rank of the Christian host ; and fighting in battle by the apostle's side, he had shared his dangers, and stood high in his esteem. Nor had he a place in Paul's heart only. He is made honourable mention of in his letters ; in that to the Colossians, for instance, where the apostle joins Demas with one of the four Evangelists—"Luke," says he, "the beloved physician, and Demas greet you." We find him in no less honourable company also in that most touching letter to Philemon, where this lover of all freedom, and hater of all oppression, and denouncer of all human wrongs throws his arms around a slave as a brother beloved—breathing a spirit that, intolerant of slavery, would emancipate every bondman, and let the oppressed go free. "There salute thee," he says, " Epaphras, my fellow-prisoner in Christ Jesus ; Marcus, Aristarchus, Demas, Lucas, my fellow-prisoners." What a galaxy of stars, and Demas shining among them ! Names of renown, these sound in our ears like David's roll of mighty men ; and the time was when Demas held such place among the champions of the cross, as, according to Scripture, belonged to Benaiah, the son of Jehoiada, who slew the lion-like men of Moab, and with no more formidable weapon than a staff encountered and conquered the Egyptian giant—" He was more honourable than the thirty, but he attained not to the first three."

Some men, as we might rashly say in our ignorance of the designs of Providence, die too soon ; but some seem to live too long—outliving not their usefulness only, which, however undesirable, a good man may do, but their honour and principles. Happy for Demas had his sun gone down at noon ! Over one who had been his friend, companion, fellow-labourer, with whom he had often taken sweet counsel, Paul lived to weep ; and to write this epitaph for his un-honoured grave, Demas hath forsaken me, having loved this present world ; a sentence that, like the scorpion, carries its sting in its tail,—" having loved this present world." Look at him ! Ovid has fancied no metamorphosis more strange or horrible. The opposite of Paul, who fell a persecutor and rose an apostle, Demas, once an apostle, has changed into an apostate; once a martyr, now a renegade; a brave soldier once, now a base deserter; a traitor now; his arms raised to pull down the pillars of a church they had helped to build. May we not cry with the prophet, How art thou fallen from heaven, O Lucifer, son of the morning! Scripture is silent on this man's future course; the curtain falls where we see him as a dishonoured knight, with the spurs he had won hacked from his heels—as a deserter, with the facings plucked from his dress, and drummed out of the regiment. But if ancient tradition speaks truth, Demas, as might be expected, went from bad to worse, sank lower and lower, from one depth of wickedness to another; till he closed his infamous career as the priest of a heathen temple—offering sacrifices to dead stocks and stones. What a fall was there? Unhappy man! whether he died amid the recollections of other and better days, stung by remorse and howling in despair; or died in sullen defiance of the Saviour, like Julian, when, overcome in battle by the Christians, he caught the blood from his fatal wound, and, tossing it up in the face of heaven, cried, expiring in the effort, The Nazarene has conquered!

Such is the story of Demas. As instructive as it is sad. Let no man wonder now that John Bradford, living in a street along which criminals in his time were led to execution, was wont to say, as from his windows he saw them passing on to the gallows, But for the grace of God, there goes John Bradford! The fall of such an one as Demas, like some tall cliff which, undermined by the waves, precipitates itself with the roar of thunder headlong into the boiling sea, must have startled the Church at the time, and wakened from their slumber those that slept in Sion; and still, as if its echoes were yet sounding round the world, let us listen to its warning. It teaches the highest of us, to take heed lest we fall; the happiest of us, to rejoice with trembling; and all of us, to watch and pray that, keeping our garments unspotted from the world, we enter not into temptation.

II. Consider the cause of Demas' fall,—he loved this present world.

Sailing once along a Highland loch where the crag goes sheer down into the water, our attention was turned by the boatmen to an immense table of rock. Tilted up on its narrow edge, it stood there threatening destruction to any who ventured below it; appearing ready to topple over at the touch of an infant's finger, and leap with a sudden plunge into the bosom of the lake. How came this gigantic stone to assume that upright attitude? No brawny arms of shepherd lads had raised and balanced it there. No earthquake, rolling along those mountains, and turning its stroke upwards, as earthquakes sometimes do, had started this mass from its bed and poised it so. Nor had the lightning, leaping from its cloud on the mountain summits, struck the crag, and, splitting it, raised this giant fragment from its bed. That was the task of a much more quiet, feeble, simple, and secret agent. When Jehovah revealed himself to the prophet, it was not in the earthquake, or in the roaring hurricane, or in the blazing fire, but in a still, small voice; and the power that rent that solid rock, and raised the mass tottering on its narrow base, was of a kind as quiet, gentle, and unobtrusive. Borne on the wings of the autumn wind, or dropped by a passing bird, a little seed had fallen into a crevice of the rock. Sleeping the winter through, but finding shelter and congenial soil, it sprang with the spring; and fed by dews and rains, the tender shoot grew. In time it lifted up its head, and spread its branches above and its roots below—worming them into fissures, wrapping them round and round that stony table, which, as they grew and thickened, it raised slowly from its bed. And then, one day when the seedling had grown into a tree, a storm, acting on leafy branches that caught the wind like sails, turned that tree into a lever, and, heaving on the rock that had received the seed into its heart and the fatal embraces of its roots, raised the massy table from its bed and poised it on the edge of the dizzy crag; and there it stood erect, waiting another storm to be hurled into the mossy waters of that wild, dark mountain lake.

As that shall fall, so fell Demas from his lofty

o

place; so have many fallen; ay, and so, unless we are restrained and sustained by the grace of God, the best of us would fall. It is not the world, observe, nor its money, nor its honours, nor its enjoyments that the Bible condemns; but the love of them. Beware of that! At first it may seem little, small as a tiny seed, but let it get a lodgment within you, and, fed by indulgence, it grows there, so silently, perhaps, that while it is worming itself deeper in, and wrapping its strong roots round and round your heart, you may never suspect the hold it is getting of you. That appears when the hour of temptation comes, whatever form it may assume; and the man falls, to the astonishment of many, perhaps to his own. When persecution came upon the Church, how did it act on Demas? as the storm on the rock that had lodged the seed in its bosom, and which, but for the tree that sprang from it with wide-spread branches and embracing roots, had stood unmoved by tempests, let them blow their worst. Turning Demas into a beggar, casting him into prison, or bringing him to the scaffold, persecution might destroy what of wealth, pleasure, health, and life was his; but had he not loved them, allowed them to take root in his heart, and occupy the place that belonged to God, persecution had never destroyed him. Never; and when Paul the apostle stood with his gray head before the crowd that had assembled to see him die, Demas had been at his side; one chain of love, as of iron, binding them; as they had fought, they had fallen together; their blood had mingled in the same stream; their heads rolled on the same scaffold; one chariot had borne both martyrs to the skies; and over their mangled remains, carried by devout men to burial, a weeping church might have raised one monument to their memory—its inscription, these words of David, They "were lovely and pleasant in their lives, and in their death they were not divided."

It is another part of that lament which best suits this case of Demas—"How are the mighty fallen, and the weapons of war perished!" He was laid in an apostate's grave—not excepting a drunkard's, the most hopeless of any; and, ere we close it over him, let us, like soldiers marched at a military execution by the dead body of a comrade who has been shot for treachery, take a last look of this unhappy, guilty man. He loved the world; and what has it brought him to? what is that world to him now, for which he denied his Saviour and forsook his servants? what now profits him a world, for which he bartered his immortal soul? He was a preacher; nor the last who has turned back in the day of battle, and abandoned his principles when they had to be suffered for. He had been a preacher, perhaps an eloquent one; but he never preached a sermon such as he preaches now—himself the sermon, and these words his text, Love not the world, neither the things that are in the world. If any man love the world, the love of the Father is not in him.

III. Learn the lessons this case teaches.

Put not your trust in princes, says David, nor in preachers, says Demas—by his example. The ornament of the pulpit may become its disgrace; and He, who will not give his glory to another, may rebuke the idolatry of the people by shattering their idol, or, rather, by allowing the idol to shatter itself. On the very throne where Herod sat, arrayed in royal apparel, making an oration at which the people shouted, It is the voice of a god, and not of a man, the angel of the Lord smote him. His flatterers saw their god eaten up of worms. And what more excellent studies than he and Demas for any who are in danger of being intoxicated with popular applause, and of turning giddy from the height of their position? An apostle once, an apostate now; the object once of good men's affection, but now of bad men's contempt, once beloved by the Church, despised now even by the world, and, worse still, by himself; a blazing star quenched in night, how does Demas warn those who are high placed, not to be high-minded, but to fear. It is safest to carry a low sail in a strong wind, even when it blows in our favour. Blessed are the poor in spirit; for theirs is the kingdom of heaven. The humble are to be exalted; those who lie at Jesus' feet are those who shall lie on his bosom.

Then, again, what a lesson does Demas read such as, by their family circumstances, their pious friends, or otherwise, are placed in conditions the most favour

able to their spiritual welfare? He associated with
the holiest society out of heaven. The bosom friend
of one in heart the purest, and in soul the loftiest,
noblest man the world ever saw, and a fellow-labourer
with him in the ministry of the gospel, Demas was in
circumstances less likely than are any of us to get
engrossed with the business, or burdened with the
cares, or entangled with the pleasures of the world.
Notwithstanding, he fell—drawn away by the love of
the world from the love of Christ. And what need,
then, have Christians much less favourably situated,
to watch and pray, and guard their hearts? This
story sounds in my ear like the voice of the old pro
phet, " Howl, fir-tree ; for the cedar is fallen."

Do you feel at ease, considering yourselves in small
danger of suffering such persecutions as led to the fall
of Demas? It may be so ; but let me warn you that
the world has trials more testing and severe than these.
Its smiles are to be dreaded, perhaps, more than its
frowns, its subtle sophistries more than its sharpest
sword. Let its love but once get into a man's heart,
and it has a tongue to persuade him that vice is virtue,
and virtue vice. Look at the sentiments of such as
make a profession of religion, and yet love the world
—fearing the Lord, and serving their own gods. According to them, a stern regard to duty, integrity,
purity, is preciseness, and the holy observance of God's
day is Pharisaism ;—on the other hand, conformity to
the fashions and practices and gaieties of the world is

not being "righteous overmuch;" a godless indifference to religious matters is charity and catholicity; looseness of principle is liberality, and freedom from the trammels of sectarianism; flattery and fawning are politeness, or, to profane the Scripture expression, are to be courteous; low cunning is caution; cowardice in the cause of God and truth is prudence; treachery to public principle is a wise regard to our own interests; dishonesty and fraud are cleverness in business; murder is an affair of honour, and seduction one of gallantry; hoarding money is carefulness; and the avarice that eats like a cancer into the heart, destroying alike the love of God and the love of man, is such frugality as Christ commended, and, indeed, commanded, when he said, Gather up the fragments that remain, that nothing be lost. And thus, when the love of the world has entered our hearts, the devil, clothed like an angel of light, walks in at its back.

In old times the sailors, a race given to superstition, told among other stories of the sea one of a strange island that lay in waters where no breakers beat, nor storms blew on its quiet shores. Yet they give it a wide berth whenever they, as they supposed, approached its neighbourhood, holding it in greater dread than the rugged coasts of our stormy climes. It rose from the deep a mass of magnetic ore, with powers of attraction fatal to the mariner. Once within their influence, the ship was drawn nearer and nearer; at first slowly, silently, gently, almost imperceptibly, but with ever-increasing speed; till, on a close approach, every iron bolt drawn from her timbers, without a crash, or sound, or any-thing to alarm the waking, or to wake the sleeping, she fell into a thousand pieces; and the whole fabric dissolved, crew and cargo sank together—down into that quiet sea. Fable as that was, so goes the religion, such as it is, of him who, drawn to the world, yields up his heart to its fatal attractions. It draws him on and on, further and faster on, till at length the catas-trophe arrives—his principles give way before some great temptation, and he is lost. What a wreck it made of Demas!

Watch, therefore, and pray while you watch, against this insidious enemy. If you find yourself beginning to love any pleasure better than your prayers—any book better than your Bible—any house better than God's—any table better than the Lord's—any person better than your Saviour—any one better than your soul—a present indulgence better than the hopes of heaven—take alarm. The evil is begun, and it does not mend the matter that its beginning is small. It does not need a large hole to admit a serpent with poison in its fangs, nor a large leak to let in the water that sinks the ship and drowns her crew. Despise not the day of small things, be they for good or evil. Behold, how great a matter a little fire kindleth! Beware how you allow Satan, or any one else, to lodge the love of the world in the smallest cranny or crevice of your heart. Give your hands to the world, but keep your heart for God. It is a very good world if kept in its own place; like fire and water, a useful servant, but a bad and most tyrannous master. Love it not, and yet love it. Love it with the love of him who gave his Son to die for it. Love it with the love of him who shed his blood to save it. Love it with the love of angels, who rejoice in its conversion. Love it to do it good, giving your tears to its sufferings—your pity to its sorrows—your wealth to its wants—your prayers to its miseries—and to its fields of charity and philanthropy and Christian piety, your powers and hours of labour. You cannot live without affecting it, or being affected by it. You will make the world better, or it will make you worse. God help you by his grace and Holy Spirit so to live in the world as to live above it, and look beyond it; and so to love it, that when you leave it, and the fluttering heart has beat its last stroke, and the bosom has heaved its last long sigh, and the last quiver has passed from your lips, and no breath dims the mirror, and all is over, you may leave the world better than you found it!

XIII.

THE EVIL OF SIN.*

WHEN the ostrich, scouring along the sandy desert, finds that it cannot escape the huntsman, it is said to thrust its head into a bush, and remain there, quite tranquil, to receive the death-blow. Poor senseless, stupid bird, it seems to fancy that the danger which it ceases to see has ceased to exist. But men, as well as brutes, do so; and not by one degree more rational than the composure of a bird at whose folly they themselves would be the first to smile, is the peace of those who, that they may enjoy the pleasures of sin, shut their eyes to its evil, and refuse to look that, and their own danger, in the face. I do not deny that they, having persuaded themselves that sin is a trivial thing, and by no means, to use the language of Scripture, "exceeding sinful," enjoy a sort of peace. They have laid the flattering unction to their souls that God is all merciful—that they have not been

---

* This and the following four papers, were originally published in a volume entitled " Saving Knowledge," partly by Dr. Guthrie and partly by Dr. Blaikie. These five chapters comprise Dr. Guthrie's part.

great sinners—that they have done no one harm,
but themselves perhaps—that many people are worse
than they—and that however they may have sinned,
the prayers and penitence of a death-bed shall set
all right. But I have seen the administration of an
opiate produce a similar effect—casting a man into
so deep a slumber that he felt no pain. But for the
low whispers of the attendants, the solemn stillness
of the room, and the anxious countenances of those
that were watching by his side, none would have
fancied that a mortal decease was raging in his vi-
tals, and hurrying him on to the grave. And not
more different this sleep from tired nature's health-
ful slumbers, than the peace of the ungodly from his
who is resting by faith on Jesus, and has made his
" calling and election sure."

Nor is it only exemption from " the stings " of conscience a man may enjoy who shuts his eyes to the
evil of sin. He may enjoy positive happiness of a
kind ; and be to appearance blither and in better
spirits than better men. What of that ? So is yon
drunkard, who has drowned all his sorrows with his
senses in the flowing bowl—the ragged wretch who,
untouched by the sad looks of the broken-hearted
wife and children that sit cowering, shivering over
some miserable embers, stands on the floor of his
dismantled home, and casts idiot smiles on the
wreck around him. I do not deny that there is

pleasure in sin. Were it not so, there would be fewer sinners. But when I look at its end—that " the way of transgressors is hard "—how justly may it be compared to the delirium of sailors who, when the bonds of order are broken, and all further effort to save themselves and their ship are abandoned, hoist the spirit cask on deck, and maddening their brains with drink, go down into the deep amid shouts of laughter and songs of merriment. Even so, many, intoxicated with the pleasures of sin, go down into perdition.

There is a state worse, more hopeless perhaps, than either of these. They stand in great danger of damnation who shut their eyes to the evil of sin, but they in greater who, practising iniquity till con-science grows seared and dead, have ceased to feel its evil. Such in some cases is their apathy that it seems as if God had cast them off, and said, pro-voked by their long-continued resistance to the re-monstrances of conscience and of his word and Spirit, " He is joined to his idols, let him alone." There lies our danger if we are trusting for salvation to a death-bed repentance. People think they will be very much alarmed at the approach of death. There is no greater mistake: the greatest wonder death-beds show, and ministers see, being not the calmness with which a believer dies, but the insen-sibility, the deep, unmoved, and unmoveable apathy with which others meet death. " There are no bands in their death—they are not in trouble as other men," as the Bible says. By their dying-bed—no place for flattery, or " healing the hurt of the daughter of God's people slightly "—they have been told the most alarming truths; I have thundered the law of Sinai in their ears; I have set forth a dying Saviour with the love of Calvary before their eyes, but it produced neither a response nor emotion. Fearing nothing, if hoping nothing, they have gone to their " own place " more calmly than many a saint who dies in Jesus' arms, and leaves earth for heaven.

It is said of the rich man in the parable that " in hell he lift up his eyes, being in torment." Alas, it is too late—too late then to get our eyes opened; and therefore I shall try, with prayer for God's blessing, to set before my readers some considerations calculated to demonstrate and illustrate the *evil of sin.*

There is a cruel deception often practised on the dying. They are left to indulge hopes of life after their case is hopeless; the friends who were parties to this deception—if friends they can be called—thereby laying up for themselves a source of unavailing regrets. If people are true Christians, it is of no moment, or at least of little moment, that they should know themselves to be dying: but if otherwise, the sooner they know the worst the better; for who can tell but God may call at the eleventh hour? There is something more culpable and cruel than concealment of the truth. The dying are not left to deceive themselves, but are deceived. Every, the most remote, allusion to death is positively forbidden: ingenuity is taxed, by schemes of future pleasure, books of light reading, and amusements, to divert the mind from solemn thoughts, and keep them " cheerful," as it is called: as new and more fatal symptoms arise, they are carefully concealed: they may be shed without the dying chamber, but no tears are allowed, nor sorrow on any face within it; and so the play, the pitiful tragedy, goes on, till the poor victim of mistaken kindness is hurried away into an unexpected, and perhaps unprepared for, eternity. Verily, " the tender mercies of the wicked are cruel."

But that expression applies with still more force to those who, called to be ambassadors of Jesus Christ, shrink from setting forth the inherent evil and awful punishment of sin—that, in the words of Scripture, " it is an evil and a bitter thing to sin against the Lord!" Some will not tolerate any allusion to hell, beyond the most distant — and that with bated breath. They cannot abide to hear of it; denouncing him as a gloomy preacher who, not for his own pleasure but others' profit, ventures on this awful and most sad subject to declare the whole

counsel of God. They say, " Prophesy unto us
smooth things." The storm rages, the ship is sinking ; yet they deem him an intruder on their peace
who attempts to wake them, crying, " What meanest
thou, O sleeper? arise and cah upon thy God !"
There are certainly more agreeable topics—the
goodness of God, which should lead us to repentance—the love of Christ, which should sweetly constrain us to live to Him who died for us—the joys of
heaven, which by virtue of their superior attractions
should withdraw our affections from the things that
are seen and temporal to those that are unseen and
eternal. No doubt also it is not so much by driving
as by drawing that sinners are ordinarily brought to
Jesus : and it is a far more agreeable task to melt a
hard heart by arguments of kindness, than attempt
to break it by arguments of fear—to work with the
fire than with the hammer, God's word being com·
pared to both. Yet the same apostle who, scatter-
ing Christ's blessed name as thick on his epistles as
God has done stars in the nightly firmament, sought
to constrain men by the love of Christ, persuades
them also by the terrors of the Lord. He who asked, " Despisest thou the riches of his goodness, and
forbearance, and long-suffering, not knowing that
the goodness of God leadeth to repentance?" also
asked, " Thinkest thou, O man, that thou shalt escape the judgment of God?" " Knowing the terror

of the Lord," said St. Paul, " we persuade men."
Hence his tears, and these touching words, " I have
told you often, and now tell you even weeping, that
they are the enemies of the cross of Christ, whose
end is destruction." No wonder he wept. The
wonder is that we can read with so little emotion
what fell in trembling accents from the Saviour's
lips—of a worm that never dieth, and a fire that is
never quenched. Why are we so callous? Why is
not our pity so moved, and our hearts melted, and
our fears awakened for poor careless sinners, that we
might adopt the language of the Psalmist, and say,
" Rivers of waters run down mine eyes, because they
keep not thy law !"

The way of transgressors is indeed hard; and we
see the nature of sin plainly revealed in its dreadful
effects. For there are two methods by which we
may arrive at the nature of anything ; we may either
analyze its properties, or discover them by studying
its effects. Taking, for instance, a deadly drug—I
may, on the one hand, by analysis, find it to be composed of elements highly deleterious and fatal to
life ; on the other hand, I may take the shorter and
more impressive method of administering it to some
of the inferior creatures, and see the virulence of the
poison in the violence of its effects—horrible convulsions and a speedy death. Some poisons are so
deadly that a grain or a few drops of them is as fatal

as a ball through the brain, or a knife stuck into the heart. To such a poison sin may with truth be compared; and nothing but their ignorance or disregard of its deadly nature would allow men to tamper with it, or speak lightly of the smallest sin.

It may be difficult for analysis to convey to some any sense of the evil that lies in all sin; but, surely, that may be understood by contemplating its effects. A child could understand the force latent in a cup of water, on seeing it, when converted into steam, rend asunder a plate of iron, or a mass of solid rock, or the power of lightning, if he saw it in the thunderstorm leap dazzling from the clouds, and striking some stately tree, rive its trunk, and scatter its leafy glories on the ground; or the venom of the cobra's fang, on seeing the reptile raise its hooded crest to strike, and him it struck reel, and fall, and die at his feet. Let sin, in like manner, be tried by its effects; and who, with a mind enlightened, can look on the sad change it has wrought on man, on the divine beauty it defaced, on the favour it forfeited, on the happiness it wrecked, on the curse it has entailed and the fire it has kindled, on the misery it breeds in time and perpetuates in eternity, without seeing " sin become exceeding sinful." Look at Eden! Man's disobedience there, his plucking the forbidden fruit, may seem to some a trivial offence; but does the misery it brought on Adam, and entailed on his posterity throughout all generations, justify such a term? Put a case:

Suppose some day, when passing the house of one revered for his piety, and universally respected for his character, and known to be the gentlest and kindest and most affectionate of fathers, you saw him driving from his door the son and daughter he had loved, and cherished, and lived with in sweetest fellowship—with sad but stern voice ordering them out of his presence, you would stand amazed; but you would neither need him, nor any one else, to assure you that before he had driven forth these weeping ones to want, and shame, and sorrow, they had been guilty of some most aggravated crime—an offence no father could pass by, or palliate, or lightly pardon. But the love God bore to His human children has far transcended any that beats or burns in a father's or mother's bosom, as the heavens rise above the earth; and who can see Him drive them from His presence, order them away, without feeling that there must be a guilt in sin which we have no line to fathom nor powers to comprehend! There had been no place of woe otherwise, for God has no pleasure in the death of him that dieth, nor is He willing that any should perish; nor otherwise had His beloved Son, betrayed by a friend, disowned by the creatures of His hand, and deserted by His Father and

God, bled on the accursed tree. If sin was not exceeding sinful and hateful, a less noble victim had
satisfied the demands of justice, and a less dreadful
expiation upheld the honour of a broken law. How
deep the stain which it required the blood of God's
own Son to wash out! How heavy the burden beneath which He sank, whose arms sustain the universe! What sorrows those which forced from His
patient lips this cry, " My soul is exceeding sorrowful, even unto death !"—the still more mysterious
complaint of Calvary, " My God, My God, why hast
thou forsaken me ?" If the virulence of a disease
may be measured by the violence of its remedy, or
the greatness of a debt by the sum paid for the discharge of the debtor, the evil that is in sin is as im-
measurable as the love for which, with all his glowing piety and power of language, St. Paul found no
fitter expression than this, " Oh, the height, and
depth, and breadth, and length of the love of God,
it passeth knowledge !"

A bitter thing, whether we contemplate its consequences here or hereafter, in this world or the next,
sin undoubtedly is. It is more. That may be called
bitter which, in a moral sense, is not evil—inherent-
ly and necessarily evil. Extreme poverty is bitter,
as where a parent looks round on hungry and hol-
low-eyed children when there is neither fire on the
hearth nor a morsel of food in the house—" When

they cry for bread, and their mother has none to give them." Yet there is no moral evil in poverty; it is no crime; on the contrary, "hath not God chosen the poor of this world rich in faith and heirs of the kingdom?" It is a bitter thing, also, to lie under the hand of acute disease, tossing on a bed of pain, vainly turning from side to side for relief, counting the long night's lazy hours; when it is night, weary for the morning; and when the morning comes, wearying for the night. Yet, in a moral sense, there is no evil here; on the contrary, while the outward man perisheth—strength turns to weakness, beauty to ghastly pallor, and symmetry to deformity—the inward man may be renewing day by day. It was a bitter thing for martyrs to suffer for righteousness' sake; to pine away in lonely exile; to perish on a scaffold; to be bound and burned at a stake. Yet, in a moral sense, it was not evil; on the contrary, Christ pronounced them "blessed" who suffer; winning a martyr's crown, great is their reward in heaven.

Let us beware of looking on sin as we might on disease, or poverty, or persecution—our only dread its bitter consequences. Take these away; let death come, but not as a grim messenger summoning men to God's awful presence; let the grave give up its dead, but not to judgment; let there be a place of happiness, but none of misery; and many would see nothing in sin to shock their feelings or deter them from committing it—from drinking up iniquity as the ox drinketh up the water. But what an imperfect view of sin is theirs—imperfect as his of the crimes of robbery or murder who, were there no society to point the finger of scorn at him, nor prison to hold, nor judge to try, nor gallows to hang him, would steal your property, nor scruple to take your life. I believe no man can measure the depths of evil that are in sin; but he certainly has no adequate idea of them who, though sin should cease to be punished, and universal salvation were proclaimed from the skies, so that there were henceforth no hell, nor judgment, but heaven for all and hell for none, would cease to regard it as an evil thing— " this abominable thing that I hate," saith the Lord.

All the guilt that lies in foul rebellion against the mildest and most merciful of earthly monarchs—in disobeying the kindest, and grieving the best of fathers—in ingratitude to a generous benefactor—in returning cursing for blessing, evil for good, and hatred for favours, in wounding a heart that loves us and the hand that was stretched out to pluck us from destruction—in refusing to please One who, though rich, for our sakes made Himself poor; took our debts on Him and paid them; took our burdens on Him and carried them; and bearing disgrace to crown us with honour, saved our lives at the expense of His own ;—all that evil, multiplied a thousand and a thousand times, there is in sin. It is a horrible crime committed against a gracious God and a loving Saviour—to say nothing of the injuries our sins have inflicted on ourselves, and the irreparable wrongs they may have done to others. It is from such views that true repentance springs. Are they ours ? Different from the remorse of yon haggard and hardened wretch, who, at the door of a prison or the foot of a gallows, when his sins have found him out, sees their evil only in their punishment; it is not where the lake burns to consume, but Jesus bleeds to save, sin is seen in its greatest evil, and felt by God's people to be their deepest grief. " They shall look on him whom they have pierced, and mourn as one mourneth for an only son, and be in bitterness as one is in bitterness for a first-born." The importance of correct views of the evil that lies in sin cannot be exaggerated. To inadequate ideas of that may be traced the very imperfect conceptions some entertain of the necessity and great work of the atonement—of Christ as our substitute, bearing our griefs and carrying our sorrows, and so opening up a passage for the ocean of divine love to flow out in the blessings of redemption on this lost and guilty world.

" Let every man," says the Apostle, " prove his own work ;" and here, I may now remark, we have an admirable test whereby to try the genuineness of our faith and repentance. If our only motive for abstaining from sin lies in the dread of punishment, our obedience, such as it is, springs not from the love of God, but of ourselves. It is entirely selfish; and having no regard to Him whatever, it is in fact but a continual breaking of the law, " Thou shalt love the Lord thy God with all thy heart, and with all thy soul, and with all thy mind, and with all thy strength." Our case is like that of a servant who has a kind master, but obeys, not because he loves his master, but only his wages,—of a son, who, but for the dread of the rod, would treat a father's wishes with insolent contempt, and openly defy his author-ity. How can God set any value on such obedi-ence? He Himself has answered the question, " A son honoureth his father, and a servant his master; if then I be a father, where is mine honour? and if I be a master, where is my fear? If ye offer the blind for sacrifice, is it not evil? and if ye offer the lame and sick, is it not evil? Offer it now unto thy governor; will he be pleased with thee, or accept thy person, saith the Lord of hosts?" The test, therefore, by which to try the genuineness of our faith and repentance lies in this question, Would we sin were no punishment to follow?—in other words, " Shall we continue in sin that grace may abound?' So Paul puts the question; and how does he answer it? Filled with holy horror at the impious thought, and speaking for all who have undergone a saving change, he replies, "God forbid!" Does his emphatic exclamation find an echo in our breasts? Does sin appear to us so exceeding sinful that we would not commit it though we had read our names in the book of life, and felt as sure of heaven as if already there? Then, notwithstanding all our transgressions and shortcomings, we may take the comfort of these blessed words, "Ye are washed, ye are sanctified, ye are justified in the name of the Lord, and by the Spirit of our God."

These views of sin are no doubt calculated to humble us in our own esteem. Humble us? Let the Spirit of our God open our eyes fully to its exceeding sinfulness, and, overwhelmed by a sense of guilt and shame, we shall exclaim with Job, "I abhor myself, and repent in dust and ashes." Some, indeed, vain of themselves and of their own doings, maintain a self-complacent spirit, nor stand abashed in the presence of Him before whose glory, as a man screens his eyes from the blaze of the sun, angels veil their faces. How different from a humble Christian's the attitude of yonder Pharisee! See how, like the bird that, strutting proudly on the lawn, unfurls its gaudy tail to display its beauty to the sun, he presents himself for the admiration of God and man. "I fast," he says, "twice in the week,

I give tithes of all that I possess. I thank thee that I am not as other men, or even as this publican."

But it is no evidence that we are abhorred of God, that we have been brought to abhor ourselves, on the contrary, "The sacrifices of God are a broken spirit; a broken and a contrite heart, O Lord, thou wilt not despise." " I," said St. Paul, " am the chief of sinners ;" " I," said David, " was as a beast before thee ;" " I," said Ezra, "am ashamed, and blush to lift up my face to thee, O my God, for our iniquities are increased over our heads, and our trespass is gone up unto the heavens ;" and so certainly does a man grow humbler as he grows holier, that it is with self-esteem as with the column of mercury in the tube of a barometer—the higher we ascend, it sinks the lower.   What more striking illustration of this than heaven itself affords ? There, purified from all conceit and pride, perfect both in humility and in holiness, the saints, as if unworthy to wear on their heads what Jesus won on his cross, cast their crowns at his feet. There, with eyes death has purged, in purest rays serene, they see God—the true mirror in which to see ourselves. For, as the best way to estimate the feebleness of a taper is not to measure the small space its rays illuminate, but to hold it up against the sun, and see its flame grow dull to blackness in the blaze of its burning beams or as the best way to correct an exaggerated im pression of the magnitude of the pyramids is not to measure their dimensions, but to transport them, were it possible, to the foot of some lofty mountain, the snow-crowned monarch of the Alps or Andes; so the best way of measuring ourselves is to measure ourselves with God. Seeing our littleness in His greatness, our vile ingratitude in His boundless goodness, the impurity of our lives in His ineffable and unspotted holiness, it is easy to understand how the best have been the humblest men; and how one, so distinguished for piety and beneficence as Job, should have exclaimed, " I have heard of thee by the hearing of the ear, but now mine eye seeth thee : wherefore I abhor myself, and repent in dust and ashes."

If this attempt to set forth the evil of sin has awakened, or deepened, any sense of my reader's need of a Saviour, if it has made him think less of himself and more of Christ, it is well. Self-abasement before God—the pledge that the publican went down to his house justified—has characterized not Job and David—not prophets and apostles only, but the elect of God in every age of the church. Read the life of any eminent saint; and from the glowing panegyric of his biographer turn to the page which records the man's opinion of himself; and how low the estimate, how different the language ' The two seem to describe distinct persons; yet, dissimilar as are the portraits, one man sat for both. What hard things he has written against himself, what confessions of guilt and sin he has left, at whose death men exclaimed, "A prince and a great man has fallen this day in Israel"—by whose grave a weeping church has raised the cry, "My father, my father! the chariots of Israel and the horsemen thereof." For example, how did Knox, the man above all other men whose name, as the greatest and bravest of her sons, is dear to Scotland, regard himself, estimate the mighty work he had lived to do? The poorest, vilest, most useless, never lay lower at the foot of the cross—there, tempted to indulge in self-satisfaction, he passed the last night of his life in mortal conflict with the enemy of souls, conquering, though the battle lasted through all its weary hours, by the blood of the cross. And who, to quote but another case, has not heard of John Wesley—how much, not England only, but the whole world owes to him, to his poetry and his piety, to his love for Christ and love for souls, to his burning zeal and apostolic labors? With his praise in all the churches, and a fame spread wide as the world itself, what estimate did he form of himself? what hopes sustained him in a dying hour? "I have been reflecting," he said, "on my past life; I have been wandering up and down between fifty and sixty years, endeavoring in my poor way to do a little good to my fellow-creatures; and what have I to trust to for salvation? I can see nothing which I have done or suffered that will bear looking at.' I have no other plea than this—

> " ' I the chief of sinners am,
> But Jesus died for me.' "

XIV

MAN'S INABILITY TO SAVE HIMSELF.

TO a young man who came, saying, "Good Master, what shall I do to inherit eternal life?" our Lord replied, "Go thy way, sell whatsoever thou hast, and give to the poor, and thou shalt have treasure in heaven; and come, take up the cross, and follow me." A hard saying that! To an aged saint a very difficult duty,—how much more to a babe in Christ, to one but entering, if entering, on the Christian life! It is not raw recruits and beardless boys, but veterans, men inured to war, to the flash of bayonet and the roar of cannon, that generals send to the front—where bullets are flying, and men are falling thickest. What man would order a sailor boy, the first day he trode the deck, to climb the shrouds, and reef the topsail in a storm, when the ship, caught in a hurricane, was plunging and tearing through the sea? Yet so our Lord dealt with this youth—putting him to a trial which the most advanced Christian would find it hard to bear.

Let us fancy ourselves in his circumstances. What a surprise to be called, all of a sudden, to part with our whole property, to leave home with its many tender ties, the scene of happy memories, the grave of beloved parents, the society of kind friends, the respect of the world, and the reputation of wealth, to descend, at one step, from affluence and comfort, to follow one himself so poor that he had no place where to lay his head! We cannot fancy the shock and the recoil we ourselves should feel, and not wonder that our Lord laid a load so heavy on a back so young.

But the apparent harshness in this case, as in many others, ceases when we know all its circumstances. What looks cruel comes out then as the truest kindness. We should make the greatest mistakes if we pronounced judgment on a remedy in ignorance of the disease it was meant to cure. You enter, for example, the theatre of an hospital. A pale, weak, wasted sufferer, with terror and anxiety in his face, is borne in, and laid on a blood-stained table. His arms are pinioned; and into the quivering flesh of him who needs rest rather than pain the surgeon buries a knife;—deaf to his entreaties, unmoved by his groans. This seems cruel, but it is not so. We have only to see the morbid mass separated from a form it had long tortured with pain, and was hurrying to an untimely grave, to see that the knife was both in a kind and skilful hand—that there was need of the knife, and life in the knife.

Even so, on turning to St. Matthew's account of
this case, our Lord's apparent harshness changes
into true kindness; all which seemed stern and hard
entirely vanishing. He, who came to Jesus seeking
eternal life, had no sense of his own inability to
save himself; but fancied that he had only to be
told how, and he could do it. In his account of
the transaction, Mark represents him saying, " Good
Master, what shall I do to inherit eternal life ?"—a
form of the question not very different from the
jailor's, when, seizing a light, he burst into the dungeon, and cast himself at the apostles' feet, to cry,
" Sirs, what shall I do to be saved ?" Had that
been the young man's question, springing up in his
heart as in the jailor's, from feeling himself lost,—a
poor, lost helpless sinner,—this, doubtless, had been
Christ's gracious and quick reply, " Believe in me,
and thou shalt be saved." But the question, as
more fully given by the Evangelist Matthew, is not
simply, " What shall I do to inherit eternal life ?"
but—a very different one—" What *good thing* shall I
do to inherit eternal life ?" Eternal life was a prize
which, with some directions from Christ, he deemed
himself able to win. Nor any wonder; for such
was his ignorance of the nature of sin, of his own
guilt and weakness, and how, spiritual in its nature,
the law of God is violated as well by desires as by
deeds, by wishes as by works, that to the repetition

of the commandments he replied, with the most per-fect self-complacency, " Master, all these things have I kept from my youth."

What is to be done in this case? It resembles that of one who, drugged with opium, has sunk into a deadly stupor; and to whom a stimulant has been administered without any good effect. The light is flashed on his dull, dilated pupils, but in vain; his pulse beats weaker, his breathing comes thicker, his lethargy grows more and more profound. Another and stronger stimulant is required. Unless he is roused he dies. So with this young man. He must be awoke to a sense of his real condition. He per-ishes otherwise, in his ignorance and sins. His case requires the strongest, and his salvation will justify the most painful remedies. For never, till he sees that he cannot save himself, will he repair to Jesus, and fall at His feet, to cry, Lord, save me; I perish!"

It was for that blessed purpose our Lord bade this man lay down the world, and take up the cross; His object being to make the man feel his need of Divine assistance and a new heart; and that, for all his talk about another world, he was glued to this one. But this could only be accomplished by put-ting the man to a trial. When in a calm, sunny day the ship rises and falls on the billows, she seems as free as the waves she rides—nor till the wind rises and swells her drooping sails, and, making no prog-

ress, she plunges and pitches like a steed under spur
and rein, do we discover that beneath the water, unseen, and till then unsuspected, an anchor, with its
iron arms, grasps the sand, chaining her to the earth.
So, also, it is, when, turning her eye to the sun, and
inspired with some love of freedom, the eagle, spreading out her wings and springing from the perch, attempts to fly, but has hardly mounted ere she drops
down again, that we discover the noble bird to be a
miserable captive, and see the chain that binds her
to the earth. And our blessed Lord bade this man
break loose from the world, and mount to heaven,
to teach him by his very failure that he could not;
that he had no power to save himself; that salvation is not of blood, nor of the will of the flesh, nor
of the will of man—but of God : that, in his own
words to Nicodemus, " Except a man be born of
water and of the Spirit, he cannot enter the kingdom of God." And that doctrine I now proceed to
illustrate.

This doctrine, I may, by way of introduction, observe, is evident from this, that the saved are all
debtors to the free choice and grace of God.

A man of taste, wishing to stock a garden, waits
till the seed he sows has sprung, and the plants that
spring from it have flowered ; and then, rejecting
the rest, he selects for his parterres the flowers of
fairest hue and finest forms. To stock an orchard

he pursues a similar course; waiting till time has
proved their character, he selects the best trees,
leaving such as are barren, or produce only inferior
fruit, to be burned as fuel—the only thing they are
fit for. Now, if man saves, or is capable of saving
himself, it were reasonable to expect that in bestow-
ing on men everlasting life, God would have pursued a similar course. But amid all the dark mysteries that invest this subject, it is plain that He did
not. It is not on our merits, but on His mercy, the
choice turns; else what does the Apostle mean who
says, "Not by works of righteousness that we have
done, but according to his mercy he saved us, by
the washing of regeneration and renewing of the
Holy Ghost, which He shed on us abundantly
through Jesus Christ?" Not waiting till time has
developed their character, as time does that of flowers and trees, God chooses those who are to be heirs
of grace before their character is or can be formed
—before their baptism, even before their birth; nor
only before their birth, but before that of time itself
—ere there was a man to sin, or a world to sin in;
ere sun shone, or any angel sung. "Blessed," said
Paul, with adoring gratitude, "be the God and Father of our Lord Jesus, who hath blessed us with all
spiritual blessings in heavenly places in Christ, according as he hath chosen us in him *before the foundation of the world.*" Chosen us, be it observed

not because we are holy; but making our holiness to be, not the cause, but the consequence of His choice—not the root it springs from, but the fruit it bears; " chosen us," he adds, " that we should be holy and without blame before him in love."

This truth—humbling to our pride, but placing our hopes on an immovable foundation—receives very remarkable and distinct expression in the reason which God assigned to Paul for requiring him to remain in Corinth. Steeped in the grossest idolatry, proverbial above any other in the world for unbridled licentiousness, the Apostle, who had succeeded in converting but a handful of its inhabitants, was about to leave that city; thinking that there no more good was to be done. Fancy his astonishment when God, appearing to him in a vision, said, " Be not afraid, Paul, but speak, and hold not thy peace, for I am with thee; for I have *much people* in this city "—serving now at heathen altars, slaves now of the grossest vices, nevertheless they are my people; and here you are to abide, from these vile dust-heaps to gather out my jewels, from these dark depths of sin to bring up my pearls— they know not me, but I know them—they have not chosen me, but I have chosen them; not for their merits, but out of my mercy chosen them before the foundation of Corinth, or of the world itself. If God's ways are equal, unless there was one rule for the sinners of Corinth and another for us, none, therefore, are chosen from regard to their merits, or saved through their own ability—salvation being all of grace, pure and undeserved, as was once admirably brought out by a humble, unlettered Christian. Strong in faith, though not expert in argument, she answered the cavils of some who tried to puzzle her, as he who said to the Pharisees, " This I know, that I once was blind, but now I see," — she replied, " This I know, that I never should have chosen God, unless God had first chosen me !"

I remark that our inability to save ourselves is evident from these, among many other considerations :—

1. We cannot plead guiltless of sin. Guiltless ? What man so ignorant as to refuse his assent to the words of John, " If we should say that we have no sin, we deceive ourselves—we make God a liar, and the truth is not in us !" In yonder temple, from which the crowd is rushing, priests, scribes, Pharisees, old and young, hustling each other in their haste, and leaving but our Lord, who stoops writing on the sanded floor, and a woman He has saved for time at least—let us hope, she going to sin no more, for eternity — who had remained behind ? Why this hot haste from the house of God ? No fire has caught its beams; nor are its walls of mighty stones, rocked by an earthquake, cracking to their

fall. Nothing but this has happened—a guilty woman has been dragged before Christ for doom ; and
He has pronounced the doom, but in this unexpected form, " Let him that is without sin cast the first
stone at her !" Him that is without sin ?—no hand
is mouldering, nor shall any moulder in the dust to
meet that condition, and execute the fatal sentence.
For however irreproachable we appear in the sight
of men, and more than irreproachable, respected, esteemed, and praised we may be of men, where in
pew or pulpit is he who could hold up his hands
before God, and say, " These hands are clean !"
We have all sinned ; and since spiritual as well as
temporal death has passed on all men because all
have sinned, we are as unable to save ourselves as a
dead man to leave his coffin, and return with the
mourners who have carried him to the grave.

2. Our utmost efforts fall short of a perfect service. Such God's law requires ; but who has ever
reached, or even approached it ?—who has satisfied
the law, as summed up in these grand and lofty
words, " Thou shalt love the Lord thy God with all
thy heart, and with all thy soul, and with all thy
mind ; and thy neighbor as thyself?" Not St. Paul.
He says, " When I would do good, evil is present
with me.—That which I would, I do not, and that
which I would not, that I do." And where Paul
failed, who can hope to succeed ? To him who, in

the splendour of his gifts and graces, shone without
an equal when he lived, nor has had any successor
since he died, dare any of us say, Stand aside, Paul,
I am holier than thou? But suppose we could,
what of that? The robe that, blanched by dews
and rain and sunshine, seems so white beside the
mould some hoary sexton flings from an open grave,
turns dull and dingy laid on a bank of snow; and
who, though he may seem an angel in the company
of reprobates, of the profligate and profane, could
stand comparison, side by side, with God's Son or
God's holy law? Whom would not the contrast
humble?—from whose lips call forth the language
both of confession and prayer?— our confession,
Job's, "If I wash myself in snow-water and make
my hands never so clean, yet shalt thou plunge me
in the ditch and mine own clothes shall abhor me"
—that our confession, and this, the Psalmist's, our
prayer, "Enter not into judgment with thy servant,
for in thy sight shall no man living be justified!"

3. As sinners we are without excuse. Ere the
judge condemns a man found guilty of a capital
offence, he asks him what he can say why sentence
of death should not be passed on him. And were
He who is not willing that any should perish, but
whenever He condemns "condemns reluctant," so
to deal with us, what should we say to excuse our
sins and escape their punishment? If the plea avails,

we save ourselves; otherwise we cannot. Now men make excuses to their conscience, and also to their fellow-men; but let us try what value these would have at the judgment-seat of a righteous God.

First, They plead sorrow. But though their sorrow were as deep, and true, and godly, as their continuing in sin proves it is not, of what worth is this plea in the eye of the law? Some wretch by his crimes brings himself to the bar of his country—and there, pale, and sorrowful, and sad enough many have looked—but, though he pleads for his life with tears, sorrow never baulked the gallows of its due. Waste and riotous living have brought many to bankruptcy, but sorrow never satisfied the demands of defrauded and indignant creditors. Sorrow acquits no criminals: sorrow pays no debts: sorrow heals no wounds: it never restored to injured woman her fair name and character, nor recalled to life the dead, whose gray hairs a prodigal had brought down to the grave. Sorrow cannot repair the wrongs we do to our fellow-creatures, still less those we do to God. "Offer it now to thy governor, will he be pleased with thee, or accept thy person? saith the Lord of hosts."

Second, They plead that they have not been great sinners. This was the Pharisees' plea—" I thank thee, O God, that I am not as other men, nor even as this publican." What that was worth, we know from this, that the poor publican, who stood afar off, and beat on his breast, and cried, "God be merciful to me a sinner," went down to his house justified; but not the other. The Pharisee's was not Paul's plea. Glorying only in the cross of Christ, he called himself the least of saints, and the chief of sinners. Nor is it a plea to which any court of justice would attach the slightest value. Think of a man found guilty of theft pleading that he should be allowed to go free, because, when he stole your purse, he did not take your life! Worthless anywhere, such a plea is nowhere so worthless as at the bar where Divine justice sits enthroned; and all who reject the Saviour, rejecting mercy, shall be tried by a law whose stern terms are these, "Cursed is every one who continueth not in all things written in the book of the law to do them."

Third, they plead the strength of temptation. This plea, like the others—a refuge of lies, is neither new nor true. It is not true; for who can deny having committed many sins they might have avoided: yielded to many temptations they might have resisted? It is not new; having been tried in Eden, and found wanting. "Hast thou," said God to Adam, "eaten of the tree whereof I commanded thee that thou shouldst not eat?" To excuse himself, he pleaded temptation—"The woman whom thou gavest to be with me, she gave me of the tree, and I did eat." "What is this that thou hast done?" said God, turning next to Eve. Taking up the same ground, she also pleads temptation as her excuse— "The serpent beguiled me, and I did eat." Vain subterfuge; Eden was lost, and our world buried in the ruins of the fall! Now the plea which did not excuse their sin will still less excuse ours. For, however we may plead its strength, there is no temptation we might not resist—in the hottest furnace walk unhurt, and go dryshod through the deepest sea. "My grace is sufficient for thee," is God's own sure and blessed word; and, however hard the fight or heavy the burden, we had but to seek His grace, to boast with His servant, Paul—"I can do all things through Christ, which strengtheneth me." Never has it been for want of faithfulness on His part, but of faith on ours, that this His grand promise has seemed to fail—"When thou passest through the waters, I will be with thee; and through the rivers, they shall not overflow thee: when thou walkest through the fire, thou shalt not be burned; neither shall the flame kindle upon thee."

Fourth, We are of ourselves unable to embrace the salvation which God has provided. "Believe in the Lord Jesus Christ, and thou shalt be saved," is indeed glad tidings; but faith itself is the gift of God. Some, it is true, fancy that it is an easy thing to believe, and that we can turn our minds, as our steps when they have brought us to the brink of a precipice—turn our hearts, as the steersman the ship, which, by a prompt movement of the helm, he guides clear of the thundering reef, and sends away in safety, ploughing through the foam, on another tack. But a lost sinner—whose proper figure is a vessel without masts or rudder, drifting at the mercy of the wild waves on a rocky shore—has no power of his own to turn from sin and the error of his ways. Were it otherwise, our Lord's words had been literally, universally fulfilled—"I, if I be lifted up, will draw all men after me." Are they so? Alas! in how many churches is He lifted up every Sabbath, nor draws one?—offered every Sabbath only to be wickedly rejected?—his servants, grieved at man's mad obstinacy, returning to their Master with the old sorrowful complaint, "No man hath believed my report, and to none is the arm of the Lord revealed!" Could man change his heart and habits, it is incredible that any should perish with God's word in their hands; not as certainly, but more certainly, than such as never had the offer of a Saviour. Here is a man who knows that if he goes to Christ, he will go to heaven; and if not, that he shall be sent to hell— who knows that Jesus is *the way*, the only way to true happiness and holiness in this world, and salvation in the next—who knows that he must die, and that in the hour of robustest health, there is but a step between him and the grave—who knows, therefore, that if he put off salvation for a single hour, that hour may be a whole eternity too late—when, with all those powerful motives to turn this moment to Christ, that man stands unmoved, how true the words of Jesus, " No man can come unto me except the Father which hath sent me draw him !"

No doubt it is in the power of all, after a fashion, to use the means of grace—by that I mean to read the Bible, and say their prayers, and go to church. But, oh, what need for prayer that a Divine power may accompany these, since, without the influences of the Holy Spirit, they will be found to harden rather than to soften the heart !   Experience proves this ; and that he is less likely to be saved who has sat from childhood under a Gospel ministry, than one on whose eyes ' the glorious Gospel of the bless-ed God ' opens with the novelty, and freshness, and astonishment, a man, born and brought up in a coal-pit, would feel when gazing for the first time on the star-spangled sky. Wesley and Whitefield reaped their largest harvests on neglected fields ;—those, adown whose begrimed cheeks, as they preached, the starting tears ran white channels, being miners and peasants and colliers, men who heard the terrors of hell and the love of God, for the first time in their lives, set fully and affectionately before them. The heart grows callous through unsanctified familiarity with Divine things—even with danger itself. And thus, as the veteran of many a battle-field waits the advance of the foe and the crush of musketry with a calm, intrepid bearing, in like manner familiarity with spiritual danger begets such spiritual indifference that the law thunders and a Saviour entreats in vain—making it evident that men are no more to be driven from sin by the fear of hell, than drawn from it by the hopes of heaven. Put this to the test. Let the subjects of our experiment be a little child and an old man. How easy it is to awaken the fears, and touch the conscience, and bring tears to the eyes of childhood! But those only who have tried it, as I have done, can know, and those only who know it can believe, how difficult it is to reach the conscience and shake the confidence of graceless and gray-haired age. I am not depreciating the means of grace. Far from it. On the contrary, I recommend a diligent, but a devout, use of them, with earnest prayer that through an outpouring of the Holy Spirit the means may be made the channels of grace. Without that, the church we attend, and the sermons we hear, and the Bible we read, and the sacraments we partake of, will but harden our hearts—even as familiarity with funerals is apt to make us think not more but less of death, until, often treading that path which others shall one day tread with us, we can carry a neighbor to the gates of another world, and leave him there, to return to the business and pleasures of this without one suitable and serious thought.

In closing this chapter let me remark, The deeper our sense of man's inability to save himself, we are the more likely to be saved. Do not despair. Deliverance is often nearest when it seems most distant. "Man's extremity is God's opportunity," is one true proverb. "The darkest hour is before the dawn," is another: and many a poor, distressed sinner's experience has been that of a crew tossed for long days on the stormy deep. They had lost their reckoning; enveloped in an impenetrable mist, their poor bark was driving they knew not where: at length they catch the dreaded roar of breakers; louder and louder they are heard thundering on a rugged shore. Unable to do anything to save themselves and avert a fatal issue, their hearts sink within them, when suddenly, as if God's own hand had drawn aside the curtain, the fog-bank parts to show them a spacious harbour, opening out its arms to receive them on the bosom of its calm blue waters. So the hope of Christ has opened to many who, finding that they had no hope in themselves, were crying, "Sirs, what must I do to be saved?" A paradox though it seems, there is greatest hope when our case looks most hopeless. "The Lord," it is said, "shall judge his people, and repent himself for his servants when he seeth that their power is gone, and that there is none shut up or left." So it fell out with Abraham. Not till he and Isaac had climbed the mountain, not till the altar was built and the victim bound, not till, with a last long look, and a last warm kiss, and a last sad farewell, the father had raised his arm to strike, was that arm arrested—did the angel, hovering over the scene, descend to stay the bloody sacrifice. It was so likewise when Israel was captive in the land of Babylon, and their harps hung mute on its willow trees, and God's own holy house lay in desolate, silent ruins. Their deliverance never seemed farther distant than when most near. Never was their captivity more galling, their misery so insulted, or their humiliation so complete, as on that night, when Belshazzar, mad with wine and wickedness, called for the vessels of the sanctuary, and turning them into drinking cups, caroused with his wives and concubines, his princes and his lords. Yet that was the very night on which the tyrant's doom was written, and the deliverance of the captives begun. Israel by the shores of the Red Sea; the three Hebrew martyrs in the fiery furnace; Daniel cast into the lions' den ; Peter in chains and asleep in prison —these cases, all admirable correctives to despair, show us how God often waits till things are at the worst. He saves at the uttermost—when with all power all pride is gone. Nor shall these words have been written in vain, if any of my readers, convinced of their inability to save themselves, shall turn to Christ—like the disciples when, abandoning all further effort to keep their boat afloat and reach the land, they threw up their oars, to throw themselves on the power and love of Jesus, and wake Him with the cry, " Master, carest thou not that we perish?" Now He does care that we should not perish. He died that we might not perish. And he who died for us with love time can neither change nor cool, longs to save us. His arms open to embrace us. Heaven opens to admit us. Angels stand ready to rejoice over us. So venturing, as well we may, on Christ's boundless power and boundless kindness, let us fall at His feet to cry, " Lord, save me, I perish !"— or with the man of old, " Lord, I believe; help thou mine unbelief !"—for whosoever cometh unto Him, He will in no wise cast out; and whosoever believeth in Him shall not perish, but have everlasting life.

XV.

THE WORK AND GLORY OF THE SAVIOUR.

AMONG other objections which infidels have taken, but vainly taken, to the divinity of the Bible, one has been the mysteries it contained. Here, driven from one post to another, some have taken their last stand; intrenching themselves in that as in a strong and impregnable position. The Bible, they affirm, cannot be a revelation from God, because it contains unintelligible statements; doctrines which man finds it impossible to comprehend. To such an objection it would not be easy to find a more conclusive reply than the answer of a plain, humble Christian. Dexterously turning the infidel's artillery against himself, he converted his objection to the Scriptures into an argument for their truth. "Not comprehend?" he replied; "I would not believe the Bible to be the word of God, if it contained nothing but what I could fully comprehend!"

There is great force in this remark. For the Bible were unlike the other works of God, if it came in all respects within the grasp of our limited understandings. There are mysteries in God's works as great as any to be found in His word. Take an example. In reproaching the children of Israel for their wilful and wicked ignorance, Jeremiah exclaims, " The stork in the heavens knoweth her appointed times, and the turtle and the crane and the swallow know the time of their coming; but my people know not the judgment of the Lord." In birds of passage, which always travel with the sun, every summer brings us visitors from southern climes; and, as they roost amid the palm-groves of Asia, or sport on the banks of the Nile, how do they know that, in a few more days or weeks, the snows shall have melted from our fields, and ice-bound streams, set loose, will be rushing merrily to the sea, and the sun shining through long summer days on our distant isle? By what means do they know, not only when to come, but how to come? What a mystery is there! In sailing to a remote foreign land, man has to provide himself with chart and compass. Now he takes observations in the heavens, and now sounds the ocean with deep-sea lead; by day and night the steersman stands silent by the helm, and the watch tread the deck; and yet, notwithstanding all their science, and skill, and care, men often miss the desired haven, and perish, wrecked amid the angry breakers of an unknown shore Look now at a voyage of a bird of passage! For many hundred or thousand miles it cleaves its course through the pathless air, without compass, or chart, or pilot to guide its flight; onward it goes through the wildest storms, through densest fogs, and the darkness of starless nights; yet—a fact well ascertained, but a mystery inexplicable—it returns over seas and lands and rivers and mountains to the very spot and home of its birth! What more inexplicable in the word of God than we have here? It is past finding out. How absurd, then, to make its mysteries an objection to the divinity of the Bible! If not in these things only, but in the painting of every flower, in the shaping of every leaf, in the shooting of every blade of grass—

> "God moves in a mysterious way,
> His wonders to perform,"

need we start at finding mysteries in the great work of Redemption?—at an Apostle, as he contemplates it, holding up his hands in wonder to exclaim, "Great is the mystery of godliness, God manifest in the flesh?" This grand mystery, the person of Him who was both God and man, we have already under consideration; and we would now turn with believing, loving, adoring eyes to contemplate His Work and Glory.

In the cell where a captive had lain long immured, I have seen the successive days of his imprisonment scored with a nail on the naked walls—as each passed, and brought his sentence nearer to a close, he marked it off; giving God thanks that another day was gone. Alas for them who, rejecting the mercy of a gracious God, are cast into outer darkness! No such employment occupies their attention, or alleviates the misery of their lot. The crown never fades on the brow of saints—the joys at God's right hand are for evermore; and for evermore also is their doom, who, preferring their sins to Jesus, resist alike the sweet attractions of His cross and the awful terrors of His law—their worm never dieth, and their fire is never quenched.

In eternity there are neither years, nor days, nor hours; yet there have been two hours in time which are drawn out, if I may say so, over the length of eternal ages. One, that hour, pregnant of evil when Eve, tempted of the devil, plucked the forbidden fruit, and the fall ensued. The sea wastes its fury on the shore, and after raging for a while, falls asleep like a fretful child; continents limit the range and ravages of earthquakes; the grave, where the wicked cease from troubling, and the weary are at rest, sets bounds to the power of the oppressor; but limited in its influence to no place, or age, or race of men, the shock of that fall was felt throughout all the world. Nor shall its consequences cease with the world, and with time. When this old world shall be no more, and time shall be lost in eternity, and death itself shall die, that unhappy hour shall live in the memory, and be felt in the misery of the lost.

The other hour, pregnant with greatest good, a the first was with greatest evil, to the world, one which, more than any in the whole course of ages, has occupied the attention and excited the expectations of earth, and hell, and heaven too, was that our Lord pointed at when He said, " The hour is come when the Son of Man should be glorified.' There, as is plain from the words that follow, " Verily, verily, except a corn of wheat fall into the ground and die, it abideth alone; but if it die, it bringeth forth much fruit," Jesus refers to His approaching death. In that hour, His great work, to to use His own last words, was " finished," and the head He bowed in death was crowned with its brightest glory.

1. There were circumstances of visible glory attending our Lord's death. Apart from the spiritual blessings which flow to us from it, and apart also from the revenue of glory Christ derives from the Church, both in earth and heaven, which He has redeemed by His blood, there never was a death like His. It is as true that never man died as He died, as that never man spake as He spake. Rays of Godhead streamed through the darkest scenes of

His humiliation; or lent these such splendour as the sun imparts to the edges of the murky cloud that conceals His face. Jesus was born, like any other child, but the fruit of a virgin's womb. Angels attended and celebrated with songs the great event. Humble as was His birth-place, a new star rested above the stable; and divine worship, offered by the manger where He lay, gave dignity to the lowly scene. His hands were rough with labor; but at their touch eyes received their sight, and the dead were restored to life. His voice had been heard in the wails of infancy, and also in dying groans; but it quelled the roaring storm, and burst the ancient fetters of the tomb. His eye was quenched in darkness, fixed and filmy as He hung on the tree; but it had read the secrets of man's heart, and penetrated the veil of futurity. He did not walk the world in costly robes, or in imperial purple; but the hem of his garment, at the touch of faith, cured inveterate disease. He did not tread on luxurious carpets; but His step was on the billows of the sea. Unaccustomed to luxuries, His simple drink was water from the well; but water changed to wine at His bidding. No lordly halls received, or sumptuous banquets entertained, His guests; but the few fishes and five barley loves of the mountain-feast were sufficient, in His hands, to satisfy the wants of thousands, and leave, of fragments, twelve baskets over.

The glory that shone through many of the most humiliating scenes of His life was still more apparent in its closing hours. Men had left nothing undone to heap shame on His dying head, and aggravate by disgrace the bitterness of death. To pour contempt on His kingly claims they crowned His brows with thorns; in mockery of His omniscience, when they had blindfolded, they buffeted Him—asking whose was the hand that struck Him; in ridicule of His omnipotence, when they had nailed Him to the cross, they challenged Him to leave it—crying, with gibes and insults, and a cruelty His dying face had no power to soften, "If thou be the Son of God, come down!" "He saved others; himself he cannot save." Yet even in this dark hour, when He was sinking into death under a cloud of shame and ignominy, see how the Son of Man was glorified! To the Pharisees who, as He approached Jerusalem amid a gleam of passing popularity, and attended by a mighty crowd that hailed Him as their King, had asked Him to silence the hosannas of the people, He had said, "If these should hold their peace, the stones would immediately cry out." No empty boast! By-and-by that multitude melted away like a snow-wreath—like a flock of sheep when, crouching to the spring, the lion, with a bound and roar, leaps into the fold, the disciples have fled; and, save a dying robber that confesses our Lord, all men hold their peace. But now events happen more wonderful than ancient story relates of a dumb son who had followed his father to battle. Seeing him struck down, lying on the ground with a sword pointed at his breast, they tell how, under the sudden impulse of affection and of alarm for his father's life, he burst the string that tied his tongue, and cried out in terror. So when at Jesus's death all men held their peace, dumb nature spake. The rocks, whose bosoms, less hard than man's, were rent, cried out on earth; the sun, veiling his face from a scene on which insensate men looked without emotion, cried out in heaven; the dead, disturbed in their graves by so great a crime, cried out from their open tombs; and the temple, with its veil, though touched by no mortal hands, rent in twain from top to bottom, added its solemn testimony to theirs; and dying amid these strange, impressive, and transcendent wonders, in that of His death the hour had come when the Son of Man was glorified.

2. Christ's death afforded the fullest display of His mercy, grace, and truth.

Not that they had not been displayed before—as in the wilderness, through which the pillar, symbol of His presence, their grateful shade by day and their light by night, guided and guarded the wandering host—as by the sea, whose waves rushed foaming and thundering together at His word to engulf beneath their waters the pride and power of Egypt—as on that desert with its barren sands covered day by day, for forty years, with corn dropped from dewy skies—as beside that gray rock which poured streams from its flinty bosom—as on that awful mountain which flamed like a volcano at His touch, and, striking the boldest with awe, shook with His thunders and trembled beneath His feet. In these, and in many other events, the forefathers of those who rejected our Lord had been the witnesses of His glory. He was the God of Sinai— the Captain of the Host—the Angel of the Covenant; and for ages they had read in the Bible, and celebrated in the songs of the sanctuary, the wonders He had done in the days of their fathers, and in the old times before them.

Yet not till, veiling His divine splendors, the Son of God appeared in the form of a man, and, giving Himself up to death, expired amid the agonies of a cross, were His love and mercy, His pity, His purpose, and His power to save, fully disclosed. It was when Moses smote the rock that its hidden treasures were unsealed; and the people, pressing eagerly forward—sons bearing aged parents on their shoulders, and mothers infants in their happy arms—heard the sweetest music in its liquid murmurs, and drank life in its cold gushing stream.

It was when the alabaster box was broken that its value became known, and its aroma, rising from the head and feet of Jesus, was diffused throughout all the house. It is when the clusters of the grape, borne with songs from the vineyard by bright and happy maidens, are crushed in the wine-press, and trodden under foot, that they yield the wine which, used for sacred and also common purposes, was said to "make glad the heart both of God and man." Nor were Christ's gracious attributes, His love to poor sinners and His power to save them, fully disclosed till His dying hour; till He entered the garden where, sinking under the load of a world's guilt, He cried, "My soul is exceeding sorrowful, even unto death;" till He hung on that cross where He poured out His precious blood a sacrifice for sin—dying the just for the unjust.

Had Jesus never died, nor heaven, nor hell, nor earth had ever known how He loved: nor had we, unable to imagine the degree and extent of His divine compassion, been constrained to exclaim, "O the height and depth, the breadth and length, of the love of God!—it passeth knowledge." No exaggeration this! Allying us more closely to God than the angels are—since His Son took not on Him the nature of angels, but the nature of man—and making these heavenly spirits our ministering servants, this love is "higher than heaven;" saving in us those more guilty than devils are—since the devils never once rejected the Son of God, nor turned a deaf ear to the voice of mercy—this love is "deeper than hell;" and infinitely surpassing any earthly affection, the measure thereof is "longer than the earth, and broader than the sea."

The full and crowning expression of the love wherewith God loved us in that, while we were enemies, He gave up His Son to die for us, and wherewith also His Son loved us in being willing to be given, at Jesus' death the hour arrived when, completing the great work of atonement, He was most fully glorified. He had been despised and rejected of men : He had been called an impostor, a blasphemer, a glutton, and a wine-bibber ; neglected of His own creatures, He had seen their doors shut in His face, and been left, when the fox sought his hole and the bird dropt into her nest, to find a bed on the cold ground; persecuted in His cradle, He had been persecuted to His grave. But now His sorrows are past, and His shame rolled away for ever. He dies, but as a conqueror—crowned with the rich spoils of victory ; a victim, but a victor also—crushing the head of the serpent that had bit His heel, and in the penitent thief whom He bears aloft to heaven, giving us a proof of His pity for the guilty, and of His willingness and power to save even the chief of sinners.

12

3. By His death, our Lord conquered hell, and death, and the grave.

It was the curse of Canaan, the descendant and representative of Ham, that he should be the servant of servants; but it is the crowning glory of Jesus that He became the conqueror of conquerors: spoiling principalities and powers, like a victor returning from the wars with monarchs and princes and captains bound to his chariot, He made a show of them openly. For forty days the haughty Philistine came forth to challenge the armies of the living God; crying, as he stalked out into the intervening meadow, and shook his plumes and spear in triumph, 'I defy Israel! Give me a man that we may fight together!" And since the fall, when Satan worsted our first parents, and laid their honor in the dust, for forty long centuries he had proudly held the field. No man had proved a match for him. In Noah, and Abraham, and Moses, and David, the very chiefs and standard-bearers of God's host had fallen; before his power and devilish subtlety, one after another bit the dust : nor had any been delivered from his cruel hand, but as Israel, when God, making a way of escape for His people, opened the gates of the sea, and snatched them from the grasp of Egypt.

But now the hour has come when this proud adversary of God and man has his challenge accepted.

David's Son is buckling for the fight; angels are gathered on the battlements of heaven to watch its fortunes, and see the issue; each advancing from its own ranks, the Prince of Light and the Prince of Darkness meet. Foiled at all points, met with his match now, and more than his match, Satan is baffled and borne back: and yet—for such was the divine decree, the claims of justice, the price of victory—our Champion falls; but falls like Samson. He bows Himself on the pillars of His adversary's kingdom—by His own death destroying Death, and him that had the power of death, that is, the Devil. The Devil!—he had seduced angels from their loyalty, and had raised the shout of victory within the gates of Eden. Death!—he had plucked the crown from the brows of kings, and darkened the eyes of seers, and sealed the lips of prophets, and mocked the skill of man, and crushed the strength of giants: and, as Solomon says, in the war with him, men had found "no discharge." But how do the fortunes of battle change when Christ, our champion, the Captain of our salvation, comes into the field! Calling out, "O death, I will be thy plagues! O grave, I will be thy destruction!" He takes the prey from the spoiler; and not only in our souls, washed in His blood and sanctified by His Spirit, redeems the jewel, but the casket too—for that purpose descending into the realms of the grave, with garments rolled in blood. The brow that bled beneath a crown of thorns now wears the diadem of victory; and now, where the eyes of men saw but a ghastly spectacle, a mangled body suspended on a tree, with the setting sun lighting up its dead, defaced, and pallid countenance, faith beholds the triumph of redeeming love—the crowning work and glory of the Son of God; and pointing to that sacred form which has death and the serpent lying crushed beneath its feet, she addresses men and angels, saying, " Sing unto the Lord, for he hath triumphed gloriously : thy right hand, O Lord, hath dashed the enemy in pieces."

The work of our Saviour was essentially and preeminently that of a surety or substitute. Some affirm that Jesus died merely as an example, to teach us how to die. Others, repudiating the proper idea of an atonement, and emasculating a doctrine which they profess to hold, regard his death as nothing more than an expression of the love of God to a fallen world. But unless our blessed Lord assumed our nature that He might, besides fulfilling the requirements of the law, bear in some proper sense, and in our room and stead, the punishment due to sin, by what rule are we to interpret the language of Scripture? Were it otherwise, what language more misleading, more calculated to mislead, than these declarations?—" I am the good shepherd; the good shepherd giveth his life for the sheep; I lay down my life for the sheep "—" God commendeth his love toward us, in that, while we were yet sinners, Christ died for us "—" If, when we were enemies, we were reconciled to God by the death of his Son, much more being reconciled, we shall be saved by his life "—" Surely he hath borne our griefs, and carried our sorrows; he was wounded for our transgressions, he was bruised for our iniquities; the chastisement of our peace was upon him, and with his stripes we are healed."

As is plain from these words, Jesus had to endure in our stead the penalty due to sin, and die for us, as the bleeding victim of old for him who offered it on the altar. Therefore it was, that they who knew not what they did when they crucified the Lord of glory, knew not what they said when they cast this cruel taunt in His face, " He saved others, Himself he cannot save!" This was true; but not for the reason they supposed. He could have saved Himself —descending from the cross to take summary vengeance on His foes; or, as Samson did with the ponderous gates of Gaza, carry it away—rise before their astonished eyes, and bear it to heaven as a trophy of His power. What then? Alas! we had been left to perish.

The case may be in some measure illustrated by what happened in the terrible dilemma in which two miners once found themselves. They were engaged blasting a rock in the bowels of the earth. The chamber for the powder bored, they charge it; and having lighted the hissing match, they take to flight, hurrying to the bottom of the shaft, to throw themselves into the basket, and give the signal to be drawn up out of reach, not of danger only, but of death. Alas, the wheel turns not. The man at the top of the shaft is able to raise one, but not both. Every moment the fire may reach the powder, and blow them into eternity. There they sit; pale, speechless, helpless, looking each other in the face, and death staring grimly at them both. Both must die, unless one, sacrificing himself to save his comrade, leap from the basket. It was done—promptly. nobly done. They were, and yet were not, in equal danger. One is a man of God; the other a graceless, prayerless profligate. Calmly addressing his wicked companion, "I know," said the first, "if you die, you go to hell; but knowing in whom I have believed, death shall be gain to me." So bidding the other farewell, a Christian hero, he leaps from the basket; and leaving it to rise, sits down to pray and die. Here, though I may remark that this man himself escaped death by a singular providence, he saved the other, but himself also he could not save; and as there was there a physical impossibility of saving both, there is here a moral one. The jus-

tice of God which awarded the penalty of death to
sin must be satisfied: the law of God which required perfect obedience must be magnified: the substitute or the sinner therefore must die; and Jesus
died, the just for the unjust, that we might be saved—
that whosoever believeth on Him might not perish,
but have everlasting life.

The object of our faith, to whose righteousness,
rejecting all confidence in our own, we trust, Jesus
is also to be the object of our imitation—our pattern as well as our propitiation. Therefore they
that are Christ's live not *to*, any more than they live
through, themselves; the rule of their life, the motto
blazoned on their banner, not self-indulgence, but
self-denial. The spectators who, drawn to roof and
window by the roar and tumult, looked down on the
passing crowd as it hurried on to Calvary, knew
Jesus by the cross on His shoulder, and the thorns
on His bleeding brow. One eagerly pointing Him
out to another—some with scorn on their lips,
others with a tear in their eye—Yon is He, they
cried, who looks so meek, and patient, and gentle,
with a cross on his back and crown of thorns on his
brow! And still we may know the servant by the
Master's livery. Who is mocked by an ungodly
world? who blesses them that curse Him? who returns good for evil? who is patient with the bad?
who toils and labors, spends and is spent, lives and

perhaps dies for others, forgetful of himself? By the tokens whereby they recognized the Master, I recognize the man. If we can sit at ease while others are perishing around us—if we can lie on a flowery bank, basking in the gladsome sunshine, without taking any interest in others, or stretching out a hand to pluck them from the torrent that sweeps them on to ruin, it matters not to what church we belong. We belong not to Christ—we are none of His. As much as to murderers, adulterers, drunkards, and thieves, "Depart from me, I have never known you," is the language He shall hold to all whose life-maxim is expressed in such words as these, "Am I my brother's keeper?"—let souls perish, so I be rich—let others suffer, so I enjoy myself—"Soul, take thine ease, eat, drink, and be merry." Unless the same mind be in you that was in Jesus Christ, ye are none of His. Paul said, "Christ liveth in me"—language which His humblest, weakest follower can hold as well as that great apostle. The beautiful incarnation of all that was lofty in aim, tender in sympathy, generous in heart, pure in life, self-forgetful, self-denying, Jesus Himself, is the fair copy which Christians, through the aids of the Holy Spirit, are to attempt to imitate. "If any man," He said, "would be my disciple, let him take up his cross, deny himself daily, and follow me '

XVI.

THE WAY OF SALVATION.

SOME Scripture terms are forensic. Such are the expressions *justified* and *condemned*. Employed in courts of law, they call up to our minds the scene of a trial—the crowd of eager spectators; the prisoner standing alone, pale and anxious, at the bar; the judges seated aloft in imposing state; the heavy indictment; the long array of witnesses; the sudden and breathless silence, amid which—all bending forward to catch their words—the jury re- turn into court with their verdict; the verdict itself, the Not Guilty or Guilty, that sends the accused away to life and liberty, or, falling from reluctant lips, and going like a knife to his heart, sends him to the scaffold and seals his doom. The expressions "justified" and "condemned," therefore, forewarn us of a day when, with God for his judge, an assem- bled world for spectators, and heaven or hell for his destiny, every man shall be put upon his trial; judged according to the deeds done in the body, whether they were good or evil. "It is appointed,"

12*

says an Apostle, " unto men once to die, but after this the judgment. '

A solemn, but a certain prospect!—for none may hope to escape this ordeal.   Universal as the sentence, judgment is inevitable as the scythe of death. It is often wonderful to see how human justice tracks the steps and doublings of a guilty fugitive, like a sleuth-hound ; and how, with an arm that stretches over broad continents and seas, she will drag him to her bar from his hiding-place in the ends of the earth.   Yet, cases ever and anon occur where the gallows, if I may use the expression, is cheated of its due, and the perpetrators of crimes that have struck society with horror escape detection, or elude the keenest pursuit.   But escape from God and His judgment is impossible. Reconciled to Him through the blood of His Son, and recognizing their Saviour in the Judge before whose face—as He comes with ten times ten thousand angels—the heavens flee away, God's people would not escape though they could ; and as to His enemies, who vainly cry on the mountains and rocks to cover them, they could not though they would.   What says one who may be supposed, under a sense of guilt and dread of punishment, to have been racking his fancy for a way to elude the presence and escape the justice of God ? "Whither," he asks, " shall I go from thy Spirit ? Whither shall I flee from thy presence ? If I ascend up to heaven, thou art there; if I make my bed in hell, behold, thou art also there; if I take the wings of the morning, and dwell in the uttermost parts of the sea, there shall thy hand lead me; if I say, Surely the darkness shall cover me, even the night shall be light about me." Nor do God's own words, any more than these, leave a chance, the shadow of a hope, the smallest loophole of escape, to impenitent and unbelieving sinners. To alarm them, to persuade them to abandon their sins and embrace the Saviour, He uses the boldest figures. Speaking of the wicked, He says, " He that fleeth of them shall not flee away; and he that escapeth of them shall not be delivered; though they dig into hell, there shall mine hand take them; though they climb up to heaven, there will I bring them down; though they be hid from my sight in the bottom of the sea, there will I command the serpent, and he shall bite them."

Another great difference between the administration of Divine and human justice, lies in this, that while none shall escape God's judgment, its sentence, once passed, whether for good or evil, is irrevocable. A very weighty and solemn consideration ! As the tree falls, so it lies; they that are filthy shall be filthy still, as they that are righteous shall be righteous still. At an earthly tribunal hope sustains the criminal, when, pity taking the place of horror, every eye regards him with sorrow, and the voice of the judge trembles with emotion, as, amid an awful silence, he pronounces the words of doom. What though the "condemned cell" receives him now? He reads above its gloomy door no such words as Dante has inscribed on the gates of hell, " Let them who enter here leave Hope behind!" Abandon the wretch who may, hope does not; but goes with him from the bar, shining into his heart like the sunbeam that falls through his grated window on the floor. In other cases justice has relented somewhat of her sternness. Why may she not in his? So, down to the last post, and the last day, and the last hour, clinging to hope as a drowning man to a plank, many whom earthly tribunals have consigned to death, have illustrated and verified the saying—

> "As long as life its term extends,
> Hope's blest dominion never ends."

But despair, more terrible than the devils old painters represent dragging away the lost, seizes those whom God condemns—let me say, condemns reluctant. He is not willing that any should perish; He " so loved the world that He gave up His only begotten Son, that whosoever believeth in Him might not perish, but have everlasting life;" yet, the great white throne once set, the books once opened, the sentence once passed, " He hath forgotten to be gracious, and his mercy is clean gone for ever," it is idle quarreling with that truth: "Shall not the Judge of all the earth do right?" and in our imperfect knowledge of the Infinite and of His ways, to challenge them is for the lay to say to the potter, Why hast thou made me thus? It is certain that with salvation purchased at an enormous cost, and not only freely offered, but earnestly and affectionately pressed on the chief of sinners, we shall not have to blame God, but ourselves, if we are lost. It is not by God's hand, but our own—not from within, but from without, the door of heaven is barred. "Ye will not come unto me," says Jesus. Now, taking God's word as it stands, what is the plain, practical conclusion to which the irrevocable nature of the sentence leads, but this, that unlike such as are arraigned at man's bar, we are to apply for pardon, not after, but before our trial—before death has summoned, or the Judge has sentenced us? It is too late then. Then, in the words of the bridegroom to the foolish virgins, "The door is shut!"

History relates the story of a man, a sagacious and far-sighted man, whose example it is our safety, our salvation to follow. He had committed heinous crimes against his sovereign and the state. He knew his life to be forfeited; and that if, allowing events to take their course, he waited to be tried, he was certain to be condemned. The case is exactly ours. In these circumstances he repaired to the palace to fling himself at the feet of his sovereign, and making full confession of his crimes, to beg for mercy. Through the clemency of his king, and the intercession of a powerful friend at court, he found mercy; and, with a full pardon in his bosom, signed by the king's own hand, left the royal presence a happy man. In course of time, the day of trial arrives, gathering a great concourse of people. He repairs to the place. Ignorant of his secret, anxious friends tremble for his fate; and the spectators wonder at his calm and placid bearing as he passes the scaffold where they think he is so soon to die, and enters the court, certain, as they fancy, to be condemned. He steps up to the bar as lightly as a bridegroom to the marriage altar; and, to all men's surprise, looks boldly around, on the court, his judges, and his accusers. At this, however, they cease to wonder when, after listening unmoved to charges enough to hang twenty men in place of one, he thrusts his hand into his bosom to draw forth the pardon, to cast it on the table, and find himself, amid a sudden outburst of joy, locked in the happy embraces of his wife and children. Let us go and do likewise. The bar of Divine judgment is a place not to sue for mercy, but to plead it. Appearing there robed in the righteousness of Jesus Christ, justified, forgiven, in our hands a pardon signed

and sealed with blood, we shall look around us un-
dismayed on all the terrors of the scene—to ask with
Paul, " Who shall lay anything to the charge of
God's elect? It is God that justifieth; who is he
that condemneth ?"

I remark that the way of salvation lies in being
justified, not through our own, but imputed righteousness.

" All we like sheep have gone astray "—" The
Scripture hath concluded all under sin "—" By the
offence of one, judgment came upon all men unto
condemnation "—" Death passed upon all men, for
that all have sinned "—" Cursed is every one that
continueth not in all things written in the book of
the law to do them "—these, the words of Scripture,
sound like the clank of fetters. In the face of such
declarations, what folly is it in a man to attempt to
beguile his conscience; to quiet its fears; persuad-
ing himself that, safe in the mercy from the justice
of God, he has no need to be alarmed at the prospect of death and judgment! Would that these
words spoke as pointedly to our hearts as they speak
plainly to our ears! Guilt has been incurred; there
is a judgment to come, and a pressing necessity, if
there be a way of escape, that we should take it;
take it now; take it at whatever cost—as our Lord
says, plucking out a right eye, and cutting off a right
hand, and losing our life that we may find it.

There is such a way; but certainly not by the works of the law. In perfect harmony with Him who pronounces our "righteousness to be filthy rags," Paul says, "By the deeds of the law shall no flesh be justified;" and in that sets up such a notice as turns one back from a road where, though once frequented, the grass, growing rank and tall, has obliterated every footmark. Ever since the Fall, the gate to heaven by the law has stood shut, nor once turned on its hinges; the rust of long ages there, and over it a notice—"No passage this way." Yet, blessed be God, there is a way of return to His favor, forgiveness, and the kingdom of heaven. Harlots, publicans, and sinners have found it; and why may not we? To make it, God's Son became a man, taking to Himself a body that He might be capable of suffering;—eyes to weep; a brow to bleed beneath the thorns; feet and hands, that, with the iron driven through the quivering flesh, He might hang, a sacrifice for sin, on the accursed tree. He was made under the law for the very purpose of answering its demands, both in the way of doing and of suffering. He became a man for the very purpose of being a man of sorrows; and shared in our nature for the purpose of suffering in our stead. There is a story of a brave sacrifice once made to save the life of a king. The battle had gone against him. Separated by accident from his followers, he was hard bested; a swarm of foes pressed on him— their swords ringing on his helmet, and each eager to obtain the honours that were to reward his capture or death. He dies unless some one will die in his room. A chivalrous follower sees the peril; spurs his horse into the thick of the foe, shouting, as he whirled his bloody battle-blade above his head, " I am the king!" and thus turned against his own bosom the swords that had otherwise been buried in his master's. A generous, heroic sacrifice! yet but a faint shadow of what He offered who laid down His life a ransom, not for His friends, but His enemies; dying, the just for the unjust, that we might be saved.

Distinguished in death as in His life and divine nature from all other men, our Lord Jesus Christ, in dying, did not pay the debt of nature, or, as it may be properly called, the debt of sin, for Himself. He did not die because He was a sinner, but a substitute; because He was a debtor, but a surety—all the sufferings borne by Him from His cradle to the grave being ours, the payment of debts incurred by us and undertaken by Him. Fulfilling all the precepts it enjoined, and paying all the penalties it required, He rendered a perfect obedience to the Divine law. This constitutes His righteousness, or merits; and since God is pleased to accept that in lack and place of ours, there can be no condemnation for those who, rejecting all confidence in their own righteousness to trust in His, are in Jesus Christ, and prove themselves to be so by walking, not after the flesh, but after the Spirit.

How there not only *is*, but *can be* no condemnation for them, I may illustrate by the case of two Greeks whom friendship had bound in the most endearing ties. One condemned to die for some offence, wishes, ere he leaves the world, to go away that he may arrange his affairs, and see his family, and bid them a last farewell. In these circumstances, and with a love deserving such a garland as David, saying, "Very pleasant hast thou been unto me, my brother Jonathan; thy love to me was wonderful, passing the love of women," laid on the grave of Jonathan—his friend undertook, in case he did not return, to suffer death in his stead. The offer was accepted; and was nearly attended with a tragic result. The day of doom arrives, but not the criminal. Nor was it till the very hour arrived, and the procession, with his surety ready to die, had reached the scaffold, that he, detained at sea, by adverse winds, appears; shouts to them from afar to stay the execution; and forcing his way through the crowd, leaps on the scaffold to push aside his substitute, and, like a brave, true man, bare his own neck to the sword. Touched by the display of such tender and rare affection—the joy of the one that he was in time to save his surety, the grief of the other that he had lost the opportunity of dying for his friend—the people, yielding to a generous impulse, and in honour of such noble friendship, decreed that neither should perish. But suppose that things had fallen out otherwise, and that the substitute had suffered the penalty of the law before the true criminal had time to reach the scene, and arrest the stroke. What then ? Why, the law had nothing to say to him. Though guilty, he was free ; and, as he looked with weeping eyes on the pale face and dead body of his generous friend, he could raise his head to look around on spectators, officers, and executioner, saying, " Who shall lay anything to my charge ?" Nor had his prayer been granted though, unwilling to survive his friend and prolong a life that had lost its relish, he had implored death at their hands. Since his surety had paid the penalty, the justice that demanded his death before would refuse it now. The demands of the law had been satisfied ; and had an angry crowd, suspecting that he had wilfully delayed his return, attempted violence against his person, the very sword that had been buried in the bosom of the substitute had been drawn in defence of his. The death of innocence had saved the life of guilt.

Now as, on such a supposition, it had happened in that case, it does happen in the case of all who, through faith in our surety, the Lord Jesus Christ, receive the righteousness that makes the sinner just. His perfect merits imputed to them—His work and sufferings accounted theirs — the justice that demanded their condemnation once demands their acquittal now; the law, with all its requirements, now fully satisfied, is no longer against, but for them; all God's attributes are on their side now; and so, instead of fleeing from justice, like Adam when he fled for shelter to the bush, they claim protection now from their enemies—Satan, and hell, and fear and guilt—as much from Jehovah's justice as from Jehovah's mercy. No creditor can righteously demand that a debt be twice paid; nor magistrate that a crime be twice punished; nor sovereign that a tax be twice exacted. And "shall man be more just than God?" Is that justice on the part of man? and "Are not my ways equal?" saith the Lord. Jesus has once for all paid the debt of His people to the uttermost farthing; fulfilled their duties, and made full atonement for their crimes. And hence their joy and peace in believing; hence the happy confidence with which, like the dying Wesley, when his spirit was hovering on the verge of another world, they who have made their calling and election sure, can sing—

> " I the chief of sinners am;
> But Jesus died for me.'

Regarding the method of salvation by faith in the righteousness of Jesus as a way, here are some of its peculiar and gracious and happy features, borrowed from the lights of prophecy.

It is a *high way*.

A highway, or the " King's highway," as it used to be called, is distinguished from private roads by an important difference. Gates, walls, and warnings may exclude from these all but members or visitors of the family to whose mansions they lead ; but this is free to the public—the whole public. Here, no man challenges my right to walk, or, holding the gate in hand, and saying " Back, back," compels me with wearied feet and disappointed hopes to retrace my steps. Here, no distinctions of noble or mean, of rich or poor, of virtuous or vicious, of good or bad, of sect, or rank, or party are recognized. Here all classes—master and servant, the peer in his robes and the beggar in his rags—meet on common ground ; the road below as free to every foot as the air above to birds of every wing.

Nor less free is salvation by faith in Jesus Christ. Not that men, encroaching as well on the prerogatives of the Sovereign as on the rights and privileges of His people, have not wickedly attempted to restrict the blessings of grace. For example—denying the free use of the Scriptures to the laity, claiming for her priests a monopoly of spiritual power, and, for her adherents, the exclusive benefits of the kingdom of heaven, this Popery does. And other churches, retaining her spirit, though they repudiate her name, show themselves hardly less exclusive. Some confining the flow of grace to the channel of what they call "Apostolical Succession;" others regarding their own as the only true and faithful church, without whose pale, often of the narrowest limits, there is little hope of a blessing either on sermons or sacraments, take from salvation by faith in Christ's righteousness the characteristic features of a highway. But in the face of invitations so free as these,—" Ho every one that thirsteth, come ye to the waters,"—" Come unto me, all ye that labour and are heavy laden, and I will give you rest,"— in the face also of declarations so gracious as these, —" Whosoever cometh unto me I will in no wise cast out,"—" Whosoever believeth in me shall not perish, but hath everlasting life,"— it is bold, and nothing less than impious presumption to attempt to dam up the living waters of the sanctuary, and confine to the narrow limits of their own sect or party the benefits of Christ's death. God be praised, they cannot. They may as well prescribe a narrower course for the great sun as he goes forth in the heavens to shine on every land; or control the tides, that, rising to celestial influences, roll over the bosom of the ocean to visit every continent and wash every shore. Inviting all, without respect to birth or baptism, to character or church, addressing as much the vilest sinners, the outcasts, the scum and dregs of society, as those whose virtues have won universal esteem, Jesus says, " Look unto me and be ye saved, all ye ends of the earth "—" I am the way "— " I have set before you an open door." And neither deterred by the voice of bigotry nor scared by the fears of guilt, let us crowd the gates of mercy ; enter—enter joyfully in. Blessed be God, He who shutteth and no man openeth, openeth and no man shutteth.

It is a *plain way.*

The Bible has had innumerable commentators. Some, by their books or sermons, remind us of him who lighted a candle to show the sun ; and others, like the fog-bank through which the sun shines shorn of his beams, " darken counsel by words," and make what was clear obscure. By their labours, some have diluted, while others, making their sermons or commentaries a vehicle for error, have adulterated the truth of God, the wine of life. But however this may be, more pens have been worn, more breath spent, more printing-presses employed, in explaining the Bible than all other books whatever ; so that were all the books collected which have been written to throw light on the Scriptures, they would— not excepting that of Alexandria, which it took many weeks to reduce to ashes—form the largest library the world ever saw. Are we to infer from this that the way of life is obscure? By no means? All that it is necessary to know in order to be saved, it is easy to know. "The wayfaring men, though fools, shall not err therein," says the Prophet; and without disparaging the labours of pious and able divines to explore the mysteries and shed light on the obscurities of the sacred volume, the simple Bible, blessed by God, has proved to unlettered thousands a safe and sufficient guide. Whatever genius and arduous study it may require to rise to a place in the temple of fame, many a humble Christian, hardly able to spell his way through the Word of God, has reached one in the temple of heaven. Thousands so deficient in talent or energy as never to have been able to make their way in this world, have found their way to a better one; nor are there wanting interesting and well-attested cases of imbeciles, who, though destitute of capacity for ordinary knowledge, have known Him whom to know is life eternal—so plain the way through child-like faith in Christ—so easy as well to the unsteady gait of simpletons as to the tottering foot of childhood, as to verify the words, "The wayfaring men, though fools. shall not err therein." With this simple answer to the great question, "What shall I do to be saved?" "Believe on the Lord Jesus Christ, and thou shalt be saved,' none need be excluded from heaven because of ignorance; as with virtue in Christ's blood to cleanse the chief of sinners, none need be excluded because of sin. It needs no learning to learn this way.

What has the Church seen? God ordaining strength out of the mouth of babes and sucklings; grey-haired men learning wisdom at the feet of childhood; the death-beds of the humble poor like the very gates of heaven; the child learning the way to life on a mother's knee; the thief learning it on his dying cross; the mantle of prophets falling on ploughmen; heaven revealing its glories to humble shepherds; rude fishermen of Galilee called to the apostleship; grace polishing the roughest men; roaming savages tamed by the voice and sitting at the feet of Jesus, clothed and in their right mind. Simple faith in Him is all that is required—such confidence as the little child, lying in its mother's arms, hanging on her neck, looking up in her face, reposes in the power of a mother's arm and the tenderness of a mother's heart.

It is a *holy way*.

> " Just as I am, without one plea,
> But that Thy blood was shed for me,
> And that Thou bid'st me come to Thee,
> O Lamb of God, I come."

As is expressed in these well-known and beautiful

13

lines, we are to go to Christ as sinners — guilty, polluted, wretched, miserable sinners. We are to go as we are; not, however, to continue as we are, but to obtain deliverance as well from the power as from the punishment of sin. Regarding it as a disease, hereditary in our family, deadly as the leprosy, and as loathsome in its features as it is fatal in its issue, the Church may be regarded as an hospital— but by no means an hospital for incurables. To those asylums where pity seeks to shelter the hopeless and alleviate the sufferings of lingering but inevitable death, the gospel presents no counterpart. With a physician in Christ, of whom I can say that He never refused a case, never charged a fee, and never lost a patient, it opens its doors to receive the sick, men and women, even in the very hour and article of death; but it is to cure them — send them out healed; through the sanative and sanctifying influence of the Holy Spirit, cured of "whatsoever manner of disease they had."

Neither requiring nor recognizing any merit in us, but resting our acceptance with God entirely on the merits of His Son, the gospel does not dispense with personal holiness, nor afford any pretext to such as say, Let us continue in sin, that grace may abound. The same authority that declares, Whosoever believeth on the Lord Jesus Christ shall be saved, declares that without holiness no man shall see God. A prominent feature that, of salvation by faith in the righteousness of Jesus Christ—" it shall be called," says the prophet, " the way of holiness : the unclean shall not pass over it." In regeneration, this way is entered on by a holy change; in the saints of God, it is frequented by a holy company; and in that pure and blessed heaven, above whose portals is written, There entereth nothing here to hurt or to defile, it conducts to a holy place.

Where are you going? said Malan, of Geneva, to an English lady who was introduced to him. I am on my way to visit Rome, was her reply. Oh, he answered, that is not what I mean; startling her with this plain, pointed question, Is it to heaven or to hell, madam, you are going? Abrupt, indiscreet, perhaps, as such a mode of address may be considered, the question is one which every person should put to themselves—proving their own work, trying the foundation of their hopes, and giving all diligence, as the Apostle says, to make their calling and election sure. For this object, what better, plainer, surer test than the holiness which the Scriptures invariably associate with true living faith? There sanctification and justification are inseparably connected; and what God hath joined together, let none attempt to put asunder. To live in the unrestrained, unrepented indulgence of any sin, and talk of faith in Christ, and indulge in hopes of heaven is a mockery and a miserable delusion; one of the strongest proofs that "the heart is deceitful above all things, and desperately wicked." To be holy as God is holy, to be perfect as our Father in heaven is perfect, to have the same mind in us that was in Jesus Christ, though not yet the attainment, is the aim and wish, the object of the prayers and efforts of every child of God—No holiness, no heaven, being an adage as true as the more common saying, No, cross, no crown.

It is a *safe way.*

"He laid his carcase in his own grave, and they mourned over him, saying, Alas, my brother!" That grave received one who was returning to a home he never reached. Contrary to his instructions, this prophet of God had ate and drunk in Bethel to learn, that when he left the path of duty, he left the path of safety. On his way homeward, a lion, the messenger of divine wrath, met and slew him. This was no accident, but a special providence—as appeared from the circumstance that the beast which he rode was found standing fearless on one side of his body, and the lion that had killed him quietly on the other; yet such accidents were not uncommon in the lands of the Bible. Jacob, for instance, when the coat of many colours was produced, all stained with blood, instantly and bitterly exclaimed, It is my son's coat, an evil beast hath devoured him; Joseph, without doubt, is rent in pieces. So also David, describing the greatness of his danger, says, " My soul is among lions;" and hence, also, the figure employed to describe the difficulty or peril of an enterprise, " There is a lion in the path !"

Blessed be God, this cannot be said of the path opened to heaven by the blood of Christ. " No lion shall be there," says the prophet, " nor any ravenous beast shall go up therein; it shall not be found there"—words these that, describing the state of those who are justified through faith in the righteousness of Jesus Christ, assure us of their safety, of the care the Lord takes of them; preserving them; defending them; and securing this, that come what may in the form of trials and temptations, they shall not come short of eternal life. Were it otherwise, what though salvation were freely offered, and offered to all, if any honestly seeking and pursuing it might nevertheless perish ! What though Christ died, if any for whom He died could be plucked out of His hands ! Farewell then to the peace that passeth understanding; farewell to the calm tranquility that is careful for nothing, but by prayer and supplication, with thanksgiving in all things, makes its wants known unto God. It is with cautious steps we tread the grass where the serpent lies coiled, ready for the spring; it is with beating heart, and anxious eye, and hushed and breathless silence, travellers skirt the brake where the lion, watching for his prey, lies crouching for the leap; and, if exposed without protection to such dangers, how is the pilgrim to Zion to go up with songs? how is he to respond to the glorious call, Rejoice in the Lord alway, and again I say, Rejoice?

"Let not your heart be troubled," said Jesus; ye believe in God, believe also in me." So He says to His people; and what says He of them?—"I give unto them eternal life, and they shall never perish." There were lions once in the way. Satan was one— a roaring lion walking about seeking whom he might devour: but he is chained now, and able to do little more than roar against the saints; he may alarm, but cannot harm them. The justice of God also was once a lion in the way: but the Good Shepherd having given His life for the sheep, justice has been satisfied, and now the lion and the lamb dwell together. Death also was once a lion in the way; but sin, the sting of death, atoned for, he has lost his terrors; direst foe is changed into truest friend; death has become gain, and in its darkness faith hails the aurora of eternal day. No doubt, they who are united by faith to Christ, accepted and forgiven of God, have evils to endure in this life; a sore battle to fight; perhaps heavy burdens to bear. But though they may be cast down, they cannot be destroyed. With Jesus at the helm, their ship may be tossed on the billows, but it cannot founder. In reward of what He did and suffered for them, God hath promised to His Son what He promised to His servant Paul, " I have given thee all them that sail with thee !" so—as when the ship took the ground, and her masts went by the board, and the waves made a clean breach over her, some swimming, some on boards, some drifting through the wild sea on broken pieces of the ship, all that company escaped safe to land, all who believe in Jesus shall reach the heavenly shore. I say, therefore, with Paul, Wherefore, sirs, be of good cheer !

> "Through Him all dangers we'll defy,
> And more than conquer all."

XVII.

MADE HOLY.

" SIRS, what must I do to be saved?" — the cry of the lost, though prior in point of time, is not prior in importance to this, the question of the saved, "What must I do to be sanctified?" To be sanctified—in plain English, to be made holy—is, to use the admirable definition of the Westminster Assembly's Catechism, "the work of God's free grace, whereby we are renewed in the whole man after the image of God, and are enabled more and more to die unto sin and live unto righteousness." But since—to borrow an illustration from a familiar object—it requires as much skill in contrivance and power in execution to restore the image to a coin from which time has effaced the features as it did to impress it there originally, even so to renew man in the image of God is plainly a work as great and divine as it was to form him in that image at the first. In point of fact, this is a new creation; and to Him therefore who, when creating Adam, said, "Let us make man in our image," David turned his face in prayer to cry, " Create in me a clean heart, O Lord, and renew a right spirit within me !"

He who has lost the image of God is like a man who has lost his life—he has neither the will nor the power to restore it. So far, for instance, as Lazarus' power and will were concerned, his dead body, having neither, would have remained in the grave to the day of judgment : nor had the current of the dead man's blood begun again to circulate, nor his heart to beat, unless the voice, which said, " Lazarus, come forth," had been that which, at the beginning, called our world and all others into being. Spiritual is as much as natural life the gift of God : and to raise man from a state of nature into a state of grace, to convert a sinner into a saint, is a work, though it may seem less surprising, not less great and divine than it would be to change a dog into a man, or a man into an angel. St. Paul knew this. Therefore he offers no unnecessary prayer at the throne of grace, imposes no unnecessary task on God, and fosters in his Thessalonian converts no unnecessary humility, when he prays on their behalf, ' The very God of peace sanctify you wholly !" —and speaking of God elsewhere to the same church he says, " Who hath from the beginning chosen you to salvation through sanctification of the Spirit and belief of the truth." Nor than Him, as through Jesus Christ the God of peace, who accomplishes this work by the effectual operation of His own Holy Spirit—is there any other source of sanctification. None else is recognized in the Scriptures, or realized in the experience of believers.

There are, as I shall afterwards show, means of sanctification. These it is our duty and privilege to use diligently. But we are never to lose sight of this—that, apart from the influences of the Holy Spirit, these are vain; altogether vain; nor able of themselves—to borrow a figure from our Lord—to do more than cleanse the outside of the cup and platter; to whitewash the building, leaving it, however, as much as before, a dismal, doleful sepulchre, full of dead men's bones and of all uncleanness. No mistake can be more fatal than one which people, not outwardly vicious, are very apt to fall into—that, namely, of mistaking, not only reformation for regeneration, but outward propriety of life and conduct for sanctification of the heart. Beware of this—the error, the fatal error, into which the Pharisee fell. Correct—perhaps even strictly correct—in his outward demeanour, fasting twice a week, and giving tithes of all he possessed, he stands well in his own esteem; not doubting that he held as high a place in God's esteem, when his eye falls on a poor publican who stands afar off, and, beating on his breast, cries, " God be merciful to me a sinner," this miserable formalist, this whited sepulchre, gives thanks that he is not such as that man. Ah, could he have seen at that moment the proud, ungodly heart that lay concealed beneath this fair exterior, and could he have heard at that moment the judgment heaven pronounced on his case, how amazed had he been! —as much astonished as Belshazzar, when, from the fiery letters on his palace wall, Daniel read out his doom—" Mene, Mene, Tekel, Upharsin, Thy kingdom is divided; God hath numbered thy kingdom and finished it." While many may, to their own great loss, neglect the means of grace, let those who use them beware lest, proud of that, satisfied with doing so, they get puffed up with spiritual pride, and stand in the same condemnation as the self-righteous Pharisee. Regularity in prayer and the reading of God's holy word, attendance on public worship and the other ordinances of religion, the practice of the various moralities and charities of life, are commendable, and indeed indispensable; but these cannot create a clean heart, nor renew a right spirit within us. The Ethiopian cannot change his skin, nor the leopard his spots; nor anything these hearts of ours but the grace of God. Without that, without the power and blessing of the Holy Spirit, the means of grace are wells without water, clouds without rain.

The necessity of this great work, a work which

has God for its author, man for its subject, and for its object his restoration to the image of God, is plain, almost self-evident. Take a simple illustration. In virtue of her royal prerogative, the Queen may pardon all the criminals—the thieves, robbers, murderers, malefactors, scum and dregs of society—which our prisons hold. Let her do so, and every jail would be at once thrown open. But this, illustrating the adage, that it is not always *right* for people to do what they have a *right* to do, would be justly regarded as a public calamity: and every man who had any regard to the safety of his person and the security of his property would take the opening of the prison-doors as a warning to shut his own. Not only so, but ere we would allow the tenants of the jail to enter our houses and mingle with our families, we should require to be satisfied that their habits and hearts were changed — that the drunkard had become sober, the thief honest, the liar true, the vile pure; that they had undergone, in short, such a change as is pictured forth in this lovely vision of the time, when God shall pour out His Spirit upon all flesh, and " the wolf shall dwell with the lamb, and the leopard shall lie down with the kid, and the calf, and the young lion, and the fatling together; and a little child shall lead them; and the cow and the bear shall feed, and their young ones shall lie down together; and the lion shall eat straw like the ox, and the sucking child shall play on the hole of the asp, and the weaned child shall put his hand on the cockatrice' den ; they shall not hurt nor destroy in all my holy mountain, for the earth shall be full of the knowledge of the Lord, as the waters cover the sea."

Now suppose that the doors, not of our prisons, but of hell itself, were thrown open — which shall never be, for their worm dieth not, and their fire is not quenched — but suppose they were, would the gates of heaven open to receive its inmates ? No. Over them these words stand inscribed, " There entereth nothing here to hurt or to defile." The door by which Manasseh and the woman that was a sinner, by which the thief of the cross and Saul the persecutor, have entered into glory, would be shut in their face ; as, indeed, from the holy nature of its society, heaven would be the last place where they would seek to be admitted. God would not, and could not, receive such as, though pardoned, were still unsanctified ; and from their company every spirit of the just made perfect, even their own father and mother, would shrink with holy horror. If so, it is plain that it is not enough to be pardoned, to be justified. We require also to be sanctified, to be delivered from the power and purified from the love of sin. Glory be to God, this has been provided, amply provided for. We are, as an Apostle says, complete in Christ. He who, by dying in their stead, has delivered His people from the punishment of sin, bestows the gift of His Holy Spirit to purify them from its love and deliver them from its power. Thus, with one hand, Jesus closes the gate of hell, and with the other throws open that of heaven; and thus those who believe in Him, who cling to Him as all their salvation, and who seek Him as all their desire, receiving with a title to the "inheritance of the saints" a meetness for it, shall not only not perish in the lake of fire, but shall enjoy everlasting life in the kingdom of heaven. So, to John's question respecting those whom he saw arrayed in white robes, with crowns on their heads and palms in their hands, the angel replied, "These are they which came out of great tribulation, and have washed their robes and made them white in the blood of the Lamb; therefore are they before the throne of God, and serve Him day and night in his temple; they shall hunger no more, neither thirst any more, for the Lamb which is in the midst of the throne shall feed them, and shall lead them unto living fountains of water, and God shall wipe away all tears from their eyes."

In regard to the nature of this work, I remark:

I. Sanctification consists in the mortifying of our sinful nature.

An Apostle says, "They who are Christ's have

crucified the flesh with the affections and lusts;" and it is hardly necessary for me to say that, by the term "flesh," he does not mean this mortal body, but that corrupt nature which our first parents transmitted to all their children. Its character may be seen in its works; and what these are, when fully developed, may be read in its awful catalogue—

adultery, fornication, uncleanness, lasciviousness, idolatry, witchcraft, hatred, variance, emulations, wrath, strifes, seditions, heresies, envyings, murders, drunkenness, revellings, and such like; of the which I tell you before," says Paul. "as I have also told you in time past, that they which do such things shall not inherit the kingdom of heaven."

Of all natural deaths which man can suffer, or violent ones which he can inflict, none is perhaps more violent than crucifixion. Struck down by a flash of lightning, or deprived as suddenly of life by any other cause, man dies without a touch of pain. Such an advantage is this to those who have made their "calling and election sure," who are ready at any time to meet the bridegroom, that we, not believing in "extreme unction," have never been able to sympathize with that passage of the Liturgy which teaches the worshipers to say from "sudden death," as well as from "battle and murder, good Lord, deliver us!" To a good man sudden death is sudden glory; but for that very reason such a death is not suited to describe sanctification — in other words, the destruction of his depraved and corrupt nature in a child of God. Those, again, who die, as most men do, of disease, suffer usually so much pain as to make it one of the special enjoyments of heaven, that "its inhabitant never says that he is sick," that there is no death there. Yet the pain of such death-beds is not very formidable, and it is chiefly because the "dark valley" opens on another world, and "after death the judgment," that many are so averse to enter it. Were men assured that there is no hell there, no punishment there, no place but heaven there, thousands who regard death as the king of terrors, would be as willing as they are now reluctant to die ; and, therefore, an ordinary death—apart from the consideration of its solemn issues—is usually attended with so little suffering as to offer no adequate figure of the pain and agony inseparable from the mortifying of the flesh. It is therefore to crucifixion, whose intensely painful and protracted agonies the Apostle himself may have witnessed, that St. Paul turns for a figure strong and bold enough to describe the death of sin — that death to which all who are Christ's must of necessity, and, rather than lose Him, will of choice, submit.

Believers are thus spoken of as being "*crucified* with Christ,"— a term that calls up to our minds that manner of death which our blessed Lord endured for us. By the side of the dying, in the last struggles of expiring nature, I have seen the features frightfully contorted, the body frightfully convulsed; but the appalling spectacle had this comfort, that the sufferer was unconscious, happily insensible as the spirit was breaking out of its mortal tenement, to the throes and pangs of dissolution. Such, however, was not the death which Jesus suffered when, to atone for sin, He took its direful punishment on Himself; and in the great love wherewith He loved us died, the just for the unjust, that we might be saved. Behold the Lamb of God! Loaded with infamy and with the tree, He sinks beneath the heavy burden, and falls exhausted, fainting on the street—unpitied save by some women, who, to the everlasting honour of their sex, bewailed and lamented Him. No kind hands are there to make His bed in His sickness; nor weeping friends to smooth His pillow. Rudely throwing Him down on the cross, cruel and malignant enemies drive the iron through His hands and feet—till, weakened by loss of blood and long-protracted tortures, He yields to the power of death, and bowing His blessed head gives up the ghost! And what agony His, as raised aloft on the cross, He hung by these torn, tender members!

I do not say, it were too much to say, that all who are Christ's, in renouncing the pleasures of sin, suffer pain to be compared with His, or equal to that of any who die on a cross. There may be such cases. The roots of sin are not drawn out sometimes but by a fearful wrench. We see people who prefer their sins to the enjoyment of health; to the possession of property; to a good reputation; to the regard of friends; to the interests of their children; even to life itself! The poor drunkard, for instance, rather than part with his vicious indulgence, will part with all these, and drain the cup, though at the bottom of it he sees the loss of character, a beggared family, death in this world, and damnation in the next. For him, in some cases, to renounce his habits may require greater resolution than martyrs, who walked with firm step and cheek unblanched have brought to bloody scaffold or burning stake. All I mean to assert is that, as crucifixion implies not the destruction only, but the painful destruction of the body, so they who are Christ's will destroy the flesh, denying themselves to all ungodliness and worldly lusts, though that should cost them sufferings equal to what he endures who cuts off a right hand; or plucks out a right eye; or expires amid the agonies of a cross.

This should certainly suggest the important practical question, whether we have ever taken our sins, and nailed them to the cross? But the question being, not whether our corruption is destroyed, but whether it is being so? not whether it is dead, but whether it is dying? for men to allege, as some do, that they are denying themselves this or that other sinful pleasure is something, but not enough. The Pharisee himself could do so. He gave thanks to God that he was not an extortioner, nor in many respects as other men. But what will such pleas avail? What would it avail a robber, to plead, and justly plead, that he is guiltless of the crime of murder; or the drunkard, that he is not a thief; or the covetous, that he has committed no overt act of dishonesty; or a man of revengeful temper, that he has not actually injured the property or the person of any who have done him wrong? Sanctification embraces the whole man; and the question is not so much whether we have mortified the flesh in this or in that respect, as whether sin in every form has ceased, I do not say to dwell within us, but to have dominion over us? And if we have been enabled through divine grace, though with sore pain, to deny ourselves to pleasures which we once indulged in— and to deny ourselves to them, not because they destroyed our health, or wasted our property, or had lost their power over us through age or change of circumstances, but because they were offensive in the sight of a holy God, because they dishonoured our blessed Lord, because they wounded our consciences, and because they were ruining, not so much this dying body, as our precious souls—then are we crucifying the flesh. This is to be sanctified, to die to sin, and live to righteousness.

The gradual nature of this work will form the subject for future remarks; but I may observe before parting with the figure of crucifixion, that the destruction of indwelling sin, like death on a cross, is not only a very painful, but is also a slow and lingering process. No doubt cases—very remarkable cases—have occurred where the "old man" was slain by, so to speak, a single blow : the crucifying of the flesh being begun and finished within the brief time a man survives who has been nailed to a cross. It was so with the penitent thief. But his case forms no rule. On the contrary, the exception, here as elsewhere, proves the rule—his conversion and his sudden sanctification, all accomplished within the space of some two or three hours, being as extraordinary an exhibition of divine grace, as the resurrection of the saints in the neighbouring tombs was an extraordinary display of almighty power.

Divines have distinguished, and very properly, between justification and sanctification. They call the first an *act*, the second a *work* of free grace ; and this they do because justification is accomplished in a moment, while sanctification, less like a flash of lightning than the morning light which shines more and more unto the perfect day, advances by progressive stages, and may take even long years to finish. Therefore, it is said in the Westminster Assembly's Catechism—one, I may remark, which, though most in use in Scotland, was chiefly the work of Englishmen—that they who are sanctified are "enabled *more and more* to die unto sin and live unto righteousness." Hence they are said to be *crucified* with Christ—the most appropriate of all figures—seeing, as we read in Martyrologies, that some condemned for their Master's sake to their Master's death hung for days in protracted agony, ere they exchanged the cross for the crown of martyrdom.

Experience proves that our depraved and sinful nature is not so easily destroyed as many seem to suppose; especially such as have the unspeakable folly to place their hopes in a death-bed repentance. When the convert has dragged the "old man" to the cross, and nailed him there, how often does he find that his enemy is not only not dead, but, tenacious of life, seems hardly dying! The "flesh" wars against the spirit; the "flesh" makes strong and obstinate resistance to grace: and but that the believer is upheld by God's Spirit, but that God according to His promise fights against them that fight against Him, the "flesh" would triumph in the end; nor could God's people say, as, blessed be God, with

Paul they can, " We are troubled on every side, yet
not distressed; we are perplexed, but not in despair;
persecuted, but not forsaken; cast down, but not
destroyed." Alas, how often does the carnal nature,
which we had almost hoped was extinguished, revived by the breath of some sudden temptation,
flame out anew, like fire smouldering in the ashes '
Some besetting sin, long denied indulgence, against
which we have prayed, and watched, and wrestled,
appears to be dead; the " old man " hangs motionless, to appearance lifeless, on the cross; when, like
the convulsive movement of a body from which bystanders supposed the life was gone, in some bad
word, or bad deed, or bad thought, the " old man "
lives again, and the " new man " learns to his sorrow
that the flesh he had crucified is not yet dead.

The entire death of sin—a consummation devoutly to be wished for—is a blessing reserved for
the close of life. We cannot indeed be too diligent
in mortifying sin, in crucifying every limb and member of the flesh. Still if a man will—as every man
should—examine himself and " prove his own work,'
the question is not whether sin is altogether crucified, but is crucified at all?—is whether, though it
be not with a perfect hatred, we really hate it —is
whether we are delivered, though not completely,
from its power?—is whether it has ceased to *reign*,
though it has not ceased to *remain* within us? It

is slow work dying on a cross, but slower still dying to sin. No vile serpent, no venomous reptile, so tenacious of life as a bosom sin! However, take comfort, Christians; God will perfect that which concerneth us—a hope which, thanks be to God, shows the believer a Father's reconciled countenance shining on him through the darkest cloud; a hope which will enable you, while confessing with Paul, "The good that I would, I do not; but the evil which I would not, that I do," in almost the same breath to exclaim, "I thank God through Jesus Christ our Lord . . . . there is no condemnation to them who are in Christ Jesus, who walk not after the flesh, but after the Spirit!"

II. Sanctification lies in conformity to the mind of Christ.

These bodies of ours are liable to an amazing number of diseases; for, though there is but one way by which we enter the world, there are a thousand doors by which to leave it. So insecure indeed is the citadel of life, it lies open on so many sides to attack, that there are none of our organs but may become the seat of a painful and fatal malady. To protect us, to cure disease, men have ransacked the herbs of the field and the bowels of the earth; but have found in neither what they sought in both, any *elixir vitæ*, any remedy against death, any specific of sufficient virtue to cure all manner of diseases

But such a power resided in the hand of Christ. The cures wrought by its simple touch were as magnificent as they were many. Not less sovereign than sudden in action, it gave eyes to the blind, voice to the dumb, ears to the deaf, motion to the withered arm, rest to the palsied limb, and life even to the dead. In the blessed hands his enemies nailed to the cross the world saw what had been esteemed a dream at length realized—a remedy for all manner of diseases; a cure for death itself. Where Christ was, there was need neither for drugs nor doctors.

And were God to impart the same mind to all men that was in Jesus Christ, equally unnecessary were all the ordinary means of checking and curing our moral diseases. Let God so pour out His Spirit on all flesh as that all men shall be transformed into the image of Christ, and the father might break his rod; the sovereign lay aside his sceptre; the soldier sheath his sword; justice discharge her courts; and with prison-doors thrown open, and no house-door barred, we should sleep in peace—fearing injury from others as little as we had done from Christ himself. St. Paul says, " Looking unto Jesus, the author and finisher of our faith, who, for the joy that was set before Him, endured the cross, despising the shame, and is set down at the right hand of the throne of God—and let us consider him that endured such contradiction of sinners." He lived more than thirty years on earth, nor injured any one; accused of many crimes, He committed none; He suffered innumerable wrongs, but never inflicted any; into no eye did He ever bring a tear, nor send a pang through any heart; shedding blessings around Him wherever He went, He could have crowded the hall of judgment with living evidences of His power and goodness; nor, though in their thirst for His blood they suborned men to swear away His life, could those to whom Judas betrayed his Master find a single person to convict Him of a single crime.

In every relation of life our Lord presents a perfect example: as a child, He grew in wisdom as in stature; and, subject to Joseph and Mary, He whom angels obeyed, obeyed them—as a man, He went about doing good; consecrating His powers to the glory of God and the happiness of mankind, He was eyes to the blind, and feet to the lame, and life to the dead; He made widows' hearts to sing for joy, and earned the blessing of thousands that were ready to perish—as a master, He was kind, considerate, gentle; treating his disciples more as friends than servants, what a beautiful contrast did His demeanour offer to the haughtiness with which many treat and trample on their inferiors—as a benefactor, He shrunk from ostentation, and, unlike the Pharisees, who, to attract attention and win the praise of men,

14

dispensed their charity to the sound of trumpets, He did good, as the poet says, by stealth ; charging those whom He blessed to conceal the name of their benefactor—as a lover of God, He delighted in hold- ing communion with His Father, and made it His meat and drink to do His will—as a worshipper, He, who could best dispense with them, devoutly attended on all the ordinances of religion ; though giving life to dead souls through the baptism of His Spirit, He sought baptism by water at the hands of John : and though Himself the object of prayer, He prayed without ceasing, and, often spending the who.e night on His knees, gave to devotion the hours which the world gave to sleep—as a sufferer, who can be compared to Him ? By that cross where He was dumb, opening not His mouth but to say, " Father, not my will, but thine be done !" remind- ing us of those plants that lend sweet odours to the hand that bruises them, yonder where He prays that His murderers might be forgiven, we lose sight of the faith of Abraham, the meekness of Moses, and the patience of Job. Like stars at sunrise, these pale and vanish in the dazzling effulgence of this Sun of Righteousness !

Such was Christ, and sanctification lies in con- formity to His temper, mind, and life. In all these things He has set us an example that we should fol- low His steps ; and since we are assured that unless the same mind—though it may be only in the bud, in the seed, in the feebleness of infancy—be in us as was in Jesus Christ, we are none of His, *that* becomes a test of Christian character. Without conformity to Him, we are no more to be called Christians than a body without life is to be called a man. Attire the dead like a bride, and with its crown of flowers and sparkling jewels, the corpse but looks the ghastlier; whitewash the sepulchre, and, full of dead men's bones and all uncleanness, the inside seems the fouler; let Judas kiss his Master, and we recoil the more from his treachery—it appears the baser and the blacker. Even so the form of religion without its power, the body of religion without its spirit, a sanctimonious profession with an unsanctified heart, instead of recommending any to God, only renders them more hateful in His sight. Be assured that it is those, and those only, who reflect Christ's image, and whose hearts are tuned to harmony with His own, that are saved by sanctification of the Spirit and belief of the truth. He who died for His people lives in them; renewing them by His grace, imbuing them with His Spirit, and moulding them into the fashion of His own heavenly image. He so helps them to die to sin and live to righteousness, that they also can use the bold language of Paul and say, " I am crucified with Christ; nevertheless I live, yet not I, but Christ liveth in me; and the life which

I now live in the flesh, I live by the faith of the Son of God, who loved me and gave himself for me."

Let all Christians, then, seek to purify themselves even as Christ is pure; or, as it is otherwise expressed, seek to be perfect as their Father in heaven is perfect. But this is an object, let me say, that cannot be attained in any measure but by daily, unceasing efforts, as, to use a figure of Scripture, they mount up on eagles' wings. Bird of the keenest eye, bird of the broadest wing, bird of the highest flight, let her suspend her efforts, and she does not hang sustained by her plumage—poised in the empty air. Ceasing to rise, the eagle begins to sink, drawn down from the skies to the earth by virtue of its strong attraction; and to a soul which naturally, according to the words of David and to all experience, " cleaveth to the dust," this world offers attractions we cannot overcome but by keeping the wings of faith and prayer in constant play. To be holy, to be meet for heaven, we must cultivate every Christian grace with diligence. God is no patron of sloth and idleness, to do for us what we can do for ourselves. In the cultivation of the soul as of the soil, we are to be fellow-workers with Him. Sanctification is the work of His Spirit; but the work of His Spirit in co-operation with ours. He holds the helm, but we are to pull the oars. He sends the showers, but we are to plough the field,

and sow the seed,—looking up for the blessing, and drawing it down with this prayer of David on our lips, " Let the beauty of the Lord our God be upon us, and establish Thou the work of our hands upon us; yea, the work of our hands establish Thou it!"

III. I go on now to say that sanctification, while the work of the Spirit, is accomplished through the use of means. There is,—

1. Prayer. In their joys and sorrows, in their trials and triumphs also, the children of Israel, during their sojourn in the wilderness, present a striking picture of the conduct and fortunes of Christ's Church on earth; and in nothing more than the use their history teaches us to make of, and the confidence it teaches us to place in, prayer. We have many remarkable examples of this; and none more to our present purpose than what is related as having occurred in Rephidim. It has been often observed that a season of great privileges is a prelude to great trials, as if God intended by the one to prepare his people for the other. For example, the three disciples who were honoured to bear Christ company on the mount of transfiguration, were the very three He chose to be the painful witnesses of His humiliation in the garden. Again, the Apostle Paul is called up into the third heavens, to hear and see things of unutterable glory; but he leaves these and the company of angels to be buffeted by a messen

ger of Satan—a warning to God's saints to carry
their honours meekly, and look out for storms on the
back of sunshine. So was it with Israel in that valley, where, from a rock cleft by the rod of Moses, a
river flowed with life in its welcome streams. Seated on its banks, as the people recalled the misery of
yesterday,—the whole camp in mutiny, and mothers
fiercely pressing on Moses with dying infants in
their arms, and this cry on their lips, " Water,
water, give us water!"—they were probably singing,
The Lord hath done great things for us, whereof we
are glad! At that moment a storm unexpectedly
bursts on their heads. The clash of weapons and
shouts of war break on the sweet, peaceful scene.
The whole camp resounds now with the cry," To
arms! to arms!" and seizing their weapons, with
Joshua at their head, the braves of Israel sally forth
to meet the sons of Amalek, who, approaching the
host by stealth, have fallen on it like a whirlwind.
Meanwhile Moses—not that he was afraid, or a man
either to fear or flee—betakes himself to the top of
a neighbouring hill. He had other and better work
to do than fight. Joshua fights below; and he
stands above, holding aloft the rod that had erst
woke the thunders of cloudless skies; turned rivers
into blood; and, breaking the power of Egypt like
a potter's sherd, cleft both sea and rock asunder.
Symbol of prayer, it appeals to heaven for help, and

teaches the people to look there for victory. And now, that rod, and the arms which sustain it, appear to govern the varying fortunes of the battle. As it stands erect, or falls through the weariness of Moses' arms, so rise or fall the scales of victory. And so, from morning to noon, the tide of battle swaying from side to side, when Moses' arms are up Israel prevails; when they sink, fortune changes sides, and Amalek prevails. The battle was fought by Joshua, but won by Moses. Setting him on a stone, Aaron and Hur, like people engaged in united prayer, join their efforts to sustain his arms. That done, Israel wins every foot of ground; the warriors of Amalek fall at every blow; the fight becomes a retreat; the retreat a rout; till, in the light of the setting sun, Moses descends the mountain to build an altar to the Lord, and in commemoration of a victory won, I may say, by prayer, call it Jehovah Nissi, "The Lord my banner."

On the same pivot turns our success in the work of sanctification, so far as concerns our life-long conflict with temptation; the good fight we have to wage with that trinity of enemies—the World, the Devil, and the Flesh. Since prayer supplies the strength and calls down the blessing, therefore everything turns on it; therefore the Apostle speaks of "praying always;" therefore he urges his con-verts to "pray without ceasing." And as in him whose case, defying the utmost efforts of Christ's disciples, required the presence and power of their Master, there are devils in every man who are not to be cast out but by prayer—earnest and persevering prayer. By way of illustration let us look at two cases—the first teaching us what triumphs are to be won by prayer; the second, what shameful defeats shall follow and punish the neglect of it.

The king of Babylon has issued his impious decree; and this man clothed with a little brief authority has forbidden all men for thirty days, and under penalty of being cast into a den of lions, to pray to any, be it God or man, but to himself. At no time is prayer more needed than when it is forbidden— just as we have never more need to pray than when we are least inclined to do so; when hearts are cold and faith is weak. Bad times require heroes— brave, as well as good men; nor should His people ever stand up more boldly and resolutely for the cause of God than when they are likely in a worldly sense to lose rather than gain by doing so. So Daniel judged. He had never been ashamed to pray; and now, with that decree hanging like a naked sword over his head, he is not afraid to pray. It was no time for such a man as he to seek his closet and shut the door. The time was one requiring faithful men to openly hold up a banner for the truth.

So, shaking out its folds in the face of king and princes, friend and foe, death and the devil, Daniel bravely displayed it — throwing his window wide open that all might see him on his knees. Paying an involuntary tribute to his constancy and courage, his enemies watch him; he is seized; hurried from the throne of God to that of a mortal man, and from thence to the den of lions. Hungry and savage, they leap with a roar on their prey, and fight, growling, over his mangled remains? No. Prayer shuts the lions' mouths; gentle as lambs, they gambol around him, or lie crouched in sleep at his feet. Not Amalek, but Israel prevails. There was a man in Scotland once so in love with prayer that he was wont to retire to his old church in the town of Ayr and spend whole nights upon his knees, till, it was said, they grew hard as the stones he knelt on. But what made the knees callous softened and sanctified the heart; inspiring it at the same time with heroic courage. Fit mate of her, John Knox's daughter, who, on King James offering to set her husband free if he would own the king's supremacy within Christ's Church, replied, as she held out her apron, "*I would rather kep his head there,*" Welsh rose by prayer above all fear of death. A prisoner in the Bass Rock, where he mingled his psalms with the boom of the breakers that burst on his dungeon walls, that man feared only lest he should not be

14*

deemed worthy, like others, to seal his testimony with his blood, and win a martyr's crown.

Now look at another and opposite case. The supper is over; and, pledged in the wine-cup rather to die with Christ than deny Him, the disciples go thence with their Lord and Master. On entering the garden Jesus—entering now into the gloomy shadow of the cross—leaves Peter, James, and John, with instructions to pray. He returns after a little, but it is to find the hands of Moses down—the disciples are asleep. Awakening them, He repeats His injunction, but with no more success; and on a third trial, returns to find them, not praying, but sleeping. They shall sleep no more. The tramp of armed men breaks on the silent night, and torches flash on armour and flicker through the branches of the trees. They are taken by surprise—The Philistines are on thee, Samson! and to them more, in a sense, than to their Master, it " is the hour and power of darkness." Jesus triumphed over death, and sin, and hell, entering on the conflict with prayer. But they entered the battle prayerless; and so, after a brief display, a mere flash of courage, they took to flight. And how does Simon, the brave and self-confident disciple who had declared that though Christ's own mother, and the Marys, and all others, should forsake Him, he never would, choosing death rather than desertion—how does he meet this trial?

No better, but rather worse than his fellows. We have seen a brave sight—Daniel stand unmoved alike before the wrath of kings and the roar of lions alas! here—" how are the mighty fallen! the weapons of war, how are they perished! Tell it not in Gath, publish it not in the streets of Askelon!" Peter quails before a woman's eye; and turning his back on that loving Master to whom he had sworn dauntless and deathless allegiance, he now—oh, most cruel and wicked lie!—says, ay swears, "I know not the man!" Daniel prays, and grace prevails; Peter sleeps, and sin prevails. But who may not, shall not, do the like if prayer be neglected? Let him that thinketh he standeth, take heed lest he fall. Who would mortify the flesh, cast out the devil, burst the bonds of sin, walk in the glorious liberty of sons of God, and, denying themselves to ungodliness and all worldly lusts, at length perfect holiness in the fear of God, must seek their strength, their " great strength," in the use of prayer. Prayer is to the Christian what his hair was to Samson; shorn of it, he is feeble as other men.

To be sanctified, therefore, to have our corruptions subdued, to reach greater heights in grace, to grow in the love and the likeness of Jesus Christ, to be mellowing and ripening for the kingdom of heaven, let us pray much; pray often; pray, in a sense, " without ceasing." That door is always open, and is open to all.　We cannot go there too often, nor ask too much.　" He that spared not his own Son, but delivered Him up for us all, shall He not with Him also freely give us all things ?"

2 Attention to the state of our hearts.

I know an ancient fortress which one brave man could have held against a host.　Perched on the summit of a lofty rock, around which the sea goes foaming, and parted from the mainland by a dizzy chasm, over which a narrow arch, hanging like a thread in mid-air, is thrown, that old castle stood in other days impregnable.　There was but one way of approach, and *that* such as one man could hold against a thousand.　As might be inferred from these words of Scripture, Keep thy heart with all diligence, for out of it are the issues of life, it is otherwise with us.　With appetites and passions, each of which may be made an instrument of sin, our hearts lie open on many sides to attack.　Take, for example, the most innocent of these appetites, that of hunger—" Give me neither poverty nor riches," says the wise man, praying as much against the first as the second; because, though happily we know nothing of it, it is difficult for a hungry to be an honest man.　The empty sack, as the proverb says, cannot stand upright; and he tempts the poor through this appetite who used it to tempt our Lord Himself—saying to Jesus when He was an hungred,

If thou be the Son of God, command that these stones be made bread. In this, as in other ways, Satan tried with his fiery darts every joint of our Champion's armour; and only failed because, as Jesus Himself said, The prince of this world cometh, and hath nothing in me! We cannot say so! Like traitors lurking within a beleaguered city, our natural corruptions are ready to open the gates and betray us to the enemy. Hence he who would keep his heart from evil, keep it pure and holy, must plant a sentinel at every avenue by which sin may find access there—guarding against none more than the little sins, as they are called, that are like the urchins who enter by the window and open the door for bigger thieves. The man of God has his eyes to keep, and so Job said, I have made a covenant with mine eyes—his tongue, and hence the exhortation, Keep thy tongue from evil, and thy lips from speaking guile—his ears, and hence the warning, Cease, my son, to hear the instruction that causeth to err— his feet, and hence David says, I have refrained my feet from every evil way, that I might keep thy word. And since there is no gate of the five senses by which the enemy may not, unless the Spirit lift up a standard against him, come in like a flood, we have need to guard every port, and write over every portal, "Here there entereth nothing to hurt or to defile."

The work of grace is carried on within the heart It is, therefore, the state of our affections more than our outward conduct that should occupy our chief attention and engage our most earnest prayers. Let me illustrate and enforce this by an analogy. The burning thirst, the flushed cheek, the bounding pulse, the restless nights of fever, are but the symptoms of disease. That thirst physicians may allay by cooling draughts ; and opiates may dull the sense of pain, and shed sleep and sweet oblivion on the eyes of the weary sufferer. The symptoms are alleviated, but the disease is not arrested—the evil is but masked, not mastered. And that is all which is achieved in the *reformation* which sometimes passes for *regeneration ;* in that outward improvement of habits and decorum of life, which will never supply the place of sanctification in the judgment of a holy, heart-searching God. Man looketh on the outward appearance, but God looketh on the heart. I once heard physicians say, as they stood baffled by the bed-side of one fast posting on to death, We can do nothing now but combat the symptoms. Ominous and fatal words ! Divine grace, thanks be to God, does more. Let it reach the heart, and those works of the flesh, which are the outward symptoms of indwelling sin, will ere long pass away, like a plant which, cut at the root, droops, and withers, and dies. It is in the heart the change is wrought for salva-

tion; and there, as a building rises from its foundations, the work of sanctification is carried onwards
and upwards to perfection. Cleanse this fountain,
and purity will flow in all its streams. Let our heart
be turned heavenward, and our members and affections, our powers, and time, and influence, will all
follow and obey its movements—as from stem to
stern, from her keel that ploughs the wave to the
masts that rake the sky, a ship obeys the hand of
the steersman and movements of the helm. Who,
therefore, would grow in grace, would die daily to
sin, would live daily to righteousness; while they
strive to keep their hands from doing, and their ears
from hearing, and their lips from speaking evil, let
them strive above all things to keep their hearts with
all diligence, since out of them are the issues of life.

3. Living separate from an ungodly world.

With all the world in His choice, God placed His
ancient people in a very remarkable situation. On
the north they were walled in by the snowy ranges
of Lebanon; a barren desert formed their eastern
boundary; far to the south stretched a sterile region,
called the howling wilderness; while the sea—not
then, as now, the highway of nations, facilitating
rather than impeding intercourse—lay on their west,
breaking on a shore that had few harbours and no
navigable rivers to invite the steps of commerce.
Such a position rendered frequent and familiar in-

tercourse on their part with heathen nations difficult, if not impossible. Other circumstances also
tended to isolate the Israelites. The words of their
law read every Sabbath, and the blood of the pass-
over sprinkled every year on their doors, kept alive
the memory of old wrongs—reminding the Hebrews
of what their fathers had once suffered in the land
of Egypt. This was calculated to alienate them
from the Egyptians, their neighbours on the south
and west; and the Egyytians, on the other hand,
were not likely to regard the Israelites with a friendly
eye, seeing how, in the oxen and heifers of their
sacrifices, they offered up the very gods of Egypt on
the altars of the God of Israel. Their other neighbours were the Philistines and Edomites. The first,
the surviving remnant of nations whose lands Israel
had seized, had old defeats and the blood of their
countrymen to avenge; while the second, the children of Esau, were ready whenever opportunity
offered, to renew their father's quarrel with Jacob,
and fall on Jerusalem with the sword, and cries of
Raze it, raze it to the ground! Thus, besides their
geographical position, the relations of God's people
to the nations around them were singularly well calculated to keep them a separate and make them in a
sense a holy people; to expose them to the enmity
rather than win for them the friendship of the world
—a position which our Lord pronounces, and Chris-

tians find in their experience to be, the safest and therefore the happiest of the two. " When men persecute you and hate you," said our Lord, " and say all manner of evil against you falsely, rejoice, and be exceeding glad, for great is your reward in heaven."

England's great dramatist speaks o finding " sermons in stones, tongues in trees, and books in the running brooks,"—and may we not find a great truth in the very position in which God placed his chosen people ? It certainly teaches us that to be holy, or sanctified, we must be a separate people—living in the world, but not of it—as oil, that may be mixed but cannot be combined with water. Nor was this the only way God took to teach His people, and through them us, this lesson. In our looms, for example, nothing is more common than to work up into the same web materials of different textures— wool from the snowy flock, with flax from our own, or cotton from foreign fields ; nor is it uncommon for our farmers to sow different kinds of seeds in the same field ; and occasionally in our country, and very often abroad, we see different kinds of animals yoked to the same plough or cart. Very harmless customs, yet strictly forbidden to the Jews by these laws of Moses—Thou shalt not sow thy field with mixed seeds, neither shall a garment mingled of linen and wool come upon thee ; thou shalt not plough with an ox and an ass together. And what spiritual lesson were these regulations intended to teach, but this, that it is not safe for those who would live godly to associate with the ungodly; that, if we would not be partakers of other men's sins, we must live, as far as lies in us, separate from their society? "Come out from among them, and be ye separate, and touch no unclean thing: and I will receive you, and will be a Father unto you, and ye shall be my sons and daughters, saith the Lord Almighty."

We have seen an adroit debater seek by the use of ridicule to throw contempt on what he could not refute: and this has he who is fertile in wiles done with the duty that lies on Christians to live separate from an ungodly world. Satan has sought to make it ridiculous. In the hermits of old times, in the convents and monasteries of Popery, where roam, in the words of Milton,

> " Embryos and idiots, eremites and friars,
>   White, black, and gray, with all their trumpery ;"

and in the seclusive, not to say sour and exclusive, habits of some good but narrow-minded Protestants, he offers us a caricature of this duty and God's truth.

It would neither promote our sanctification, nor the glory of God, nor the good of others, to with-draw altogether from worldly society. To " depart from evil " is but a part of our duty; we are also to

" do good." " Pure religion and undefiled " walks
not in solitude ; her hands are employed providing
the orphans bread ; her feet are found at the widow's
door ; her steps are even sometimes turned to haunts
of vice ; her visits are paid, not so much to the great
and noble as to the fatherless and widows in their
affliction ; and, following our Lord, nor shrinking
from the touch of guilt, she goes forth to seek and
save the lost. The proper station for a life-boat is
not the quiet lagoon or land-locked bay, but the
shores of a stormy coast. But though true religion
seeks to strengthen her graces by exercise, and thus
effectually promote the work of sanctification, that
is a totally different thing, both in its intention and
results, from voluntary association with the ungodly ;
from courting the company and cultivating the friendship of such as are not the friends but the enemies
of God. It is not safe, as Lot found to his cost, to
live in Sodom. Who can touch pitch, and not be
defiled ? Sailors give a wide berth to shoals and
whirlpools, and we shall find it safest and most for
our sanctification to keep away from seductive influences—not so much as venturing into the stream
which has carried off their feet many who fancied
they could stem its torrent. How often have God's
people learned to their sorrow that worldly society—
cooling if not quenching their love, blunting the fine
edge of a renewed conscience, and checking their

growth in grace—has done them far more ill than they ever did it good. Who walks, as we do, in slippery places, is in great danger of backsliding· who throws himself into a crowd is more likely to be borne along with the current than to stop it; and who even bravely and nobly attempts to save the drowning must be on his guard lest, locked in their deadly embrace, he sinks to perish along with them.

It is impossible to altogether escape the temptations which the world presents; in that case, a man, as Paul says, must needs go out of the world. This has been tried. But in vain have pious dreamers fled the haunts of men, excepting in the depths of untrodden forests, in caves and lonely deserts, to enjoy uninterrupted communion with God. Alas, they carried with them in the corruption of their own hearts what often proved the worst of company; nor there did they escape him who pursued our Lord Himself to the solitudes of the desert. But suppose that hermit's cell or cloistered convents offered a perfect protection from evil in every shape and form, it were not the duty of God's people to withdraw from the world. It has need, much need of them. " Unless these abide in the ship, ye cannot be saved." Saints are the salt of the earth, and if the salt be withdrawn, how is corruption to be checked ? Saints are the lights of the world; but lights are not kindled in empty halls and unpeopled solitudes. They burn where houses stand thick and crowds throng the busy streets : or shine out at the harbour mouth through the night and tempest—guiding lights by whose welcome gleams the sailor, leaving storms behind, steers his bark into the desired haven. Let such be the aim of God's people. Living for their sanctification, separate in a sense from the world, and moving, like the stars above it, in a loftier sphere, let them shine with the lustre of holy and useful lives, that others, seeing their good works, may glorify their Father which is in heaven.

4. The hope of glory.

Hope is a medicine on which physicians place great dependence : nor is there almost any symptom they are more prompt and anxious to combat than the depression of mind which, prostrating the vital powers, goes to produce the very evil that it dreads. Imparting courage, and also strength, firmness to the troops who receive, and energy to those that make the charge, hope has braved the face of death, and won proud victories on many a battle-field. In almost every position of life hope is the prelude of of success ; as *hopeless*, on the other hand, may be justly regarded as equivalent to *helpless*. No hope, no effort—as observed ir the demeanour of an unhappy Indian who, caught in the current, perished in the Cataract of Niagara. Wearied with the chase and asleep, or forgetful of his peril, he had allowed his canoe to drift into the rapids, nor awoke to his danger till the current was sweeping it along with an arrows's speed. Roused at length by the shouts of terrified spectators, he sprang to his feet, and looking around him, took in all the danger at a glance. But he seized no oar, nor raised a cry, nor made an effort to reach the bank. With the courage of his race, and the calmness of despair, the savage bows to his fate; resumes his seat; and, folding his arms, awaits the moment, when, borne over the fall, he is buried in its boiling gulf. Hope had fled.

The Word of God furnishes two cases strikingly illustrative of the influence of hope on the one hand, and of hopelessness on the other. I refer to those of Saul and David, when each went forth to meet the Philistine. It needed no familiar spirit, nor prophet from his grave, nor accursed witch that night Saul repaired to her hut in Endor, to foretell the disasters of the coming day. Prostrate at her feet, abandoned of God and of hope, rejecting both food and comfort, Saul was already conquered. In his crushed hopes and heart coming events cast their shadow before. Paralyzed by despair, he was incapable of such efforts, either of body or mind, as the time and his danger required. Ready to fall before the Philistines as a noble oak whose roots have been severed by the axe before the first blast of the rising storm, he had not a chance in the coming battle.

What a contrast to this scene the day that saw David, in the sight of two armies that hung on opposing hills, hastening with eager eye, and flying locks, and elastic foot to meet the giant! Hope was in his bounding step; and sounds to my ear like the blare of a battle trumpet in his reply to Goliah, "Thou comest to me with a sword, with a spear, and with a shield; but I come to thee in the name of the Lord of Hosts, the God of the armies of Israel, whom thou hast defied; this day the Lord shall deliver thee into mine hand, and I will smite thee and take thine head from thee; and I will give the carcase of the host of the Philistines unto the fowls of the air, and to the wild beasts of the earth, that all the earth may know that there is a God in Israel: the battle is the Lord's, and He will give you into our hands." Brave speech! this was the voice of hope, of heaven-born hope. Sustaining David's heart, giving sight to his eyes and imparting strength to his arm, as, whirling the sling around his head, he launched the messenger of death right to the mark, that hope was the omen, and under God the means of victory.

And so it is in the Christian's conflict with sin; and indeed in all the work of sanctification. Hence, not for our peace only, but for our purity, also, the

importance of a " lively hope," of making our calling and election sure. In spiritual as in earthly
things, there is great strength in hope; and, therefore, God's people are carefully to cultivate that
grace. Carefully avoid everything that could cast a
doubt on your salvation; throw you into a state of
spiritual darkness; and bring you, as David seemed
to have been brought by his great sin, to the very
borders of despair. A well-grounded hope that,
having been made new creatures in Jesus Christ, we
are His—that with our names, though unknown to
fame, written in the Book of Life, we have grace in
possession and heaven in prospect—that after a few
more brief years, pure as the angels that sing before
the throne, we shall be brought with gladness into
the palace of the King, to be like Christ, and with
Christ, seeing Him eye to eye, and face to face—
such hopes are powerful springs of action. The
source of a peace that passeth understanding, nothing could be better calculated to wean our affections
from the world, and deepen our abhorrence of sin,
and inflame our desires to be holy as God is holy.

IV. Sanctification is a progressive work.

A connoisseur is painting, so soon as the dust of
years and neglect is wiped from a fine old picture,
can tell whose hand laid these colours on the canvas—the works of each of the great masters having
a character of their own. In like manner an anti-

quarian, though history is silent on the subject, and no date stands carved on the crumbling ruin, can tell when this tower was built, or that arch was sprung—the architecture of every age being marked by features peculiar to itself. And to pass from small things to great, so distinguished are God's works by features all their own—evidences of divine goodness, power, and wisdom—that a Bedoween, when asked how he knew there was a God when he had never seen Him, had good reason to look with surprise on the sceptic, and reply, as he pointed to a footprint in the sand, "How do I know whether it was a man or camel that passed my tent last night?"

Among other features impressed on all the works of God, none is more distinctly marked than their progressive character. It was step by step, and day by day, not all of a sudden, that our world was constructed, and creation finished—with man, his Maker's image, and his crowning work, standing on the summit of the pyramid. The Providence, also, that sustains and governs the world is no less distinctly marked by progress. Babes grow into men; seedlings into trees; the gray dawn into the rosy morn; the morn into the blaze of sunshine; and the green blades that spring from dull clods into the golden sheaves of autumn. Nothing in nature starts at once into maturity—neither the fish of the sea, nor the fowls of the air, nor the flowers of the field, nor the trees of the forest. Nor is man himself, in respect of either soul or body, exempt from this imperial law. Going away to push your fortune in the world, you leave an infant in your mother's arms, and return after long years of absence to hail the blue mountains of your native land as they rise above the wave. Hastening homewards, you stand once more amid the dear and well-remembered scenes of other days. The same trees wave over the house, the same stream with its daisied banks runs murmuring by the door; and, though time has silvered their heads, and written wrinkles on their brows, you at once recognize the faces and are locked in the arms of happy and beloved parents. But who is he that stands there, in strength and stature a mighty man?—but the infant you left hanging helpless on a mother's breast. And thus, without any previous knowledge of the matter, and looking only at God's works of creation and providence, we could predicate that sanctification, one of the greatest of His works, would also be one of progress—giving us no more reason to expect that a sinner on his conversion would suddenly grow up into a perfect saint than a seedling into a perfect tree, or the field sown to-day be to-morrow flashing with the sickles and joyous with the song of reapers Grace has its dawn as well as day; grace has its green blade, and afterwards its ripe corn in the ear; grace has its babes and its men in Christ. With God's work there, as with all His works, " in all places of his dominion," progress is both the prelude and the path to perfection. Therefore we are ex horted to grow in grace, and in the knowledge of our Lord and Saviour Jesus Christ—to lay aside every weight and the sin that doth more easily beset us, and run with patience the race set before us—to run so that we may obtain—to go on to perfection, saying with Paul, What things were gain to me, those I counted loss for Christ; yea, doubtless, and I count all things but loss for the excellency of the knowledge of Christ Jesus my Lord. I count not myself to have apprehended; but this one thing I do, forgetting those things which are behind, and reaching forth unto those things which are before, I press towards the mark for the prize of the high calling of God in Christ Jesus.

This is a view of sanctification well calculated to strengthen feeble knees and hold up arms that are ready to hang down. I am a great sinner—my head is dark and my heart is dead—my feet are ever slipping—when I would do good, evil is present with me; what I would I do not, and what I would not that I do! has been the complaint of the godly. And as a native of the plain, who climbs some Alpine summit, on finding, when he has reached the first height, that another rises before him, and after it another, and still another, each towering higher into the sky, is ready, under the depressing influences of disappointment and fatigue, to throw himself on the ground and abandon the task in despair, so, thus complaining and confessing, God's people have been ready to fall into despondency and, writing hard things against themselves, lose the blessed hope of being ever wholly sanctified.

But why should you be cast down, or your spirits disquieted within you? "It is good that a man should both hope and quietly wait for the salvation of the Lord." Descrying the day in the dawn, the man in the stammering babe, and in the seedling the stately tree with roots rifted in the rock and giant arms thrown out defiant of the storm, let His people rejoice in the Lord, and joy in the God of their salvation. It is not possible for them to employ language humbler than that of St. Paul, the great Apostle of the Gentiles. He reckoned himself "the chief of sinners, and less than the least of saints"—that he had not attained, or was yet perfect. But did he therefore go mourning all the day long, wearing a face of gloom and hanging his head like a bulrush? No. He went out to work, expecting a blessing on his labours; he went down to battle confident in God, and therefore confident of victory. They cast him into the inner prison, and he passed the night singing psalms of praise; they hunted him like a partridge on the mountains, and he rejoiced in tribulation; they, both the heathen and his own countrymen, sought to overwhelm him with persecutions, and amid perils and sufferings many he rose, like the ark, buoyant on the top of the flood; Death shook his grisly hand at him, and he defied the king of terrors—this the source of his joy and peace, of his unwearied energy in work and dauntless intrepidity in danger, the confidence that He who had begun a good work in him would carry it on to the day of the Lord Jesus. No cloud on his brow nor in his sky, I am persuaded, he exclaimed, that neither life, nor death, nor angels, nor principalities, nor powers, nor things present, nor things to come, shall be able to separate me from the love of God, which is in Christ Jesus our Lord.

This confidence is " the inheritance of the saints " —of all the saints. The blood of Jesus has lost none of its virtue, nor His Spirit any of its power; the fountain of grace is not exhausted, nor is the edge of the sword of the Spirit of God either rusted by age or blunted by use. To-day, the sun in heaven shines as bright as when his old fires first began to burn: and so does that better Sun, the Sun of Righteousness, which sheds healing in its beams—to-day, the wind sweeps field and forest with wings as strong and free as when first it stirred in gentle breezes or

tossed in storms the palms of Eden : and now not
less free and full than ever that Spirit which is as the
wind that bloweth where, and when, and how it listeth—to-day, the great sea, " where go the ships,"
after receiving, for long ages, into its capacious
bosom the mud and mire, the decay and death of a
thousand rivers, is as pure as when its billows first
broke their snowy heads on the shores of our new-
born world : and so, though ten times ten thousand
and thousands of thousands have washed away their
guilt in the blood of Christ, are the fountains of
grace and salvation.   For deliverance from the love
and power, as well as the guilt, of sin, we are " complete in Christ."   In this confidence, though with
fear and trembling, let us work out our salvation ;
God working in us both to will and to do of His
good pleasure.   Seeking the aids of the Holy Spirit,
let us aim at perfection.   Let every day see some sin
crucified, some battle fought, some good done, some
victory won ; let every fall be followed by a rise, and
every step gained become, not a resting-place, but a
new starting-point for further and higher progress ;
and, looking over the gloomy confines of the grave
to the glory that lies beyond, let us meet our last
hour and last enemy, when they come, calm " in the
sure and certain hope of a glorious resurrection "—
this our confidence, that He who hath begun a good
work in us will carry it on to the day of the Lord

Jesus; and will, while mourning friends receive our parting sigh, bring forth the " headstone "—all the angels of heaven and all the saints in glory shouting, ' Grace, grace unto it !"

XVIII.

THE SHINING LIGHT.*

"The path of the just is as the shining light, that shineth more and more unto the perfect day."—Prov. i. 18.

EVERY man's life is a path. Long in some cases, it is in others so short that many—that all those, indeed, of whom our Lord says the kingdom of heaven is—leave no impression on the sands of time other than the prints of little feet and a few brief steps. With all varieties of length, this path presents also an endless variety of scenes and circumstances. Like travellers whose road, passing over a mountainous district, now climbs to the summits of the hills, and now plunges into their gloomy gorges—some meet many "ups and downs" in life; they come out of one difficulty to encounter another; their home is saddened by successive bereavements; misfortune follows on misfortune, as do the billows on each other that come swelling in with

---

* The papers from this point to the end, were printed in the first edition of the volume entitled "Man and the Gospel," but are not in the new edition of that work.

(344)

foan.ing crests to break, and thunder on the beach. On the other hand, some who enjoy the peace of God and a good conscience, have so little in their outward circumstances to give them trouble, that their life, like a river flowing by wooded banks and through fertile fields, glides smoothly on; and they are in considerable danger of loving the world too well, of forgetting a better one, amid so much in this to gratify their desires. But, long or short, bordered with flowers or beset with thorns, life is but a pathway which has, for all the crowd that travel it, in the cradle a common beginning, and in the coffin a common end.

The grave is the end of all men. Here all things earthly — the grandest schemes, ambition's ladder, love's torch, the marriage altar, the conqueror's sword, the poet's laurels, the rich man's gold, the poor man's sorrows, woman's beauty, and manly strength—find their tomb. "One dieth," says Job, "in his full strength, being wholly at ease and in quiet; his breasts are full of milk, and his bones are moistened with marrow. Another dieth in the bitterness of his soul, and never eateth with pleasure. They shall lie down alike in the dust; the worms shall cover them."

But life is a path in another, and still more important sense. We shift the scene. Now, in place of many roads that start from a common cradle to

15*

meet again, after diverging far apart, in a common grave, we see but two; and they proceed in entirely opposite directions. They open differently—a wide gate admits to this, a narrow one to that. They end differently—these the inscriptions above their respective portals: on this, "Wide is the gate and broad is the way that leadeth to destruction; and many there be that go in thereat;" on that, "Strait is the gate and narrow is the way that leadeth to life; and few there be that find it." Solemn words, which it were well all had grace to lay to heart! On the one path or the other our feet are planted; and since every step is one upward to heaven or downward to perdition, it is sufficient to cast a solemn aspect over the glories of each setting sun, to think that it leaves us a day nearer hell, or nearer heaven. Different in character—that broad and this narrow; different in access — that wide and this strait; different in their ends—this terminating in heaven and that in hell: these roads, on which a motley crowd, kings and beggars both, may be met, differ no less in the character of those who travel them; and we are thereby furnished with tests for determining, each for himself, this grave and most important question—On which am I travelling? To which of the parties do I belong?

One of these lies in the progressive advancement of God's people in virtue, in holiness, and in all manner of heavenly graces—a distinctive feature of their character which it may be interesting and profitable to study, as set forth in this beautiful image, "The path of the just is as *the shining light*, which shineth more and more unto the perfect day."

But, before looking at the figure, let us, in the first instance, consider *Why God's people are called just.*

Of all who have lived in the world since Adam's fall, our Lord Jesus Christ alone was, in the strict and proper sense of the word, entitled to that high character—to an appellation which He obtained from an unlooked-for quarter in the darkest crisis of His history. The fulness of time has come. The hour of redemption strikes. All things are now ready— the altar and the victim both. There is the wood and the fire, and the Lamb also for a burnt-offering. Heaven and hell look on in high expectancy. The representative and substitute of an elect world, the Son of Mary and of God, stands before Pilate to be condemned to death; and pour out His sinless soul an offering for sin. At this moment, to human eyes, the fate of Jesus hangs in the balance : for though the Jews demand His execution, the Roman governor refuses His assent. Strange rumours about this same Jesus of Nazareth, how He cured the most inveterate diseases, calmed storms on the deep, cast out devils, opened the eyes of the blind, the ears of the deaf, and even the graves of the dead, have reached Pilate's ear; stirred, astonished, and awed the palace. The Roman hesitates to strike; not so much probably out of regard to justice, as because he is afraid to challenge and provoke the power of this unknown; and rouse perhaps a lion in this gentle Lamb. Besides, there is a strange calm, lofty, mysterious dignity in the bearing of the prisoner that strikes terror into the heart of his time-serving, guilty judge; making him shrink back like one who is about to take a leap in the dark—he knows not where. Indeed, once and again, he attempts to save the accused. He pleads his cause, but in vain. And now, as no way of escape seems left, either for the prisoner or himself, submitting like a heathen to the Fates, he resumes his place on the seat of judgment, and, though reluctant, is about to pronounce the fatal sentence. At this critical moment there is a stir among the crowd, through which one, wearing Pilate's livery, is seen elbowing his way. He comes in hot haste, a messenger from Pilate's wife; and ascending the steps, whispers this warning in his master's ear, "Have thou nothing to do with that just man, for I have suffered many things this day in a dream because of Him.' Strange, of all the thousands whom Jesus had blessed and cured, there was not so much as one to cry, Crucify Him not! Strange, as the only confession of Him came from the lips of a dying thief, the only voice raised in His behalf came from the lips of a dreaming woman! Yet though he was despised and rejected of men, though He came unto His own and His own received Him not, well spoke that dreamer. Let the guards unbind His arms, let Him break the strange silence that seals His lips, and He holds up His hands high above that raging multitude, before them, before the priests, before Pilate, before heaven as well as earth, before God himself, to say, These hands are clean! He, and He alone, of all that ever lived, since sin entered our world, was without sin—guile, there was none in His mouth; guilt, there was none in His heart. In Him a clean thing came out of an unclean. Though entering the world by Mary's womb, He was by birth the Just One. Though called the friend of publicans and sinners, He—holy, harmless, and undefiled, separate from sinners, as oil from the water amid whicn it floats—was in life the Just One. Though condemned as a malefactor, and crucified between two thieves, He was in death the Just One. He died, as Scripture says, "the just for the unjust, that we might be saved"—that His righteousness, the merits of His holy life and of His atoning death, being imputed to us, we might appear righteous; in other words, be reckoned just in the judgment, and therefore acquitted at the bar, of a holy God. Thus the apostle says, "justified by faith —in other words, made just through the righteousness which grace on God's part imputes, and faith on ours receives—"we have peace with God through our Lord Jesus Christ." So I remark—

It is through the *righteousness of Jesus Christ* that any, in the strict and proper sense of the term, are *just* in the sight of God.

Society divides itself into a variety of classes—an arrangement that to some extent seems as much a law of Providence as the division of the hand into fingers, or a tree into boughs, and of its boughs into branches. So we speak of the higher and lower classes, of nobles and commoners, of sovereigns and subjects, of the rich and the poor, of the learned and unlearned. Like the differences of stature among the individuals of a crowd, between even giants and pigmies, to one who surveys them from a lofty bartizan, the ordinary distinctions of society vanish in the sight of heaven; and in the eyes of Him who looks down on the world from the heights of divinity, there remains but one, only one distinction. It is that which divides the whole human family, princes and peasants both, into two great classes—the good and evil, the just and unjust—and so, for example, it is said, "God maketh his sun to shine upon the evil and the good; and his rain to fall on the just and unjust." At any rate, no other distinction but that survives the stroke of death; descending with us into the grave and making it our peaceful bed, or a doleful prison. You cannot tell the skull of a king from that of a beggar; and in the grave, beauty the most charming and deformity the most revolting moulder into indistinguishable dust. Yet Jesus knows them that are his. It is as the just they sleep in Him; and as the just they shall rise from their graves on that day when the trumpet sounds the resurrection, and it shall be said " to the north, Give up, and to the south, Keep not back; bring my sons from far, and my daughters from the ends of the earth !"

But how do any become just with God? It cannot be because they are sinless. There is not a just man on earth that doeth good and sinneth not; and the inspired author of that statement also remarks of those who may in a sense be called just, " a just man falleth seven times and riseth up again." And since the best do fall, and that not seven times, nor seventy times seven, but times and ways innumerable, notwithstanding that they do rise again, and, through the grace of God sanctifying the humbling lesson, may rise, like the fabled giant, stronger than before, then in the words of the patriarch, " How can man be just with God? If he will contend with him, he cannot answer him one of a thousand." Such being the case, the apostle argues with unanswerable logic, that by the deeds of a law which requires perfect obedience, in other words, by man's own righteousness, "no flesh can be justified in the sight of God."

The Shuhite asked, as you will find written in the Book of Job, "How can man be justified with God; how can he be clean that is born of a woman? Behold even to the moon, and it shineth not; yea, the stars are not pure in his sight. How much less man, that is a worm; and the son of man, which is a worm?" Bildad's question finds its answer, the grand difficulty of all heathen nations and ages its complete solution, in the gospel. Let this poor "worm" but creep through the dust to the foot of the Cross, and bathe itself in the blood of Calvary: and how it is changed! What a change on that which, once a creeping caterpillar, crawling on the ground and devouring garbage, now spreads its painted wings, and springs into the air to live in sunbeams and to feed on flowers! What a change on the leper, when, bending his way from the prophet's house to the banks of Jordan, he goes down into the sacred stream; and dips, and dips again, and, taking the seventh plunge, rises from the parting waters with a skin like a little child's! But a greater change is here. At the foot of the Cross, sprinkled with the blood of Christ, the sinner changes into a saint; the unjust into the just; the condemned into the acquitted; the child of hell into an heir of heaven. Putting off self-righteousness to put on Christ, he exchanges a beggar's rags for a kingly robe; once covered with iniquity as with a garment, he now stands apparelled in one finer, fairer, costlier than ever angel wore; and in the eyes of his Sovereign Judge, the believer, happy man! is without spot, or stain, or any such thing. "There is no condemnation for those who are in Jesus Christ, who walk not after the flesh, but after the Spirit."

As appears from this figure, the spiritual life of the just, the justified, the believer in Jesus, is one of *progress.*

A connoisseur in works of art, so soon as the dust of years has been wiped from an old picture, can name the master who painted the glowing canvas. So also, though time has left no record of their history, and no date stands carved on the crumbling ruins, an antiquarian can tell from its form when that arch was sprung; from their capitals, by what hands, long mouldering in the dust, these grand, impressive, silent pillars were reared on their massive pedestals. The works of all great men, and those of all great ages, are marked by properties peculiar to themselves. And features entirely their own are eminently characteristic of all the works of God; so characteristic of these that the untutored Arab when challenged to prove in God the existence of a being whom he had never touched, nor heard, nor seen, regarded the scoffer with amazement; nor deigned to return any answer to his gibes but one borrowed from the scenes of his native desert · " Just as I know," he replied, in terms worth a volume of divinity—" Just as I know," pointing to a footprint on the sand, " whether it was a man or a camel that passed my tent last night."

So distinguished by a divine wisdom, power, and goodness are God's works of creation and providence that all Nature, by the gentle voices of her skies and streams, of her fields and forests, as well as by the roar of breakers, the crash of thunder, the rumbling earthquake, the fiery volcano, the destroying hurricane, echoes the closing sentence of this angel hymn, " Holy, holy, holy is the Lord God Almighty, the whole earth is full of his glory!" But the works of God are not less marked by their progressive character than by the attributes of wisdom, power, and goodness. A work of time, the world was built story by story; and course by course the pyramid of animated nature rose from its base, till man, his Maker's image, and creation's crowning work, was placed on its lofty summit. Brief as is the history of creation compared to the large portion of the Bible which is devoted to the story of redemption, the opening chapter of Genesis, though leaving much unexplained and wrapt in impene·

trable obscurity, shows us God working onward to
His Sabbath rest by a series of successive creations;
and when we close the pages of revelation to examine those of nature, they who are skilled to read
that older record, see progress inscribed on all its
stony leaves.

Then, the Providence that governs the world is
equally characterised by progress. It is to be seen
every morning in the approach of day—not flashing
like an explosion to startle the world from sleep, but
advancing, by silent though steady steps, from the
first faint streak in the east through all the glories
and changing hues of sunrise, of amber and saffron
and gold and purple, to the blaze of the perfect day;
we see it in the growth of plants, from the pale, tender shoot which lifts a tiny head above the soil to
its maturity in the tree that, with its stately form
rifted in the rock, throws out its giant arms, and,
battling with the elements, defies the rage of storms;
we see it in the change a few days makes on the
flowers of the garden, or a few months on our corn
fields, or a few swift years in our families where girls
grow into women, and boys into stalwart men. Like
God's works of creation, and his works also of providence, redemption, while displaying all His attributes in their brightest lustre, and forming His
greatest work, is also marked by this never-failing
feature of progress. The temple of salvation was

not built in a day, or in a century, or even in a thousand years. Its foundation was laid in Eden, and at a time remote as the Fall—laid in that promise of a Saviour which God embosomed in the curse He pronounced on the cunning serpent—" I will put enmity between thee and the woman, and between thy seed and her seed: it shall bruise thy head, and thou shalt bruise his heel." Yet not till four thousand long years had come and gone did the Redeemer crown His work; and, in the dying but triumphant accents of His expiring breath, pronounce it " finished."

And it is with the work of our sanctification, the work of renewing grace in the soul, as with all God's works in all places of His dominion; " Hear, O Israel, the Lord thy God is one Lord." In this, as in all things else, progress is God's plan, and man's pathway to perfection. Let this yield comfort to some in whom grace seems but a little spark—a feeble, flickering flame, easily quenched and often ready to expire. Let them not be cast down; but pray God, with His Spirit and the breath of His mouth, to blow the smoking flax into a bright, burning, heaven-kindled, and ascending flame. The day of small things in grace is no more to be despised than the day of small things in sin: for it is commonly with Christ formed within us as it was with Christ on Mary's bosom, in the carpenter's house of

Nazareth. He grew in wisdom as in stature; at first a feeble babe, hanging on a mother's breast, clinging to a mother's side. He grew betimes into a man whose voice hushed the tempest, whose foot trode the rolling billows, from whose presence devils fled, and whose behests even the dead obeyed.

Imitating Him whom faith receives both as our propitiation and our pattern, we are by pains and prayer to grow in holiness and humility; in sweetness of temper and heavenliness of mind; in active obedience and patient suffering; in conformity to the will and delight in the ways of God. Why should we be cast down, dispirited, disheartened, and ready to abandon all efforts in an unwarrantable despair? No doubt, whether our aim be high or humble, we always come short of the mark? Yet let us be thankful, though we have not reached, if we are nearing perfection; if, like the harbour lights, we see it ahead of us, not vanishing on the stern, but growing on the bow; if our course shows marks of progress; if our spiritual life is lighting up like the morning; and we can express our experience in the words of the apostle, " We all, with open face beholding as in a glass the glory of the Lord, are changed into the same image from glory to glory, even as by the Spirit of the Lord."

As does not appear in this figure, the progress

of God's people in a life of grace may be *helped and hastened.*

The progress of those celestial luminaries that raise the tides of ocean and rule the seasons of the year, and make night and day, morning's growing dawn and evening's deepening twilight, is independent of us; both of our works and our wishes. Those heavenly bodies that roll through the fields of space, move in orbits beyond our reach; nor did man ever interfere with their machinery but on that occasion, when, for a special purpose and by miraculous power, Joshua laid his hands on their wheels— "So the sun stood still in the midst of heaven and hasted not to go down about a whole day; and there was no day like that before or after it, that the Lord hearkened unto a voice of a man: for the Lord fought for Israel." All experience confirms that observation of the inspired historian. Ah, time moves no slower for the wishes of the miserable wretch, in whose eyes, as he waits the day of execution, its sands never ran, and in whose ears its lessening hours never struck, so quickly—and the long night passes and the dawn comes no sooner for the wishes of the crew that, wrecked on the thundering reef, with a straining ship breaking up beneath and every moment threatening to ingulf them, scan the east with anxious eyes; and watching for the first streak of light, weary, and pray for the coming of the morn. The natural light which shines over our heads and brightens into the perfect day, obeys the unalterable decrees of heaven—our wishes cannot hasten its progress, nor can our indifference by one moment delay or hinder it.

It is otherwise with grace in the soul; in the life, habits, and hearts of God's chosen people. No doubt sanctification, like redemption, is the peculiar work of God—the life of grace in His people being as much His work as the light that breaks and brightens on the eastern sky when, with almighty hand, He throws open the gates of day. Yet, while God by His Spirit works in sanctification, we also are to work. In this field, as in that of the conversion of the world, Christians are honoured and are called to be fellow-workers with God—the injuction of the apostle being laid on them all: "Work out your own salvation with fear and trembling; for it is God which worketh in you both to will and to do of his good-pleasure." Hence we are exhorted to grow in grace; to grow in the knowledge and love of our Lord Jesus Christ; to labour for the bread that never perisheth; to forget the things that are behind, and press forward, onward, upward—the path we move on, progress; the end we aim at, perfection. No effort of ours can either hasten or hinder the dawn of day; but by watchfulness and prayer, by the devout use of our Bibles and the hallow ed observance of God's holy day, by waiting on Him in all the ordinances of His house and holding fellowship with our heavenly Head, and Lord, and elder Brother, we can do much to promote our growth in grace, and mature our meetness for the kingdom of heaven. Let us labour for such lofty ends. Anything beneath them is to mistake the grand purpose of life, and to peril the salvation of our souls. He who imagines that the grace of God once received into his heart, will grow in that soil without either effort, or care, or prayer of his, as without these the dawn breaks and the day brightens above his head, is grievously, fatally mistaken. Alas! his case is described by another figure, though also borrowed from the break of morn:—unlike the shining light which shineth more and more unto the perfect day, his goodness, a delusion, shall be "as a morning cloud and the early dew" that vanish away; and, dissolving into empty air, leave neither on earth nor sky so much as a trace behind them.

XIX.

RISEN WITH CHRIST.—Part I.

" If ye then [or, since ye then] be risen with Christ, seek
those things which are above."—Col. iii. 1

THERE are tracts of country in some regions
of the world where the soil feels hot to the
touch, the ground rings hollow to the foot,
and groaning mountains belch forth flames, clouds
of vapour, and streams of molten rock. There,
where the " solid earth " seems an inappropriate
expression, earthquakes occasionally occur, to bury,
not houses only, but whole cities, in their yawning
chasms. Unlike these, which are connected with
ordinary volcanic agences, was the earthquake that,
with strange signs in the heavens, distinguished our
Lord's from all other deaths. It opened graves, not
to bury the living, but set the dead free; and, wrench-
ing the bars of death asunder, exposed to the eye of
day the grim and silent tenants of the tomb.

So happened it when Jesus, God manifest in the
flesh, gave up the ghost. Our earth was struck with
terror. Seized with an extraordinary trembling, the

rocks, in whose bowels the Jews hollowed out their
tombs, were rent asunder; and such as had the curiosity and courage to look in, saw the dead—each
lying in his stony chamber. They were waiting the
hour of resurrection; nor could they rise till Christ
had risen. A king goes foremost—not before, but
after him his subjects; nor is it the feet but the head
that rises first to the surface when a man, falling
overboard, is buried in the sea. Such was the order
of events on the morning of the third day. The
angel, seated on the stone that he had rolled from
the door, is silently waiting the issue with eyes fixed
upon the tomb, when Jesus, untouched, unsummoned,
awakes; and rising to put off shroud and face-cloth,
passes forth into the morning air with the step of a
conqueror. For this hour, for the joy set before
Him, to redeem our souls from hell and our bodies
from the grave, He had endured the cross and despised the shame; and He now lives to die no more.
And as, so soon as the heart in a case of suspended
animation resumes its functions, the blood begins to
flow and pulses throb through all the body, even so
they revive with Christ, who were to show forth the
connexion between His resurrection and that of His
saints at the final judgment. Prefiguring that great
event, and leaving the graves the earthquake had
opened, many saints arose. The evangelist St. Matthew thus describes the scene :—" Jesus, when he

had cried again with a loud voice, yielded up the ghost. And, behold, the veil of the temple was rent in twain from the top to the bottom; and the earth did quake, and the rocks rent; and the graves were opened; and many bodies of the saints which slept arose, and came out of the graves after his resurrection, and went into the holy city, and appeared unto many." Our Lord's ascent from the grave was a fit counterpart to His descent from the skies; both events being characterised by manifestations of the divinity that touched with resplendent glory the darkest mysteries of His life, He left heaven attended by a train of angels, and left the tomb with one hardly less, if not more remarkable—a band whom he had restored to life, and brought out of their graves. They, the strangest assembly ever met on earth, had " risen with Christ ;" and so, in the plainest sense of the terms, St. Paul might have addressed them, saying, " If ye then," or since ye then, " are risen with Christ, seek those things which are above."

Had the apostle addressed these words to that company, they could have had little interest, and no application to us. But the words occur in a letter he wrote to the church at Colosse; and were addressed to such as, far removed from the scene of this stupendous miracle, had no more share in it than we have. We shall therefore consider them as bearing on the whole Church of Christ, in every age as well as in every country of the world. Happily combining doctrine and practice, they present two distinct points for consideration; they delineate a character and enjoin a duty. Taking these in their order, let us consider—

Who are those that may be said *to have risen with Christ.*

There is a churchyard where the passenger who reads the inscriptions on the tombs, that stand up amid the long rank grass beneath the shadow of waving elms and an old gray steeple, will find one to surprise him; which, though quaint in form, I doubt not is true in substance. Here, no angel flying through the heavens sounds a trumpet; no figure of old Time, with bald head, shoulders a scythe or shakes an hour-glass; no cross-bones rudely carved, nor sexton's spade, nor grinning skull, give point to the trite "Memento Mori." Stranger still, the monument which is raised to the memory and virtues of one person bears the date of more than one birth: with long years between, it says, speaking in name of the dead, I was born the first time on such a day, and born the second time on such another day of another year. Strange, indeed! Yet, had John Baptist's disciples erected a monument to the memory of their murdered master, it might have recorded a more astounding fact; and, to those ignorant of the work of God's Spirit, a more inexplicable riddle. For, contradiction in terms though it seems, the second birth in John's as in Jeremiah's case, went before the first—the Baptist being sanctified from his mother's womb. There, a babe yet unborn, he rejoiced in God his Saviour; " Lo," said Elizabeth to Mary, when the two cousins, both by and by to become mothers, met—" Lo, as soon as the voice of thy salutation sounded in mine ears, the babe leaped in my womb for joy."

The history of every saint on being completed, which it shall not be till the final judgment, and heads mouldering in the dust are crowned with im mortality, will contain a record of two births, of two deaths, and of two resurrections—the first visible, the second invisible ; the subject of the one change, the body; the subject of the other, which is a mat ter of faith and not of sight, the soul of the believ er. This second birth and first death, or resurrec- tion, are one and the same event. Here let me pause to say, How important an event ! and to ask, Have we any experience of it ? This change of heart is the door to heaven, the hinge on which turns our eternal destiny; without it Jesus declares that no man, however virtuous or honest, can see the king- dom of God ; promising to bestow it, God says, " O my people, I will open your graves, and cause you to come up out of your graves—a new heart also will I give you, and a new spirit will I put within you;" and what God has promised in these, and many other no less gracious words, Ezekiel was privileged to see in vision—there, where the bones of a valley, once a battlefield, orderly arrange themselves into skeletons, and the naked skeletons get clothed with flesh, and no sooner does a wind from heaven come, sweeping along to stir their hair and kiss their lips, than every dead man, inspired anew with life, springs to his feet, and the valley, before so silent, echoes to the blare of trumpets, and is filled with " an exceeding great army,"—God's host, bannered and marshalled, and eager for battle.

The words " risen with Christ," which express the condition of such as are born of God's Spirit and have passed through the first resurrection, are in complete harmony with all that Scripture and con-science reveal of our lost state by nature. The Word of God pronounces all men dead, " dead in trespasses and sins;" and the most cursory exam-ination of the subject teaches us that more is meant by that expression than the fact, alarming as the fact is, that, until justified by faith in the righteousness of Jesus Christ, we all lie under condemnation. What does he think of, for example, who lies in a condemned cell, sentenced within so many days to be taken to the place of public execution, and hanged by the neck till he is dead?—of what he

shall eat, or drink, or wherewithal he shall be clothed
—of comforts with which to surround himself—of
the pastimes and pleasures in which he may spend
his numbered hours? No. By his grated window
the wretched man sits, inditing petitions for pardon:
when the world sleeps, and all but his beating heart
is still, he creeps softly from his pallet to try the
strength of the iron bars; unlike those who neither
pray nor solicit the prayers of others, he engages
every possible interest to intercede with the Crown
on his behalf, nor leaves any means untried to make
his pardon sure. But, till awakened and converted
by divine grace, do men show any such anxiety for
salvation: or put forth one earnest effort corresponding to his? If they did, who should be lost?
None. With pardon freely offered—to be got for
the asking; with liberty proclaimed and prison
doors flung open; with God not willing that any
should perish, but that all should come to Him and
live, it is not possible to account for sinners perishing otherwise than by the fact that men, while under
the sentence are also under the insensibility of death.
Think you that unless the body stretched on the
funeral pile by the banks of the Ganges were dead,
it would lie passive there, to be wrapped in flames
and reduced to ashes? Alive, how the man would
watch the torch's fiery glare, and perceiving it touch
the pile, burst his bonds. spring from his bed, and

fly for life! Much more, were men not " dead in trespasses and sins," would they work out their salvation with fear and trembling—give all diligence to " make their calling and election sure."

Besides being marked by insensibility, death is followed by corruption. It, not the glassy eye, nor marble brow, nor rigid form, nor heart that neither beats nor flutters, is the surest, saddest proof that life has fled; and so with the grand and bold imagery of inspiration, the prophet represents the dead as talking in their graves, saying " to corruption, Thou art my father; and to the worm, Thou art my mother and my sister." And turning from the physical to the moral aspects of man's case, alas! how much corruption is in his heart to prove him " dead in trespasses and sins." Let the Holy Spirit, before he begins to cleanse it, open a sinner's eyes to its depravity, show the man himself in the mirror of God's Word, and he starts back from the glass, aghast at his own image; shocked to see that there is no grave so foul as man's heart. " Ye shall loathe yourselves," says God to His people, " ye shall loathe yourselves in your own sight for all the evils that ye have committed." Need we wonder at such strong expressions? Why? Even saintly Ezra blushed to lift up his head: and Job, eminent above all the men of his time for uprightness, cried, " I abhor myself:" and St. Paul, as if this greatest of apostles had been the greatest of sinners, feeling through the corruptions that clung to him like a living captive in a most horrible predicament — chained to one whom death had turned into a festering corpse, exclaims, " Who shall deliver me from the body of this death?" If it is so with renewed men, what must it be with those who are entire strangers to the grace of God—if such is the state of the green tree, how must it be with the dry?

I am far from asserting, though sin, like a poison carried along in the blood, has affected in a sense our entire nature, that the unconverted are without amiable, excellent, and valuable properties. I have seen flowers of lovely hue and fragrant odour clinging to the walls of a crumbling ruin, and I have seen such beauty lingering on the face of the dead as went far to deprive death of its repulsive aspect, and make it difficult to believe that life had fled. Such are the graces that belong to fallen humanity. They adorn, but cannot redeem it—pleasing man but not propitiating God. If our Lord's body in the grave, to borrow an illustration from it, might be regarded as the type of a soul " dead in trespasses and sins," these natural virtues are but the fine linen in which Joseph wrapped the sacred form, the bed of spices on which with tender hand he composed the mangled limbs. What availed the snowy fabric of the loom, and fragrance that filled the sepulchre? Death was

16*

there—the dear form was cold; the eyes were fixed and filmy; silent the voice that hushed the tempest and cheered the weeping penitent; powerless the hand at whose touch blind eyes opened and old sores were closed; and, with its features muffled in a napkin, low on the cold ground lay the head that had lain in the bosom of God. Thus Jesus was under the insensibility as well as the sentence of death; and so remained till, after three days and nights, as the Jews expressed it, life returned to the lifeless body, and His heart with all other organs resumed its functions. Then He rose; declared by His resurrection to be the Son of God with power. And they who are risen with Him, undergoing a greater change than the saints who had their graves opened at His death, and their life restored at His resurrection, are those whose souls once dead in sin have become alive through grace. Your way to spiritual life opened up, perhaps, by convictions that have rent the rocky heart and shaken soul and body too, as earthquakes shake a trembling world, have you risen to newness of life? Then cast off, like grave-clothes, the habits of sin. In the strength of heavenly grace, burst its bonds, and go forth to enjoy the light and walk in the liberty of the sons of God.

For on those who have thus risen with Christ is— The duty enjoined—*seek those things which are above*, or as St. Paul more fully expresses it in words we shall by and by consider, Set your affections on things in heaven, and not on things on earth.

When the doctrine of a resurrection was first revealed, it dazzled all eyes and blinded some. Reason started at the strange announcement; and treating its great preacher with undisguised contempt, the Athenians sneered—asking, as they curled the lip and pointed to St. Paul, "What doth this babbler say?" To throw some light on that mystery, he employed the similitude of such familiar objects as corn-seed, which is cast on the soil, and, though when buried in the furrow a dry, sapless, lifeless-looking thing, rises to push aside the clods, and clothe the fields with verdure, and fill the barns of the husbandman with golden sheaves. In other realms of nature, science finds a still more remarkable similitude in the insects that, sporting in sunbeams and flitting from flower to flower, give life to the air and beauty to the scene. Once creeping worms, after a while they wove a shroud and wrapped it round them, and, dropping from bush or tree, sought a grave in the earth, where they lay entombed till spring winds thawed and summer beams warmed the soil, and at the appointed time shuffled off their shroud, and rose into the sunny air on silken wings —in form, in food, in tastes, in habits so different, that it might be said, " Old things have passed away and all things are become new."

An image of the change on our bodies when this poor dust shall hear the trumpet, and mortality put on immortality, this is not less, but perhaps more, an image of the change wrought in our souls when the Spirit renews them at the second birth and first resurrection. Then, at least, in their dominant power, old things have passed away; and, in their bud and germ at least, all things have become new. The Bible, for example, so soon as a man is converted, reads like a new book; the Sabbath bell rings out new sounds; Jesus, 'once despised, but now invested with new and attractive graces, is prized as the chiefest among ten thousand and altogether lovely—every feeling and affection leaving its old channel, flows in a new and opposite direction; and loving what once he hated and hating what once he loved, shunning what once he sought and seeking what once he shunned, the years the renewed man spent in sin seem to him like a strange, and guilty, and frightful, and horrid dream. Yet, though perfect in nature, this holy change is imperfect in degree—many being the hostile influences to which believers are exposed here; many the temptations that assail their virtue; many the difficulties that impede their course; many the conflicts they have to maintain against the love of the world and the remaining corruption of their hearts. Therefore St. Paul urges them to withdraw their affections from things on earth, and, as those that have risen from sin to the enjoyment of a new life, to set them on things above.

Thus to rise and soar, though by no means easy, is a duty to which God's people will give earnest heed if they consult only their present happiness. The ivy which throws its arms around a hollow and rotten tree dooms itself to be crushed; and they are laying up suffering for a future day who allow affections which should be trained to the skies to be entangled with perishing earthly objects. God will not permit His redeemed ones to perish; but to save their souls He will sink their treasures—cast away the cargo to keep the ship afloat. If they choose Sodom, He will burn them out of it; to deliver them from idolatry, He will destroy their idols; and when precepts fail to teach it, He will teach them by bitter experience that " he builds too low, who builds beneath the skies." Startled by the whirring of a scared bird, the fall of a leaf, even their own shadow which the moon, shining through a glade of the forest, projects on the path, they may fear robbers who carry their fortune on their persons; but he who has his wealth in the banker's safe, walks light-hearted through the gloom of night, and whistles as he goes—careless though thieves be thick as

forest leaves. Even so, the man who has his treasure in heaven is, in a sense and measure at least,
prepared for the worst that can befall; nor, when
misfortune comes to take away his wealth, or disease to take away his health, or calumny to take
away his reputation, or death to pluck wife or child
from his loving arms, has he to raise the old, bitter
cry, "Ye have taken away my gods, and what have
I more?" He who has his affections set on things
above is like one who hangs on by the skies; and,
having a secure hold of these, could say, though he
saw the world roll away from beneath his feet, "My
heart is fixed, my heart is fixed, O Lord, I will sing
and give praise!"

I do not say, notwithstanding all its sins and
sorrows, but that there is much good in God's world.
It is a good servant, though, like fire and water, a
bad master; useful as a staff, though in the heart a
tyrant's rod; good beneath a man's feet, though on
his back a burden to make a saint groan, like Atlas.
Be careful, therefore, by setting your affections on
things above, to keep the world in its own place.
Allow it to thrust itself in between you and God,
and Christ, and holiness, and heaven, and it shall
be with your souls as with our planet when the moon
rolls in between us and the sun; though vastly inferior to that glorious luminary, yet blotting out all
beauty, hushing the voice of song, turning day into

sudden night, and striking terror into all nature, it wraps the world in the darkness of a cold eclipse. It matters little how much of the world is in our hands, if it is kept out of our hearts, and care be taken that neither business nor pleasures make us forget that heaven, not earth, is our home. Would that heaven had such a place in our thoughts as home has in the hearts of boys about holiday time, of soldiers when the weary war draws to a close, of exiles looking to see the ship sail round the headland which is to convey them and their fortunes from a foreign shore. As I have seen the twittering swallows, when their time of migration drew near, sit on house-tops pruning their pinions, and wheel in mazy circles through the air to try and to strengthen their powers of flight, so, living above and looking beyond this world, let us prepare for our departure—daily, prayerfully, assiduously cultivating that holiness which is the unfailing characteristic of believers, and which, perfected on their arrival at the gates of heaven, shall be their highest happiness and brightest crown.

But if we are to live separate from the world like oil among water—though in it, not of it—how, it may be asked, since men only do well what they do with a will, are we, with affections fixed on things above, to perform aright the secular, ordinary duties of life? If our hearts are engrossed with heavenly things, how are we to obey this other, and equally divine, commandment, " Whatsoever " — be it to sweep a floor or reform a state, hold the helm of a ship or of a nation—" whatsoever thy hand findeth to do, do it with thy might "—a way of doing ordinary work, let me observe, not more conducive to our temporal advantage than creditable to our religious profession. " With might," implies that the heart is engaged along with the head and hand ; and having, though two hands, but one heart, which, like the living child for whom the mothers wrangled, to divide were to destroy, how can we do things apparently so incompatible as to set our affections on the things of heaven and yet engage with " might " in the secularities of earth ? The two are perfectly consistent. Man standing between the celestial and terrestrial worlds is related to both ; and resembling neither a flower which, springing from the dust and returning to it, belongs altogether to the earth, nor a star which, shining far remote from this lower sphere, belongs altogether to the heavens, our hearts may be fitly likened to the rainbow that, rising into heaven but resting on earth, is connected both with the clods of the valley and the clouds of the sky.

Let this familiar example show how Christians may have their affections set on things above, and yet give diligent attention to the duties of their earthly calling. With the salt tear standing in his eye, with a mother's precious counsels and a father's pious prayers, a youth leaves home for a distant colony. At the foot of the ladder he looks to its topmost round; resolved to climb. step by step, up to wealth and honour. For this end he saves with an economy that allows no waste; works with an energy that never wearies; submits without shrinking to trials and hardships; and throws himself into his duties with a zeal that merits fortune and commands success. People, and especially his fellows whom he leaves lagging far behind, fancy that his affections, like its trees, have taken root in that foreign soil, and that his heart is wholly engrossed with the cares and business of his post. They know no better. His heart is not there. It is at home—its affections, like an elastic chain, stretching unbroken over all the lands that lie and broad seas that roll between. Visions of his father's house float around his couch, the forms of loved ones move in his nightly dreams: where palm-trees wave, he longs to see the hills of dusky pines, and thinks, when the nightingale sings from orange groves, of the larks that carol, soaring over his native fields. Fond memory dwells on the past; fancy stretches away into the future; and he sets store on honours and wealth, chiefly for the pleasures they will yield to loved ones at home. Home is the centre around which his hidden life keeps turning; the dear word stands engraven on his heart: his settled purpose, his daily thought is one day to go home. And yet, whether his office in that distant land be to sit at the head of a council, or march at the head of an army, to manage a business, to hold a pen or guide a plough, whatever his hand findeth to do he does it with all his might.

Even so should it be with us in our earthly pilgrimage. So far from doing our earthly duties worse, we do them better for having our affections set on things above—the hope of rest strengthening us for labour: the example of Christ inspiring us with ardour; and no fears of ultimate disappointment clouding our prospects and weakening us by the way. One, an exile, returns to his native land; but not to home. Ah! he finds no home. The voices are silent he hoped to hear; the cold grave holds those he hoped to see; his old friends are in the dust, nor live but in his dreams: and turning away from a generation that stare coldly on his gray hairs, he repairs to the churchyard, and, sitting down on a father's or mother's grave, weeps over the ruins of fondly cherished hopes—this the verdict on all his toil, and exile, and wealth, and honours, Vanity and vexation of spirit! But where Christ sitteth at the right hand of God, we shall find more than hope ever anticipated, imagination fancied, or love desired. Who after long years of exile goes up to the door of his old home, approaches it with a beating heart·

knocks with a trembling hand. He knows not what has happened in his absence : an empty chair may meet his eye, and to the questions that tremble on his lips the only answer may be, Dead—all dead! How different his fortune who knocks at heaven's happy gate ! It opens on scenes of surpassing glory. Arrayed in robes of light, long missed and long mourned ones hasten to meet him at the door; and lead him up through lines of shining angels to the throne where Jesus, his Saviour, seated in glory at the right hand of God, bends on him looks of ineffable affection, and bids him Welcome to the bliss of Paradise.

XX.

RISEN WITH CHRIST.—Part II.

"If ye then [or, since ye then] be risen with Christ, seek
those things which are above."—Col. iii. 1.

THE world once boasted of possessing seven
wonders; but a greater than any or all of
them is, a true Christian. His feelings, enjoyments, aims, and objects are such, that he is
more than a wonder; he is a mystery which none
but those initiated, like himself, in the mysteries of
the faith, are able to comprehend. Dying, yea, by
nature "dead in trespasses and sins," he lives; sor-
rowing, he rejoices; having nothing, he possesses all
things; poor, he makes many rich; reversing the
common proverb, that "seeing is believing," he believes more firmly in what he does not see than in
what he sees; contrary to the ordinary laws of nature, he is more powerfully attracted by distant objects than by near ones; his well, like Israel's of
old, is a flinty rock; his bread grows on barren
sands; his homeward path is at the beginning
through a tumultuous sea, and at the end through

a dark, roaring flood. He is confident of wanting nothing, yet depends on the bounty of One who depended for His own bread on others, and had not a place where to lay His head; for his joys, he looks to One who was a Man of Sorrows; and expects a crown of glory from Him who wore no crown on earth but a wreath of thorns.

If the world is right in its judgment of what constitutes true greatness, the humblest believer is a great man. What discoveries in science so important or sublime as those he makes—in the study of the Bible and of his own heart? Neither David with his sling, nor Abishai with his sword, slew such giants as he conquers and slays—in his sins. What victories does history record, or triumphal arches celebrate, so grand in their nature and enduring in their effects as those He wins—over " principalities, and powers, and spiritual wickedness?" No laurels crown his humble brow; his name is unknown to fame. Yet, mortifying his affections, controlling his passions, keeping his body in subjection, and subordinating his will to God's, this is what the wise man says of him : " He that is slow to anger, is better than the mighty; and he that ruleth his spirit than he that taketh a city."

No true greatness, there is no true faith, like a believer's. One of the grandest characters in history is Christopher Columbus; but what the bold

Italian did, when, leaving the shores of Spain, he sailed west, and still farther west, over an unknown and a boundless sea, seeking a world none had discovered, and hardly any but himself believed in, the Christian does. "He seeks a country "—and with stronger faith; since from that world in whose existence he firmly believes, and on whose happy shore he hopes one day to land, not one of the thousands that have gone to seek it have returned. Columbus appeared again in Europe, loaded with the strange fruits and golden spoils of his brilliant discovery: but, like barks that, foundering at sea, have never been heard of after they left the port, none have come back from the other world—to say, "Arise, we have seen the land, and, behold, it is very good!"

Of boundless faith, whose aims and aspirations soar like the believer's? The world which the Macedonian subdued by his arms has wondered less at his achievements than at his ambition; nor has it ever ceased to regard as one of its strangest spectacles that man of universal empire sitting down to weep, because he could find no other world to conquer. And yet there burns a loftier ambition in that lowly cottage, where a sun-browned peasant sits reading his Bible, with a roof of thatch above his head, a rough clay floor beneath his feet, and no more of the earth to call his own than the graves where his fathers sleep. He is thankful for bread to eat, and raiment to put on; he is content to possess as much as will serve for staff and sandals to the end of the pilgrimage; yet he has a heart not one, nor a thousand worlds could fill. Nothing below, however it may gratify, can satisfy his longing soul. He sets his affections on things above, and turning from all created enjoyments to God, his language is the Psalmist's—" Thou art my inheritance and the portion of my cup. Whom have I in heaven but thee? there is none in all the earth whom I desire besides thee."

Nevertheless, naturally drawn like a falling stone to the earth, the best of God's people often feel constrained, amid the attractions and distractions of this world, to cry with David, "Quicken me, O Lord, according to thy word, for my soul cleaveth to the dust;" and to help such as have risen with Christ to rise to things above, let me point out some earthly objects from which they should be careful to withhold, and withdraw their affections. Pope, the poet and moralist, has remarked, that to attack vice in the abstract, and not in persons, is safe fighting, but is fighting with shadows; and, instead of indulging in such general observations against the love of earthly things as would furnish an unhappy illustration of his remark, let us come to close quarters; and select some of those objects on which we should not, and yet on which we are prone to, set our affections.

One of these is *the adornment of the body*.

I have seen a child in ignorance of its great loss totter across the floor to its mother's coffin, and, caught by their glitter, seize the handles, to look round and smile as it rattled them on the hollow sides. I have seen a boy, forgetting his sorrow in his dress, survey himself with evident satisfaction as he followed the bier that bore his father to the grave. And, however painful such spectacles, as jarring our feelings, and out of all harmony with such sad and sombre scenes, they excite no surprise nor indignation. We only pity those who, through ignorance of their loss or inability to appreciate it, find pleasure in what should move their grief. When one is a child, as St. Paul says, they speak as a child and think as a child. Nor is it difficult also to understand how families which have lost their social position, either through injustice or misfortune, should retain, and take a pride in showing, the relics and memorials of their better days. These may secure the respect usually paid to fallen greatness; and if they do not exalt them in the eyes of others, they minister to self-esteem, and exalt them in their own.

The pride of dress, however, though excusable in those savage tribes who walk their forests daubed with paint and decked with feathers, is a passion in all other cases as strange as in some it is strong. Can a maid, says God, forget her ornaments, or a bride her attire? Yet, though this be an example of what is improbable, or indeed impossible, we might wonder that woman's attire, though sparkling with costly gems, does not cover her cheeks rather with the blush of shame than the glow of pride. The history of dress is humbling; not flattering to our vanity. I do not refer to special cases,—the hardships they endure who thread their needles with the threads of life, and die early victims to the demands of fashion; nor to those who, more vain than honest, purchase what they cannot pay for, and assume an appearance as false as the flowers they wear—nor to those who are more proud of being gaily attired than ashamed of casting their parents on public charity; nor even to those who buy their wretched fineries with the wages of iniquity, and abandon the paths of virtue for the sake of gaudy attire. Associations belong to dress, when most honestly obtained and modestly worn, and altogether suitable to the rank and condition of the wearer, sufficient to prevent it becoming an idol. No doubt robes of snowy white may raise our minds by reminding us of the fine linen of the saints, the spotless garments of Jesus' righteousness; and the spectacle of a queen at court or coronation, arrayed

17

in jewelled crown and regal splendour, may recall the psalm where the graces of His Church are set forth under the imagery of a maiden's beauty, raiment of needle-work, and cloth woven with threads of gold and blazing with costly gems. Still the oldest associations connected with dress are those of sin and shame. Sin was its beginning, as it is often still its end. It dates from the fall of our first parents, and has led to that of many of their children: and surely there is nothing, either in its root or in its fruits, to justify us setting our affections on it, or giving it any measure of attention beyond what propriety demands, or comfort and health require.

Apart from these considerations, vanity of dress is, more than anything else, "vanity of vanities." Man's soul is a spark struck from divinity; and with its expressive features and graceful symmetry, even his body presents a form of beauty worthy of the hand that moulded it; but in the matter of attire, man is as inferior to many other creatures as he is inferior in brute strength to an ox, or to a frog in the art of swimming. Let looms and needles do their utmost, the worm yield its silk, the rocks their gold, the mine its diamonds, the deep her pearls, and Nature all her treasures, to adorn the person and inflate the pride of a haughty beauty. The bird whose plume she wears, when it flashed a winged and living gem through tropic groves, was

more gorgeously apparelled than she—the difference **between** her and it, that which lies between the Almighty's hand and ours. Here the proudest beauty bends to the flower that bends its head to the wind, and is crushed by a passing hoof. How miserable the vanity that feeds on dress! How wicked, in practically regarding the question, Wherewithal shall I be clothed? as greater than this, What shall I do to be saved? How utterly contemptible, since, with taste as true as divine, our Lord, pointing to a bed of lilies whose graceful forms and glowing colours bedecked the meadow, said, " Solomon in all his glory was not like one of these!"

A story is told of one whose bosom swelled and heaved with pride as, standing before a mirror, she decked herself out for triumphs. Suddenly, though none had entered the chamber, another figure appeared in the glass. An awful form, it was wrapped in a winding-sheet, and dressed out in grave-clothes, and stared at her with pallid face and glassy eyes. And if, on recognising herself in that hideous vision, she started back, and horror seized her, and her pride was humbled in the dust, how should it wean our affections from these vanities, and secure much of our daily and all our Sabbath time for the study of ourselves in the mirror of God's holy Word, to reflect that the fairest form which draws admiring eyes shall be wrapped in a shroud, and put away in a coffin, and thrust into the grave—for worms to hold riot on its damask cheek, and nestle their loathsome brood where the lights of life and love are flashing!

I have often wondered at the amount of precious time, at the eager attention, and at the vast sums of money lavished on vain attire, as on extravagant feasts. Where many have hardly rags to cover them, and shoeless children shiver on the winter streets, and cold and hunger banish sleep from the eyes of houseless wretches, and by the tongues of hundreds, Jesus, making their cause His own, being naked, beseeches us to clothe Him, one may wonder more to see Christians gay as butterflies—fluttering about in the very pride, and height, and extravagance of fashion. How unworthy such pride and pleasures of those who have in Jesus' blood-bought righteousness a robe beside which silks lose their lustre, diamonds their brilliancy, the very snow its whiteness; and royal apparel seems filthy rags! It is enough to sadden one to think of the time, and thought, and conversation, and keen and lively interest that are wasted even by God's people on the changes, and often absurd forms of fashion. It almost makes one wish that our fashions were as fixed as the laws of the Medes and Persians; or the customs of the Arabs; or the colours of the flowers that are not ashamed to come out in the same robes year by year. "Let our adorning," as St. Peter says, "be the hidden man of the heart, in that which is not corruptible—a meek and quiet spirit, which is in the sight of God of great price:" ours be the treasure which moth and rust cannot corrupt, and thieves break not through to steal. Having in salvation "the pearl of great price," we possess a gem worth more than the costliest that ever topped kingly crown, or was fished from the dark depths of ocean. If we have put on Christ, what matters how homespun or humble our attire? What though no rings flash on fingers that shall ere long be mouldering bones, if the Father, accepting us in Jesus Christ, and regarding us as beloved for the Beloved's sake, has kissed the tear of sorrow from our eyes, and, calling for music and the dance, given forth the glad command, Put a ring on his finger, and shoes on his feet, and bring forth the fairest robe and put it on him; and let us rejoice and be merry, for this my son that was dead is alive again, that was lost is found.

Another is *money*.

When swimming a river where the current runs strong, who, however powerful his strokes, does not find himself borne a long way down, ere he reaches the other bank? It is even difficult to make one's way across a street along which a vast, eager, excited crowd is rushing, without being lifted off our feet and swept along—like a straw on the stream. Such are the contrary influences which impede, if they do not prevent, the heavenward progress of God's people. God's people are not the majority. The multitude goes the other way. And since there is moral as well as material weight in masses, devout men and women in old times, to escape being carried away by the ungodly influences of those around them, fled to cloistered retreats; or, withdrawing altogether from the society of men, passed their days as hermits amid the silent solitudes of forest or desert. Let two musical instruments be placed on the same floor, within the walls of the same apartment, if a player sit down before one of these and strike its keys, the other instrument, as if some spirit's finger had lightly touched its chords, unapproached and untouched by mortal hands, sounds out the self-same note. And such, but still more remarkable, is the influence which, by the laws of sympathy, men have in forming the opinions and moulding the manners of each other—on the side at least of worldliness and sin. Recognising the existence of this law, and the danger to which it exposes the godly in an ungodly world, the Bible says "Evil communications corrupt good manners;" David resolves, "Mine eyes shall be upon the faithful of the land, that they may dwell with me;" Solomon declares, "He that walketh with wise men shall be

wise, but a companion of fools shall be destroyed;'
and the Book of Psalms opens its divine melodies
with this grand beatitude, " Blessed is the man that
walketh not in the counsel of the ungodly, nor
standeth in the way of sinners." It is not easy to
walk on muddy streets and keep our garments clean ;
it is still more difficult to live in an infirmary, breathing its pestilential airs, and escape plague or fever ;
but it is most difficult of all to resist the immoral
influences that surround us,—to live pure amid corruption,—to be in the world, and yet not of it,—
while making and spending money, while enjoying
the pleasures of possessing or suffering the serious
inconvenience of wanting it, to walk the earth as
they the Celestial city, who, walking on streets paved
with gold, tread it beneath their feet.

We are neither to despise, nor refuse money.
Honourably come by, or the reward of honest in-
dustry, this, like other gifts of God, is without repentance. Well employed, it affords much enjoyment ; and, when applied to dry the widow's tears,
to fill the orphan's cup, to help the deserving poor,
yields one of life's sweetest pleasures to its fortunate
possessor—saving him from the pangs they suffer,
who, with the inclination, but without the ability,
to assist suffering and do the kind office of a good
Samaritan, have, though neither priest nor Levite,
to " pass by on the other side."

Nor, however applicable to cases where wealth is found dissociated from worth, to scenes where, as in the parable, sin sits robed in purple and fares sumptuously every day, while saintship is clad in rags and fed on crumbs, is the remark one made so just as it is smart: "You may see how little God thinks of money by observing on what unworthy characters He often bestows it." It is the law of a wise and holy Providence that the hand of the diligent maketh rich; God promises that riches and honour shall be in the good man's house; and many are the instances in which He has bestowed great wealth on such as were persons of great worth. We have one in Abraham; and in his history a remarkable proof of that grand man's superiority to the love of money. Entitled by the laws of war to the whole spoil of battle, he might have swept all into his own hand—enriching himself like those who, taking advantage of the laws of commerce, make fortunes out of speculations that involve others in ruin. But he refuses the gains which law puts within his reach; and out of regard to the honour of his God, the wants and the welfare of his fellow creatures, he abandons his legal claims, and, declining to grow rich on other men's losses, leaves the spoil to its proper owners—saying, "I will not take from a thread to a shoe latchet, lest thou shouldst say, I have made Abraham rich." We have a second instance in David, who did not forget on the throne Him who had taken him from the sheepfold, nor, when riches increased, set his heart on them. David was dead and buried before the temple was begun. It rose from its foundations to look on his tomb; but the house that bore Solomon's name was a monument of his father's piety. It was built with David's money; and unlike such as never part with theirs for the best objects till death parts them from it, this good king, grieved that Jehovah should dwell in curtains while he dwelt in a house of cedar, would, but that God forbade him, have raised it with his own hands—in the fruits of peace and spoils of war, lavishing his treasures on the house of God

We have a third instance in Job. No man of his day was so perfect, and few men of any day so rich. Some there are who resemble the pestilential swamp that, poisoning the air and spreading disease around it, retains in its spongy bosom all the bounties of the skies. Not so the man of Uz. He resembled rather what imparts blessings and beauty to a landscape — the lake that with flowery verdure on its winding shores, life in its waters, and heaven reflected on its unruffled bosom, discharges at its outlet the full flood of streams that enter it; making glens and plains to smile. Their recollections of prosperity abused must exasperate, rather than alleviate, the misfortunes of many; but Job draws a

17*

picture of his days of prosperity which we look on
with admiration, and he, amid changed and adverse
fortunes, must have looked on with comfort:—
" When the ear heard me, then it blessed me ; and
when the eye saw me, it gave witness of me; because I delivered the poor that cried, and the fatherless, and him that had none to help him. The
blessing of him that was ready to perish came upon
me : and I caused the widow's heart to sing for
joy."

But though, as these cases prove, money may be
found in the hand where the love of it is not eating,
like a cancer, into the heart, there is danger of gold
stealing our affections from God—as was strikingly
put by Richard Cecil to one of his congregation.
This person had suddenly and unexpectedly succeeded to an enormous fortune.   Cecil met him
sometime afterwards, and inquired anxiously about
his welfare.   The other having expressed surprise,
said, " I heard that you had been in great danger."
" In great danger," replied his friend ; " I never
was better in my life."   " Have you not succeeded
to a large fortune ?" said Cecil, adding, as the other
nodded assent, " Well, sir, I consider any man in
your circumstances to be in circumstances of very
great danger,"—there sounded the echo of Agur's
words, " nor riches, lest I be full, and deny thee. '
The larger and more sudden the accession of wealth,

the greater the danger—it being with riches as with rain. When showers fall slow and soft, they penetrate the soil, and refresh the ground without disturbing it; but, falling in waterspouts, descending in a deluge from the loaded air, they fill the river to the brim, and, bursting its banks, carry havoc and destruction along their tumultuous course.

But there are no circumstances under which we do not need to be on our guard against wealth. Its attractions are great to all, and seem to exert over some a resistless power. See what sad illustrations this sinful and suffering world presents of these words: " The love of money is the root of all evil." How are woman's virue, and man's honesty, the liberties of the slave, the dignity of rank, the purity of justice, the sacredness of the pulpit, the claims of Christ's cause and of humanity, the love of God and of man, all sucked in and swallowed up by this roaring, devouring whirlpool! No doubt, this is the basest of passions; and one with which, amid all the faults recorded against them in the Bible, the saints are almost never charged. Still let none feel secure. Let him that thinketh he standeth, take heed lest he fall, and his fate resemble that of the almost invulnerable Greek, who, fearing neither the thrust of lance nor crash of battle-axe, fell by a wound in his least mortal and meanest part.

Achilles was slain by an arrow that hit him on the heel.

To the love of money we trace the melancholy apostasy of Demas, the awful perfidy of Judas, the fatal lie of Ananias and Sapphira—all, and some of them distinguished, professors of religion. Be on your guard. Watch and pray. Their history is written for our instruction. Nor need any of His people who allow the love of money to entwine it self around their hearts, expect that in saving them God will do otherwise than the woodman who, seeking to save a tree, applies his knife to the canker that eats into its heart, or the ivy that has climbed its trunk and is choking it in its close embraces. He is a jealous God. He will not give His glory to another. While then we have, and shall have so long as we are here, in some form or other to do with money, let us beware of setting our affections on it. There are better riches—those that take not to themselves wings and flee away—those that neither moth nor rust corrupt, and thief breaks not through to steal. In these, the riches of redeeming grace, seek the things that are above; saying with Bunyan, in these rude but expressive lines,

> Our drossy dust we change for gold,
>   From death to life we flee,
> We let go shadows, and lay hold
>   Of immortality."

Another is *our living or rather dying, fellow-creatures.*

The gospel does not forbid us to give them a place in our hearts who have one in our houses. On the contrary, it teaches us by the voice of Christ to love even our enemies. " Ye have heard that it hath been said," says Jesus, " an eye for an eye, a tooth for a tooth; but I say unto you, that ye resist not evil; and whosoever shall smite thee on the right cheek, turn to him the other also. Ye have heard that it hath been said, Thou shalt love thy neighbour and hate thine enemy; but I say unto you, Love your enemies, bless them that curse you, and pray for them that despitefully use you; that ye may be the children of your Father who is in heaven, who maketh his sun to rise on the evil and the good, and his rain to fall on the just and unjust." And what is thus written with sunbeams, and sounds audibly in every falling shower, is, more affecting still, seen in the blood and heard in the groans of Calvary ; all forgiveness extended, love-felt kindness shown to enemies, being but a faint echo of Christ's answer to the blows that sent the nails through His quivering flesh, " Father, forgive them, they know not what they do !" Well, it stands alike consonant to reason and religion, that if it is right to love our enemies, much more should we love our friends · still more our families. God is not a God of confusion, but of order; and the language of the Bible is always in perfect unison with the best feelings of nature.

Duty to Christ may require a man to leave father and mother, wife and children, and to act—to use our Lord's strong figure—sometimes as if he *hated* them; but the gospel is not calculated, as it certainly was not intended, to cool, to freeze, to blight our natural affections; and, like the influences of winter on smiling, singing streams, to lock them in chains of ice. They were not saints, but sinners, of whom the apostle said, "They are without natural affection;" and elsewhere than in those streets where you see mothers buying drink to debauch themselves with the money that should feed and clothe the skeleton infants they carry in their arms, the ragged, shivering, hungry children at their side,—everywhere, indeed, sin is found blighting the affections that cling like sweet wall-flower to the ruins of humanity. Religion makes better, but sin worse, husbands, wives, parents, children, brothers, sisters—producing such an effect on the heart as a cancer on the bosom it attacks. It hardens it; and next destroys what it has hardened; and at length turns an object of love and beauty into foul and hateful loathsomeness. But piety, ever favourable to humanity, intensifies, while it purifies, the best affections of our nature. And so, did I wish to illustrate, and by examples enforce, generous friendships and domestic love, I would seek them in the Bible—there, where the old man clings to Benjamin, saying, with a voice choked by emotion, " Joseph is not, and Simeon is not, and ye will take Benjamin away;" or there where their brother, within whose bosom the tide of affection had been rising till his heart is ready to burst, no longer able to restrain his emotions, cries, " I am Joseph :" or there where David pours forth in tears and touching numbers his sorrow over the fate of Jonathan, or melts all who hear him as he goes up to his house, wringing his hands at the death of Absalom, and crying, " O my son Absalom, my son, my son Absalom ! would God I had died for thee, O Absalom, my son, my son !" The natural affections found then, as they find still, their most congenial soil in pure and pious hearts.

But while we are encouraged, rather than forbidden, to hold them dear who are near to us, we are not to allow them to usurp the place of Him who says, " Thou shalt have no other gods before me." Beware of turning household delights into household deities, household goods into household gods. The danger against which we are to guard is not such attachment to loved ones as that, when death lops off a branch, the poor tree, shaken by the blow, is left wounded and bleeding ; but such as makes gods of them, and murmuring, not merely mourning, at their loss, feels as if with them all joy, and peace, and hope, and life were for ever buried. Pliny the younger tells us that when the eruption of Vesuvius, which buried Pompeii, had covered with a pall of blackness the whole heavens, and the earth, rocking beneath successive and tremendous earthquakes, had no other light at broad noonday than the blaze of the burning mountain and broad flashes of lightning that occasionally penetrated but added to the effect of the gloom,—Pliny the younger tells us that people thought, not only that nature was dissolving, but that the very gods were dying. And if a god had died, the terror and grief could hardly have exceeded that I once saw in the case of a mother who had set her affections too exclusively on the child we had met to carry to the grave. Seated at the head of the coffin, she seemed a statue; the grand work of some master hand, to represent the deepest, blackest grief. No tears were on her blood-less cheek. Fixed on the coffin, her eyes never left it. She neither moved nor spake, as on her face one could read these words, " My heart is withered like grass." Absorbed in sorrow, it mattered as lit-tle to her as to the dead who went out, or who came in. At length the moment came to remove the body. Then, as when the heavens that have been gathering blackness break out into a blaze of flame and roar of thunder, burst the storm. The form that had looked more like lifeless marble than one animate with life, now sprung up, threw itself on the coffin, clung to it with wails to pierce a heart of stone; and, when gentle force was employed to unloose her arms, she walked to the door—patting the poor coffin; and saw it borne out of her sight with an expression of agony, which, as she fell back fainting into the arms of kind neighbours, seemed to cry, Ye have taken away my god, and what have I more!

It is not so we are to love our loved ones. We are to love our children, for instance, as they are to obey their parents, " in the Lord;" never forgetting that He who lends may resume His gifts whensoever it pleases Him; never forgetting that the fairest flowers of the family may soon wither and die; ever striving as we keep our children in their own place in the house, nor allow them to usurp ours, to keep them in their own place in our hearts, nor allow them to usurp God's: ever seeking in our nurseries to rear plants for heaven, and so train up our children in the faith, in the saving knowledge of Christ and the devout love of God, that we shall have the consolation of knowing, if death enters our house and plucks them from our arms, that our loss is their gain; that if a chair in the circle by our fireside is empty, a blood-bought throne is filled in heaven; that if there is one voice less in the psalm when we are assembled for worship, there is one more ringing sweet and clear in glory, praising Him through whose dying love and in whose blissful presence we shall join our lost and loved—to weep and to part no more.

To live thus, walking by faith and not by sight, touching the impalpable, seeing the invisible, living for eternity in time, and for heaven on earth, with our affections not where we are but where we hope to be—where Jesus is, is no easy work. But prayer, drawing down strength from the skies, makes difficult things easy, and impossible things possible. Through Christ strengthening me, said the apostle, I can do all things. So may we. Turn to that source of superhuman power. Trust to it; nor doubt but that, as those risen with Christ, you shall walk with Him, living realisations of this old, quaint, but beautiful picture :—

> " Man of lofty nature looks up
>   To heaven so calm, and pure, and beautiful.
>   He looks below, but not contemptuously :
>   For there he sees reflections of himself,
>   As a poor child of nature : and he feels
>   A touch of kindred brotherhood : and pants
>   To lead the weak and erring into heights
>   Which he so joyous treads ; nay, more, descends
>   Into the smoky turmoil and the roar
>   Of the rude world : his hands at work on earth,
>   His soul beyond the clouds, dwelling with God,
>   And drinking of His Spirit."

XXI.

EARLY PIETY.—Part I.

"From a child thou hast known the holy Scriptures, which are able to make thee wise unto salvation through faith which is in Christ Jesus."—2 Tim. iii. 15.

THERE is no person, perhaps, who makes a profession of religion but has come to some decision or other on that all-important subject. People either believe on good or bad grounds that they are already religious, or they resolve to become so at a future time. True, many Sabbaths may have been spent, and many sermons heard, and many funerals attended which have awakened no serious thoughts, nor led to such questions as these: Am I saved?—What shall I do to be saved? In the case of many, more or less in the case of all, who are mere hearers of the Word, familiarity with divine things breeds indifference; if not contempt. Under its influence they become as insensible to the most solemn threatenings of the law as the inhabitants of the Indies to the thunderstorms that, though terrific, are common there. The mercy of God, and the bleeding love of Jesus are set forth in the sermons of every Sabbath and the symbols of every sacrament, but they are as little impressed by these as by the nightly glories of the starry sky. Death is such a common event, an obituary so certainly finds a place in every newspaper, and they are so accustomed, on inquiring, to hear that this old acquaintance is dying, and that one is dead—they are invited to so many funerals, and meet so many hearses in the street with their nodding plumes and sable array —and, till more decent customs were adopted, they so often saw the mouldering relics of the dead " scattered at the grave's mouth, as when one cutteth and cleaveth wood on the earth," that they grow familiar with death ; and can hear him knocking at a neighbour's door without once thinking that, whether they are ready or unready, his hand shall soon knock at theirs.

True ; and pity 'tis 'tis true ! Yet there are occasions which awaken serious thoughts in the most careless—however they may endeavour to suppress and banish them. Some event occurs, like a clap of thunder, to rouse the sleeping conscience ; and, calling up terrible visions of death, of judgment, and of hell, she insists on men thinking of the subjects that belong to their peace ; and one of two things happens : either they conclude, on insufficient grounds, that they are saved, or, as is much more common, they resolve to be so at some future time.

In the first case, without altogether ignoring Jesus Christ and His salvation, they trust to something meritorious in their works, or in themselves. One builds much on his honesty,—his motto the adage, "An honest man's the noblest work of God;" another on his integrity—his boast this, that "his word is as good as his bond;" another on his charity— seeking no better inscription for his tombstone than one I have read in an old churchyard, "He was kind to the poor!" They have, or fancy they have, amid many sins, some virtues. These be thy gods, O Israel! Alas! that we should forget that sinners cannot get to heaven on the fragments of a broken law, as in St. Paul's shipwreck some got ashore on the planks of the broken ship. St. Paul himself has made that plain. Speaking of the works of the flesh —adultery, fornication, uncleanness, lasciviousness, idolatry, withcraft, hatred, variance, emulations, wrath, strife, seditions, heresies, envyings, murders, drunkenness, revellings, and such like — they, he says, who do such things shall not inherit the kingdom of God. And what does it matter, though men are not guilty of all, if they are guilty of one of these sins? "Cursed," says the God with whom we have to do, "is *every* one who continueth not in *all* things written in the book of the law to do them." Other

hope therefore man has none but what lies in accepting the righteousness which, wrought out by Christ
and imputed to believers, is not of works, but of
faith. And how sad it is to see men leave this solid
rock, and having to build a house, against whose
rocking walls fierce winds shall rave, and angry waters roar, build it on a sand-bank that the last flood
cast up, and the next shall sweep away.

But those I have now to do with, belong to a different class. They are convinced that they have no
righteousness of their own; yet they put off embracing Christ's—they fear, were they to die this
night or drop down this moment, that they would
be lost; yet they delay to seek a Saviour till the evil
days come, and the years draw nigh when they shall
say they have no pleasure in them. A dangerous
delay; a very desperate venture!—yet not one for
which a " heart, deceitful above all things and desperately wicked," cannot urge some specious pleas.
All who put off salvation have reasons, of a kind, to
plead for the step they take. So had those who,
with the forms of polite respect, declined an invita-
tion to the " great supper :"—I have bought a piece
of ground, says one, and I must needs go and see it,
I pray thee have me excused—I have bought five
yoke of oxen, says a second, and I go to prove them,
I pray thee have me excused—and, with less manners but more appearance of reason, I have married

a wife, says a third, and therefore I cannot come. Even so procrastinators have reasons, though not so plausible, for declining, meanwhile, Jesus' gracious invitations. But whether it is that they are so engaged on the world's business that they have no time, or are so bewitched with its pleasures that they have no inclination to turn religious, one idea is common to them all—this, namely, that not childhood, nor youth, nor manhood, but old age is the most suitable period for becoming devout. They argue thus: In old age we shall have less to do with the business of this world, and have consequently more leisure for that of the next; then this world will afford us little enjoyment—our passions, like fierce fires, will have burned themselves out; our bodies, withered and bent beneath a load of infirmities, will be incapable of debauchery or excess—and, with more time, we shall thus have more inclination to turn to religion. The vessel that, racked by storms, is falling to pieces and gaping at every seam, makes all haste to port : so will we. Unfitted by age for active pursuits, and compelled to withdraw from the giddy circle that goes its round of pleasures, we shall be left to quiet scenes and twilight hours favourable to meditation. Brought in the course of threescore years and ten to the borders of another world. it cannot fail to occupy much of our thoughts · nor when the head has turned gray, and the hands are palsied, and the limbs shrunk and tottering, and ears are deaf and eyes are dim, can we miss to recognize these as the heralds of the grim king, and hear the voice that says, Be ready, the Judge is at the door !

Is this our hope? Hope tells a flattering tale It is a wild fancy—a mockery and baseless delusion. See how God, with one blow of His hand, one sentence of His Word, dashes the fabric to pieces! Talk of old age, gray hairs, passion quenched, life's quiet evening, and sands running to the threescore and ten!—what if He should say, Thou fool, *this night* thy soul shall be required of thee?

To uproot an idea which stands in the way of all attempts at, and hopes of, early piety, I observe that conversion is more *difficult* in old age than any other period.

At whatever age it takes place, this change is properly the work of God—"not by might nor by power, but by my Spirit, saith the Lord of hosts;" or, as our Saviour said to Nicodemus, "Except a man be born of water and of the Spirit, he cannot enter into the kingdom of God." Be he Jew or Gentile, old or young, learned or ignorant, with many or few religious advantages, no man can become a partaker of the present or future blessings of grace unless he is born again; is changed into the divine nature; is renewed in spirit; has Christ formed within him: is, in short, so far as his motives and affections, principles and practice are concerned, made a new creature in Jesus Christ. Regarded as a work of God, this change, I admit, cannot be more difficult at one age than another. With equal ease the great ocean bears ships and sea-weed on its bosom, the earth carries mountains and mole-hills on its back; and still more are all things equally easy to God—to preserve, for instance, an angel or an insect in life, to kindle a sun or a glow-worm's fire, to create a world or a grain of sand. And as it had been as easy for divine power to raise Adam, who had been dead four thousand years, as Lazarus, who had been dead only four days, or to raise Lazarus after four years as after four days in the tomb, it is not more difficult for God to convert an old than a young sinner. The dying thief was saved in the jaws and very throat of death—he stept into heaven from the edge of hell: John Baptist, again, was born the second time before being born the first, being sanctified from his mother's womb—and both these events were equally within the compass of His power, to whom nothing is impossible—who has in either or in any case, but to say and it is done: to command, and it standeth fast. Therefore let none despair.

Nevertheless, since we are fellow-workers with God, there is a sense in which the difficulties of conversion increase with years—every year adding

18

strength to our sinful habits; deepening, as by the constant flow of water, the channels in which they run.

Take a sapling, for example. It bends to your hand, turning this or that way as you will. When seventy springs have clothed it with leaves, and the sun of seventy summers, ripening its juices, has added to its height and breadth, who is strongest? Now, it scorns not your, but a giant's strength. Once an infant's arm could bend it; but, with head raised proudly to heaven, and roots that have struck deep in the soil and cling to the rocks below, now it braves winter's wildest tempests. They may break its trunk, they cannot bend it; nor is it but in death that it lays its head on the ground. Every year of the seventy, adding fibres to its body and firmness to the fibres, has increased the difficulty of bending it. That was less easy the second year than the first, and the third than the second; till, as time went on, what was once easy grew difficult, and what was once but difficult became impossible. Who, wishing to give it a peculiar bent, would wait till the nursling had become a full-grown tree, or stood in its decay, stiff and gnarled hollow in heart and hoar with age? None but a fool. Yet, with folly greater still, we defer what concerns our conversion, a saving change, and our everlasting welfare, till long years have added to the power, and strengthened the roots, of every wicked, worldly habit. Oh, that men were wise, that they understood this!

Human life, to borrow an example from it, furnishes many, and some very melancholy, illustration of this growth and power of evil habits. Take the case of the poor drunkard, for instance. The rust of years eats into other chains, making it easier to snap them asunder; but the links of his grow stronger with time. Other cups may quench thirst, his but increases it: till the love of drink becomes, not a passion, but a madness; and, deaf to all arguments, and less blind than careless to all consequences, he holds out the goblet in palsied hand to cry, "Give! give!" The day was when that wreck of honesty and manly strength—that sad ruin of grace and womanly beauty, was filled with sorrow and remorse; but these feelings became more and more enfeebled, while drinking habits, fed by every new indulgence, increased in strength—making reformation less hopeful by every day's delay. And now, like a boat swept on in a foaming rapid, which neither oar nor arm can stem, with all the dread consequences full in sight—a ruined character, a beggared family, his body descending into an untimely grave, his soul to the doom of these awful words, "no drunkard shall inherit the kingdom of heaven"—he yields to a torrent that sweeps means, character, wife, children, body and soul, into one common ruin.

With such touching and terrible illustrations before their eyes, men talk of delaying to turn to God for ten, twenty, or forty years! Is it painful now to tear the world from our hearts?—when the love of it has grown with our growth, and strengthened with our strength, when it has spread its roots wider, and struck them deeper, to tear it up will demand a mightier effort, and inflict a greater pain. If sin has already so seared the conscience, that we can hear another St. Paul reason of "righteousness, temperance, and judgment," nor tremble in our seats as the Roman trembled on his throne, in what state shall our conscience be when the sins of future years have passed over it like a hot iron—searing, till, all sensibility destroyed, it becomes as hard as horn; like callous flesh, which the knife finds it difficult to penetrate, and impossible to pain? This is no exaggeration. Of all tasks, we know none so difficult as to touch the feelings, and rouse the conscience of godless old age.

Besides, will conversion be more likely and easy when age has dimmed our eyes, and the Bible is become " as the words of a book that is sealed "— when the church-bell rings for others, but not for us; and, unable to creep beyond the door, our Sabbaths are lonely and silent? Which is the better time—when, in the enjoyment of health, we can give undistracted attention to the things that concern our peace, or, when sinking under the infirmities of years, or racked with the pains of disease, we are reduced to such weakness, or suffer such torture, that we can neither pray, nor join in prayer?

Besides, second childhood, to a greater or less extent, comes with age—the faculties of the mind failing with, sometimes even before, those of the body. Like the leaves of the ash-tree, these which were the last to appear, are occasionally the first to depart; leaving the mind a more melancholy wreck than its shattered, crazy tabernacle. And where the soul, asserting its immortality, seems to grow larger, like a setting sun at the close of day, and its faculties survive amid the decays of age, it is by no means rare to see life's last hours passed in a disordered day-dream; their realities offering a striking contrast to the phantoms and fancies of the dying chamber—fancies which restore the preacher to his pulpit; the weaver to his loom; the merchant to 'change, the sailor to the slippery deck; the soldier who has no enemy now to fight but death, to the battle-field, where, deliriously shouting out the word of command, he mixes in the *mêlée*, or heads the desperate charge. What man in his right mind would select such times and scenes for working out his salvation? Which is better—to remember your

Creator now, or delay till conversion is a thousand times more difficult; sinful habits have struck a deeper root; age has dulled the mind, deadened the feelings, and seared the conscience—till you are but the wreck and shadow of what you were; and all your pitiful attempts to turn to God only recall the warning, " Can the Ethiopian change his skin, or the leopard his spots? then may ye also do good, that are accustomed to do evil."

Conversion in old age is a very *doubtful* matter.

It is doubtful whether we shall ever reach old age. Few do; and the probability is that we never shall. It is still more doubtful whether, suppose we do, we shall be more serious than in earlier years. The probability is all the other way—it being true of other sinners besides seducers, that they, as Scripture says, " wax worse and worse." But suppose that we are spared to old age, and, by the devout attention we give to the Bible, to prayer and the house of God, appear to have undergone a gracious change, it lies open to the gravest suspicion. The possibility of conversion at the eleventh hour I do not deny; still, its reality is exceedingly doubtful.

Take the case, for instance, of a convicted thief. You find him where silver plate, gold, and jewels glitter temptations on his eye. Alarmed, you reckon up your money, examine your treasures—to be agreeably disappointed. They are safe; and you naturally conclude that he has turned over a new leaf, and become an honest man. But, however willing to judge charitably, how would your confidence in him vanish on discovering that his hands were shackled, and that, though it was in his heart, it was not in his power to rob you? So far as many gross vices are concerned, such is exactly the position of hoary-headed sinners. Age has frozen their passions, and unfitted them for pleasures after which they once "ran greedily;" and so many infirmities have come with years, that a regard to health, and to life itself, forcing them to refrain from debauchery, produces an apparent reformation. A boat rotten in every plank, and gaping at every seam, has to avoid the seas and swell that others brave; and it were death to old men to venture on debaucheries in which others indulge. Thus the decorum which in some cases marks the closing years of such as had been notorious for vice, may be due to other causes than an inward, saving, and gracious change. The lion has not become a lamb when he has lost his teeth.

But here is a hoary penitent. Poor old man, he trembles to hear of death and judgment; his aged limbs carry him to what he once neglected—the house of God; the glasses through which he scans his Bible are bedewed and dimmed with tears; bitterly lamenting his sins, he warns others; and on knees unused to bend, pours forth prayers for pardon in tones of deepest earnestness. It seems cruel to entertain doubts of such a case. But what is it we doubt? Not that he is sorry for his sins, after a fashion; not but that he would give a world, which he must any way soon part from, to be saved. In this case we may cling to the hope that He who can save to the uttermost has called him at the eleventh hour; still, this sorrow may only correspond to what the felon feels for crimes which have brought him to the gallows—cut short a mad and guilty career. Sorrow for sin, and wishes to be saved? What death-condemned man does not feel these? does not bitterly lament the hour he embrued his hands in blood? does not petition the Crown to spare his life? would not give the world for a file to cut his chain—for a key to unlock his prison? Repentance for crimes at the foot of a gallows is not more oper. to suspicion than repentance for sins on the brink of a burning hell.

Solemn warnings have come from scaffolds; but no one standing on the brink of time, with the white cap on his head, and his feet trembling on the drop, as he made his last speech to the awe-struck crowd, ever uttered voice so full of warning as the recorded experience of the chaplain of a large jail in England. With the death-bell slowly tolling, he had accompanied many to the scaffold, and also prepared not a few for execution who were unexpectedly reprieved. Of these a large number seemed to be converted. Their repentance appeared sincere; and had they suffered the penalty of their crimes, he and others would have believed that, whom earth rejected, Heaven in its mercy had received—for the sake of Christ's righteousness acquitting at its bar those whom man had condemned at his. But they were spared—to lead a new life? Alas, no! Thrown back into the world, the reality of their conversion was put to the test. The glittering coin was tested, exposed to a fiery trial; and what deceived others, deceived perhaps themselves, proved counterfeit. With hardly an exception, all who seemed to be converted within the prison, under the shadow of the gallows—in circumstances to the condemned corresponding with old age and the closing days of life—returned to their former courses; went back like the dog to his vomit, and the sow that is washed to her wallowing in the mire. A melancholy fact! What a dark suspicion does it cast on late conversions? In these cases the sun that sets on this world may rise to shine in a better; but dark clouds obscure such a close of life; and so long as men will risk their souls on these desperate ventures, however trite the remark, it cannot be too often, or too loudly, or too solemnly repeated, that the Bible, which ranges over a period of four thous-

18*

and years, records but *one* instance of a death-bed conversion—one, that none may despair, and but **one,** that none may presume.

XXII.

EARLY PIETY.—Part II.

"From a child thou hast known the holy Scriptures, which are able to make thee wise unto salvation through faith which is in Christ Jesus."—2 TIM. iii. 15.

TO everything, says Solomon, in the Book of Ecclesiastes, there is a season, and a time to every purpose under the heaven: a proposition which, like a flower full blown, he spreads out into such particulars as these—"a time to be born, and a time to die; a time to plant, and a time to pluck up; a time to kill, and a time to heal; a time to weep, and a time to laugh; a time to mourn, and a time to dance; a time to get, and a time to lose; a time to rend, and a time to sew; a time to love, and a time to hate; a time of peace, and a time of war." Religion, it may be observed, has no plaec in this remarkable catalogue; and, paradoxical as the assertion seems, its absence only makes it the more conspicuous. It has no place among births or deaths, saving or slaughter, feasts or funerals, the calm of peace or the tempests of war, because, unlike these, it belongs to no season, but to all seasons, to every period and time of life. Its functions are like those of breathing, which, distinguished from eating, resting, or working, are carried on throughout all the years of our existence, nor cease even when reason sleeps and the bodily senses are all steeped in slumber.

Notwithstanding, there is a sense in which religion also has its season. As there is a time to be born, there is a time to be born again: to turn to God; to die to sin, and live to righteousness. And which of all the periods of human life will prove most favourable to that great change, is a question we can neither too soon nor too carefully determine. Interests are involved here more important far than those which belong to any, or to all those other times; to the loves or hatreds, the wars or peace, the births or burials of a life, whose joys and sorrows in a few more years will be nothing to us—no more than the suns that shine, or the storms that beat upon our grave. The great English dramatist, accepting the three-score years and ten of Scripture as the ordinary span of life, divides it into seven decades; and, borrowing imagery from the stage and shifting scenes of his own profession, represents each as an act played out on the boards of a theatre —beginning and closing his famous description thus:

" All the world 's a stage,
And all the men and women merely players
They have their exits and their entrances,
And one man in his time plays many parts,
His acts being seven ages. At first the infant,

   .   .   .

             Last scene of all,
That ends this strange, eventful history,
Is second childishness, and mere oblivion."

Without following the French, to regard all children under fourteen years as being, to use their
term, *sans discernement*, and not properly amenable
to punishment, let us here exclude infancy and mere
childhood from consideration; periods, these, when
many, hardly able to act for themselves, are plastic
as a piece of clay—taking shape and form from the
hands into which they fall. And of the three remaining periods,—youth, manhood, and old age,—
which is the most fitted for working out our salvation, for giving all diligence to make our calling and
election sure, for fighting the good fight, for running
the Christian race? The very terms of the question
supply the answer. Solomon says the first. Well,
if he is right, if in this judgment he sustains his
fame as the wisest of the sons of men, if he spake
thus in the noontide of that wisdom which dawned
in his early choice and rose like a sun on the eyes
of a dazzled world,—I need not ask, if he is right,
how many are wrong? Not but that they intend

some day or other to become religious; only **not now**, when their blood is hot, and the reins lie loose on the neck of passion, and the cup of pleasure is foaming to the brim. Were the plans and wishes of many expressed in words, they would take the very shape of the striking but shocking prayer of Augustine, Lord, convert me! but not now—not now!

They have no wish to die as they are. On the contrary, knowing, at least fearing, that they have never been converted, and are not at peace with God, they recoil from such a thought;—their type, one in whose company we once happened to be placed in alarming circumstances. The carriages flew along the iron rails; they flashed by stations, post, and pillar; and began so to sway from side to side, that my fellow-traveller, by profession a minister of the gospel, got much alarmed, and asked, "Do you think there is danger?" "Think there is danger!" I gravely replied; "we may be in eternity in another moment." Struck to the heart as by a knife, his full and florid countenance turned pale as death, while, with an emphasis no acting could imitate, and a look of horror never to be forgotten, he raised his hands to exclaim, "God forbid!" Equally dreading a present and sudden death, how many live and sin on in the hope that, after spending their days as lovers of pleasure, they shall end them as lovers of God; that they will turn over a new leaf when they are old; and that, to use a common expression, it will be all right in the end? Bubbles, fair to look on, but fragile as those the touch of a finger breaks! and the breath that blows up such vain expectations is the belief that of all the periods of human life none is so favorable to religion as old age. A great, yet not a wonderful, mistake!— one into which, on the contrary, it is very natural for unreflecting and inexperienced youth to fall. Young people fancy that when the days are come when they shall say they have no pleasure in them, —when, in other words, there are no pleasures to enjoy,—it will be easy to cease being lovers of pleasure, and become lovers of God; they fancy when they have fallen "into the sere and yellow leaf," fading sight and health and hearing cannot fail to warn them of the approach of death, and prepare them for his coming; they fancy that religion, like ivy, which gets no hold of a close and firm wall, grows best on what is old; and that as the weathered stones, the cracks and gaping rents of the shattered ruin, by offering a hold to its arms, helps it to climb till it crowns the summit and clothes the grim old tower in a green, graceful mantle, so the infirmities and decays of age will prove helpful to piety— giving it a hold on our hearts it had not obtained, but that they have been shattered by the disappointments, and trials, and shocks of life.

Alas for those who embark their salvation on such bad bottoms, such ventures, and worthless speculations! Experience is the true test here. Youth speaks from fancy, but old men from facts; and all experience—whether that of Solomon, or of others much less wise than he—pronounces these hopes to be utterly false, mere delusions. Old fruit, still hanging on the tree, comes away to the touch; but it is seldom without a wrench that old people part with life. Have I not seen, and wondered to see, how some aged saints would cling tenaciously to life, and be almost as happy on recovering as one in the green spring, or flower and summer of their days? Earthly joys are like the sun, which never looks so big as at his setting; and be it life, or children, or pleasure, or money, it is natural to love that which we are soon to lose, not less, but more.

> "I loved him much, but now I love him more.
> Like birds whose beauties languish, half-conceal'd,
> Till, mounted on the wing, their glossy plumes
> Expanded, shine with azure, green, and gold:
> How blessings brighten as they take their flight!"

Then as to the effect on man of the near approach of death, youth has to learn what experience teaches age, that death resembles the horizon. Within the lessening circle of advancing years, death may seem much nearer than once it did, and the expression, "If God spares me," may be oftener in the

thoughts and on the lips; still it presents this remarkable feature of the visible horizon that, whether
it seem near in a misty, or distant in a clear, fair,
open day, as we advance, it recedes—ever flies before us. Youths count on forty or twenty years;
and where is the old man who does not, even from
his stand-point by the grave, see one or two years, at
least some days or months, before him?

Suppose it otherwise; suppose also that the powers of the mind do not fail with those of the body;
suppose that no aged Christian ever had to complain
of the evil days when he could not pray, nor meditate, nor fix his thoughts, nor rise, as on eagle's
wings, in heavenly meditations, as once he did;
suppose that none ever blessed God on their death-
bed that they had not left their peace to seek amid
the weakness and infirmities of age; suppose that
sin may be safely yielded to till it becomes habitual;
suppose, so to speak, it were found as easy to bend
an old tree as a young one, to turn a swollen river
as a tiny stream; suppose it is not true that

> " Ill habits gather by unseen degrees,
>   As brooks run into rivers, rivers run to seas."

suppose that for once Solomon is wrong, and that of
all the periods of life old age is best for getting a
change of heart, an interest in Christ, peace with
God, a title and a meetness for the kingdom of

heaven,—yet, I say, it were well and wise not to delay, because *we may not live to be old*.

The oak lives a thousand years. The yew reaches a much greater age : a churchyard among our
Scottish mountains boasting one, specially mentioned by Humboldt, under whose green canopy we have
sat, which flourished in the days of Solomon, and
stood, white with snows or hoar frost, a mighty tree
that Christmas eve on which our Lord was born.
In contrast with the giant forms and stubborn lives
of trees that, yielding slowly to their doom, look
down on the graves of many generations, are their
leaves. Fragile and fading, these are often nipped
in the bud ; they are easily crushed ; their life does
not extend beyond a few months ; the cold of autumn is their death, and the snows of winter are
their shroud. For these reasons a leaf has been a
favorite emblem with poets, both sacred and profane, of man, of his feebleness, of his mortality. So,
when stripped of all his property, his children suddenly whelmed into a common grave, these his dead
griefs and his wife a living one, his few friends the
"miserable comforters" whose unskilful hands wid-
ened the wounds they sought to close, so spake Job :
turning to God, he plaintively expostulates with
Him, crying, "Wilt thou break a leaf driven to and
fro ?" Thus also spake the prophet who saw a picture of man his sins and sorrows, where the wind at

the close of autumn, tearing through the tinted
woods, swept off their leaves in showers, and scattered them swirling and eddying along the ground—
"We all," he exclaimed, " do fade as a leaf, and our
iniquities, like the wind, have carried us away!"

We fade as a leaf! In one sense we do, and in
another we do not. Most leaves live out all their
days, but not many men—few men the half of them.
Of all our race, nearly the half die in infancy, and
are torn from mothers' bosoms to lie in the cold
arms of death. Another large proportion drop into
the grave ere the summer of life is past. The woods
retain their foliage till days grow short, and fruits
grow mellow, and fields fall to the reaper's sickle ;
but how small the number of men who survive, in
gray hairs and stooping form, slow step and shuffling
gait, to wear the marks of age ere they follow their
companions to the tomb ? Ask that hoar old man
where are the playmates of his childhood, where the
boys who sat by him at the desk in school, where
the youths, flushed with health and full of hope,
with whom he started in the race of life, where the
guests of his board, his competitors or his partners
in business ? In the grave !—all mouldering in the
grave : save one and another who, amid new faces,
now find themselves to be strangers on this earth,
and remain the last vestiges of their generation,—
clinging to life just as I have seen a few brown

leaves hanging on the tree, and whirling in the win
ter wind when skies were dark with storms, and
fields were white with snow.

To the eye of faith this survey, these bills of mor
tality, present nothing melancholy. An early death
to those who are in Christ is but another expression
for an early deliverance; and if, in place of being
long becalmed, or tossed about by storms, and perhaps driven out once and again to sea when their
ship was in sight of land, those voyagers who make
a short passage count themselves happy, fortunate,
are not they rather to be envied than pitied who, by
an early death, escape much of the sins and sorrows
of this world ?—like birds of passage, they just light
on it, rest for a little while, and then, as if they found
nothing tempting them to prolong their stay, take
wing and soar up to heaven. Viewed in this aspect,
but for the cold, the cruelties, the hunger, the wants
and sufferings which, springing to a large extent from
parental vices, account for the circumstance, there
is nothing melancholy in the shortness of many lives,
and that nearly the half of all born die under five
years of age; leaving but a small fraction to see the
threescore years and ten. But what more melancholy, more marvellous, than to see thousands setting
at nought these well-established facts; delaying their
salvation, and, where interests of the highest moment are concerned, counting on years which not

one in a hundred of them shall ever reach? No
wise man acts with such infatuation in other, and far
less important matters.

For example. Prudent men insure their lives;
and why? Because, they answer, life is uncertain;
because there is nothing more uncertain; because
the chances are that they shall not live to be old.
And if I should be cut off suddenly, early, what,
says a man, is to become of my family? The children of this world are indeed wise in their generation. Oh that men would reason as soundly, and
act as wisely, where higher interests are at stake!
If you should be cut off suddenly and early, what
is to become of your family? Well, let me change
but a little the terms of the question, and ask him
who, reckoning on years, is putting off the things
that concern his peace, If you should die suddenly
and early, what is to become of your soul—your
precious soul!

Prudent men, again, make their will when their
bones are full of marrow, and there is not a gray
hair in their head. The deed shows their name
written with a strong and firm hand; nor is it by
their death-bed that, hastily summoned to the scene,
the lawyer, the physician, and the minister of the
gospel meet. In many respects it would prove much
more convenient, saving the trouble and expense of
codicils, to delay the settlement of their affairs to

future years—to old age, should they ever reach it
—when they shall have retired from business and
realised their fortune. Should they ever reach it!
But they know that few reach it, and that they may
never do so; and therefore, with health bounding in
every artery, and blooming on their cheeks, they sign
their last will and testament. In matters where the
interests and peace of families are concerned, wise
men repudiate delay, nor venture anything on the
chance of living to be old. Is the peace of our
souls less worthy of our care? "Set thine house
in order, for thou shalt die," said the prophet to the
king; but how much more need, with a higher foresight, that we should set our hearts than our houses
in order? We may die to-morrow—"Thou fool,
this night thy soul shall be required of thee."

Prudent men, again, by the practice of economy
and self-denial, make provision for dying in their
prime. Young, they seem to have reasonable ground
for expecting that many years are before them; and
that they may live to see their children standing on
their own feet—fighting their own battle, altogether
independent of a parent's help. Why should not
they then, launching on the tide of prosperity, take
their enjoyment of the world?—in place of being
haunted by fears of a widow and children left with
a scanty provision, why should not they anticipate a
venerable, green old age, a long day and a quiet

evening, with their children's children climbing their
knee and playing at their feet? Why? Because, they
answer, though many fancy such a picture, there are
few that sit for it. Few live to be old; nor on such
an unlucky chance will they venture the happiness
and well-being of their children—not they. Would
to God we were all as wise in what involves the
happiness and well-being of our souls! and that
every sinner without an hour's delay turned to Jesus,
to embrace Him as his Saviour, to cry, in his great
extremity, Save, Lord, I perish!

Old age is a most *unsuitable* period.

The work to which we are called, which must be
done by all in this world, and by some this day, or
never done, is well described in the words of Nehe-
miah, " I have a great work to do, therefore I cannot come down." It requires our utmost energies.
You have seen a man who had thrown himself into
the crowd that blocked up a narrow door, battling
his way through, with broad shoulder throwing the
living mass aside, as the vessel does the water that
breaks and foams and flashes from her brow—so we
are to strive to enter in at the strait gate. You have
seen the smith swinging his heavy hammer at the
glowing forge, with the veins standing out on his
brawny arms, and the sweat on his swarthy brow—
so we are to labour for the bread that never perisheth. You have seen the sinewy frame of a lithe and

young competitor in the race go by like the wind as with flowing hair, expanded nostrils, eager eye, heaving breast, and flying feet, he bends to the course—so we are to run the race set before us; so, forgetting the things which are behind, and looking to those which are before, we are to press toward the mark of the prize of the high calling of God in Christ Jesus.

Whoever sat to Solomon for this graphic picture —the keepers tremble, the strong men bow themselves, the grinders cease, the windows be darkened, the almond tree flourishes, and the grasshopper is a burden—it is plain that neither the old man he painted, nor any at his age, is fit for tasks like these. The Scriptures, whatever figures they employ, everywhere represent the work of salvation as one demanding the highest energy, powers untouched by time and unimpaired by decay. Look at the subject in the light of that figure, where the kingdom of heaven is represented as a city taken by assault. Defenders man, and assailants swarm round the beleaguered wall. It is breached; the breach is pronounced practicable; the forlorn hope lie in the trenches, ready when the bugle sounds to spring to their feet, and with a run and a dash to throw themselves headlong into the yawning chasm; but this must be bravely, quickly, vigorously done, for the breach is bristling with bayonets, and men within

stand by their guns to sweep it with showers of death.
Now when the stormers are waiting a leader whom
they expect to come with elastic step, and bold carriage, and manly form, and eagle glance, and sword
flashing in the sun, and a voice that, crying, Follow
me, rings through the ranks, and starts all to their
feet, let an old man advance, tottering on a staff,
with panting breath and piping voice, to bid them
follow,—who would follow? Amid all the solemni-
ties of an hour that should be the last to many, they
would laugh his gray hairs to scorn. Let these and
like feeble steps keep the garrisons at home; but the
assault of cities, and storming of the deadly breach,
require the pith of manhood, the fire and flower of
youth. So does the work of salvation. It is incon-
sistent with the feebleness and decay of age; for
" the kingdom of heaven suffereth violence, and the
violent," says our Lord, " take it by force."

. True, salvation is not of works. " By grace," as
St. Paul says, " are ye saved, through faith; and
that not of yourselves; it is the gift of God: not of
works, lest any man should boast: for we are His
workmanship, created in Christ Jesus unto good
works, which God hath before ordained that we
should walk in them." And since God occasionally
magnifies and illustrates the exceeding riches of
His grace by calling one, and another, at the eleventh
hour, making them, after being grafted into Christ,

19

bring forth fruit even in old age, making, so to speak, " the barren woman to keep house and be a joyful mother of children," there is no age and no case hopeless. The words, " Is anything too hard for the Lord ?' are as applicable to the new birth of an old man as to the birth of Isaac by an old woman. So fast as their tottering steps can carry them, in the last lingering lights of day, let hoary-headed sinners hasten to Jesus. He will not reject them. He might, but He will not say, When I spake ye would not hear, and when I called ye would not answer; now when ye speak I will not hear, and when ye call I will not answer; I will laugh at your calamity, and mock when your fear cometh. Fear not that—

> "As long as life its term extends,
> Hope's blest dominion never ends ;
> For while the lamp holds on to burn,
> The greatest sinner may return."

Notwithstanding this, and that the Word of God assures us that whosoever cometh unto Him He will in nowise cast out; the homage we owe to truth, and the duty we owe to souls, require us to say, that, judging by results, old age is, of all the ages of life, the least fitted for the work of salvation. No doubt we have read of hoary sinners becoming as little children, and turning to God ; but in the experience

of more than thirty years we have never met with
one such case.

At the close of a dark and stormy day we have
seen the sun break forth at his setting, to bathe the
whole landscape in a flood of glory, and having
painted a rainbow on the storm-cloud, to sink to
rest amid the odours of flowers, and the joyful songs
of groves and skies. But whatever others may have
done, we have met nothing corresponding to this
in the realm of spirits ; not one old man who lived
the life of the wicked, and died the death of the
righteous. I am not speaking of those who, in
circumstances that were more their misfortune than
their fault, had no opportunity of knowing the truth
till they were old—who, like the penitent thief, perhaps, received their first as well as last offer of a
Saviour at death ; never had Christ in their offer, as
Simeon never had Him in his arms, till their eyes
were dim, and their heads were gray with age ; — I
speak of those who have gone Sabbath after Sabbath to the house of God, whenever Christ was
brought forward, to reject Him, and cry, like the
Jews of old, "We will not have this man to rule
over us ;" who have put Him off, again and again,
with the most miserable excuses ; who have resisted
the influences of the Holy Spirit of God ; who have
wilfully shut their eyes to the truth ; who have obstinately refused to be saved ; who have spent long

years in fighting neither with the devil, nor the
world, nor the flesh, but with their own conscience;
and wounding it to the death, have at length won
the victory. Now they have no qualms in sinning;
and they may have no bands in their death. They
have triumphed; but their victory reminds us of the
saying of the king who, holding the ground after a
hard fought day, but seeing it covered with the
bodies of his bravest knights and stoutest men-at-
arms, exclaimed, Another such victory and we are
ruined! So fatal are victories obtained over conscience! Delay till your head is hoary, and your
conscience seared, and you are, as they say, " gos-
pel-hardened," and there is none to whom these
words of hope are less applicable and appropriate,
" Thou art not far from the kingdom of heaven."

Still God does not shut the door in an old man's
face. The blood of Christ cleanseth from all sin —
even from his—and the door of mercy stands open
to the chief of sinners. Only, none can come too
soon. Our position resembles his who, sole survivor
of the wreck, was seized by a mountain wave, and,
borne upon its crest onward to the cliff, was flung
into a cave midway between the top where anxious
spectators had gathered and the sea that raged and
foamed below. Over a precipice no foot could
scale, dangling above a sea where no boat could live,
friendly hands lower a rope—but, alas! the beetling

rock overhung his place of shelter; and though he
stood poised on its utmost ledge with outstretched
arms, the rope hung beyond his reach, mocking his
misery. Quick to devise and prompt to act, like all
seafaring-men, his brave friends above haul in the
life-line, and, now loading its end, they toss it once
more over the crag, but seaward this time. It has
got the motion of a pendulum, and now swinging
back, it comes in beneath the beetling cliff. With
eager eye watching its coming, he makes a grasp;
but alas! his hand closes on the empty air, and the
rope swings out again to sea. Ere long it returns,
but to be as far, or farther, from his reach; and he
now observes with horror that each time it swings it
comes less near him. A few more oscillations, and
the line dangles in the air—a life-line could he
reach it, but beyond his utmost reach. If balancing
himself on the utmost ledge, he leap to catch it at
its next approach, he may still be saved—not otherwise—nor shall this long be possible. Once more,
again it comes; and a voice seems to ring in his ear,
Now, or Never! With a prayer on his lips, and his
eye on the rope, he bends to the spring, and, rising
into the air, makes one desperate bound out from the
cliff. The line is caught; he is saved; and cheers
from above that go up to heaven greet him, when,
swinging out from below the overhanging crag, a
living burden hangs on that rope with the grasp of

death. So are we to understand the words, " Lay hold on eternal life." Such is the diligence we are to give to make our calling and election sure. For here, as there, Soon and Saved, or Late and Lost, are very near the truth. For anything, indeed, we can tell, it may be Now, or Never.

XXIII.

EARLY PIETY.—Part III.

"From a child thou hast known the holy Scriptures, which are able to make thee wise unto salvation through faith which is in Christ Jesus."—2 Tim. iii. 15.

DREADFUL is the havoc which intemperance works among us, on the finest virtues of man and woman, on the peace of families and the membership of Christ's Church. The sad miseries it produces, the fair characters it ruins, the kind hearts it breaks, the innocent children it murders by want, cold, cruelty, and neglect, the gray hairs it brings with sorrow to the grave, should make us seek to protect the young from its dangerous influences. Our hope for society lies, not in adults, but in them, in the rising generation—the position of social reformers resembling that of the priests who went down into the Jordan bearing the ark of God, and, leaving the waters that had already passed to pursue their course and find a grave in the Dead Sea, arrested the descending current. We have tried to accomplish something like this. And when for that purpose advising parents, as they valued their own peace, the safety of their children, and the reformation of society, to rear their households in the entire disuse of all dangerous, because intoxicating, stimulants, we have found them excuse themselves on the ground that children brought up in this, or in any other strict way, are afterwards much more likely than others, by the very law of recoil, to carry innocent indulgence to excess.

There is no more vulgar or pernicious error than this. It is a groundless fear—the old cry of " a lion in the way !" wherewith many excuse themselves for not doing what in truth they have no inclination to do. We appeal from them to history ; to the character as well as happy fortunes, for example, of a family whose stout adherence for successive generations to the simple and sober manners of their father, is recorded with the highest approbation in the Word of God. Commissioned to try them, Jeremiah says, " I set before the sons of the house of the Rechabites pots full of wine and cups, and I said unto them, Drink ye wine. But they said, We will drink no wine : for Jonadab the son of Rechab our father commanded us, saying, Ye shall drink no wine, neither ye, nor your sons for ever. . . . Thus have we obeyed the voice of Jonadab the son of Rechab our father in all that he charged us, to drink no wine all our days, we, our wives, our sons, nor our daughters." Three hundred years had passed since Jonadab was laid in his grave; but these, which had seen other families rise and fall, wax and wane, win and lose their character, had wrought no change on Jonadab's. Teaching us how men live after they are dead for good or evil in their manners and morals, the character which their sire had impressed on his family remained through the lapse of centuries—like features cut in granite. How many families which vice has reduced to abject poverty, sweeping some of them even from the face of the earth, would have inherited, had they been trained to virtuous practices, the happy fortunes of the sons of Rechab; and that through the ordinary operation of the laws of Providence? "Thus saith the Lord of hosts, the God of Israel: Because ye have obeyed the commandment of Jonadab your father, and kept all his precepts . . . . Jonadab the son of Rechab shall not want a man to stand before me for ever."

The case of these Rechabites demonstrates that strict training is not, as some believe, or at least allege, likely to be followed by loose living. The idea that children carefully instructed in the principles and strictly reared in the practices of piety, in a severe sobriety and holy observance of the Sabbath, are more prone than others to run into vice, cannot stand with the opinion of Solomon, "It is

16*

good for a man to bear the yoke in his youth.'
This notion, which is no less pernicious than absurd,
sounds as different from Solomon's judgment as the
ring of good money from bad. Nor can it bear the
test of experience and Scripture more than a counterfeit coin the drop of acid that bites through the
silver and lays bare the brass.

But as this notion, were it allowed to stand, would
stand in the way of the cutlivation of early piety, let
us look at one proof of it very commonly adduced.
This is the fact, as they call it, that the children of
the strictly religious, especially those of the manse,
of ministers of the gospel, have been often observed
to be more vicious than others. Cases of that kind
have certainly occurred. But it is not difficult to
account for such a melancholy result. It often happens that men discharging the functions of the sacred
ministry, or those who devote themselves to redress
the wrongs and promote the welfare of society, have
found their time and talents so taxed, so occupied,
so engrossed by the public interest, that they have
neglected their own. They have bestowed the care
which belonged to their children on the affairs of
others. As they contemplated the misconduct of
this son, and the misfortunes of that, and were reminded, by the wreck which vice had wrought on
their family, of the sad old plaint, " The boar out
of the wood doth waste it, and the wild beast of the

field doth devour it," how might they add, " They made me the keeper of the vineyards, but mine own vineyard have I not kept !" But the bad result in such cases is not due to the children being reared too strictly, too carefully, too piously. Suffering, on the contrary, from neglect, they have been sacrificed, unintended but unhappy victims, on the altar of the public good.

Nor when the children of pious people turn vicious is it wonderful that they become worse than others. The sweetest wine turns into the sourest vinegar ; the blackest shadows are cast by the brightest light; the angel that falls becomes a devil—and so, sinning against light and conscience, the prayers, counsels, warnings, and tears of godly parents, the children of the good, on becoming wicked, become more remarkable than others for their wickedness. Like Jeremiah's figs, " the evil are very evil, so evil that they cannot be eaten." And being also from their birth and position as a city set on a hill, their case attracts more attention than that of others. While others escape notice, these are observed and talked of ; and thus people fall into the vulgar, pernicious mistake that a strict and virtuous training is apt to result in a loose and vicious life.

Such is the complete and satisfactory explanation which we give of those cases that impart any semblance of truth to so gross an error. At the same time we can adduce facts to prove that it is an entire mistake. I have in my eye a district of my country sufficiently large, and containing a sufficient number of families, to form the basis of a wide and sure conclusion; and, on looking to the history of the children who went forth from its manses to make their way in the world and fight the battle of life—poor, but well, strictly, and virtuously educated—I can aver that, take them overhead, they have not done worse, but better, than others. Doing credit to their homes and virtuous training, the sons of clergymen stand above the common average, both in point of character and of the position they have won. Unhappily, some good people, by their sour tempers and severe, forbidding manners, have made their children recoil from a pious life. By rough and injudicious treatment they have broken the twig which more skilful and gentle handling, with God's blessing, had trained upward to the skies. Accustom the young to associate the Sabbath, and the Bible, and piety, not with gladness, but with gloom; train them so that their affections are not won over to the side of religion; and no wonder that, after being held in, like a horse, only by bit and bridle, when they go forth on the world with the reins loose on their own necks, that they plunge into a career of vice—as the war horse rushes into the battle. But let justice be done to religion; let gentleness temper severity; let there be as much pains taken to win the heart as to instruct the head of youth; let mothers, as of old, employ their loving, tender hands to give it a Christian shape and form; and the results will prove the soundness of the advice, " Remember thy Creator in the days of thy youth."

The importance of this will appear if we consider that youth is the *critical period* of man's life.

An infant is a bud unblown, with green impervious sheath hiding the flower within; nor, though hope may paint fair visions of the future, can any tell whether the cradle in their house holds a Cain or Abel, a Jacob or an Esau. Childhood corresponds to the next stage—the bud has now blown out into a fragrant, lovely flower; but whether, as the bud has changed into a flower, the flower shall change into fruit, the child shall fulfil the wishes and reward the care of parents, who can tell? I have seen the blast strew the ground with the hopes of the garden, and trees stand barren in autumn that had been white with blossoms, as with a shower of snow. However genial the spring, or cloudless and warm the skies of summer, there is a critical period when the two seasons shade into each other. This, which holds the fruits and future of the orchard in its hand, fulfilling or disappointing the hopes of the gardener, lies in those few days and nights when, to use a common expression, the fruit is setting

Wrapped up in its warm sheath, the flower sleeps through the winter, nor feels nor fears the frost; when, waking to the voice of spring, it throws aside its coverings, and, disclosing its beautiful form, opens its bosom to the sun and its treasures to the bees, it is full of life; and, once changed into fruit, though its sweetness may depend on the character of summer, it battles bravely with adverse circumstances, and lives and ripens in spite of cold and rain. But there is a critical time, on which its whole future depends; and that lies in the few days and nights when, in its progress from one stage to another, the flower is changing into fruit. To use a fine Scotch expression, this is *the tyning* (losing) *or the winning time.*

Such a period is youth in human life. Then impressions are received which remain for ever; then the character, like the color fixed by the mordant in cloth, is fixed; then the die is struck; then a life of virtue or of vice is begun; then the turn is taken either for God or the world; then the road is entered on which leads to heaven or to hell. The period is one which corresponds to a knoll I know, where you stand on the watershed of the country, midway between the two seas which wash our shores; and there, standing on the doorstep of a shepherd's cottage, as you turn your wrist to this side or to that, depends the course of the water you fling from your hand! whether, after long travels and many windings, it reach the east coast or the west, to mingle with the waves of the German or Atlantic Ocean. It is the youth, not the boy, as is commonly said, who is father of the man. What importance, then, belongs to this over any other period of life—what care does it call for on the part of the young, and on the part of those who are charged with their upbringing! Childhood receives impressions easily; but, like the sea that bears no traces of the birds that skim, or the keels that plough its waves, it does not retain them. Manhood, again, like the solid rock, retains impressions once made, but does not easily receive them. Now, it is in youth that our minds, like the wax to which the seal, or the clay to which the mould is applied, possess both the power of receiving impressions, and the power of retaining them. This, therefore, is the crisis of life—the time to be most careful of our company, our pleasures, and our pursuits. Then the slightest thing may fix our character, and determine our future destiny— the wax is cooling, the clay is hardening into stone, the soul is receiving its form and shape, and, as if time to some extent anticipated the irrevocable decrees of eternity. it may be said in many instances of our youth, what shall be afterwards and absolutely and universally said of our departed spirits—" He that is filthy let him be filthy still, and he that is righteous let him be righteous still."

Youth is the most *dangerous* period of life.

There is no age which may not put principle and piety to trial. Old men who shock the world by their crimes, the occurrence ever and anon of cases where vice, like a long pent-up power, overcoming at length all restraint, breaks forth like the volcano that pours its burning lava on the woods, cornfields, and vineyards that clothe its slopes—these, and many things else, warn us that we are never safe till we are in heaven, and have laid off with our bodies the infirmities that belong to them. Here, like travellers on those Alpine slopes where a coating of snow hides the treacherous ice, and one false step may prove their ruin, we walk in slippery places, and have ever need to lean on an arm stronger than our own, praying—" Hold up my goings that my footsteps slip not." In no circumstances, and at no age, can any of us afford to forget the caution—Let him that thinketh he standeth take heed lest he fall.

Still youth is of all ages the most dangerous. With its ardent temper, its inexperience, its credulousness, its impetuosity, its impatience of restraint, its unbroken passions, and feeble hands to control and guide them, it requires the utmost care and viligance. " Lead us not into temptation," should be its daily, constant, earnest, anxious prayer.

The most interesting and picturesque scenes, it has been remarked, are found in those half-highland half-lowland districts, where the wild and shaggy and savage grandeur of the mountains mingles with the rich and softer beauties of the plain; and so the most interesting period of life is that where in youth the lightness and buoyancy of childhood blends with the gravity and wisdom of age. But as it is among scenes intermediate between the mountains and the plain that the river, which winds like a silver stream through the glen, and after pursuing its calm and widening course through the plains loses itself in the sea, taking its wildest leaps, and, tearing its way through rocky gorges, now eddies in black pools, and anon rushes roaring and foaming on its way; so it is in youth, when man, subject to the turmoil and disturbances of impetuous passions, leaves the home of his birth to enter on the world, that virtue has to sustain her severest trials, and not seldom to suffer her sorest falls.

How critical, how dangerous, I will say how dreadful, the position of many launched, without father or friend to counsel or control them, on the temptations of a large city! In what a multitude of cases are large cities large graveyards of virtue, honour, and honesty; large shambles, if I may say so, to which youths fresh from the country and yet uncontaminated by vice, come up like sheep to the slaughter? Read the list of wrecks that happen yearly on our winter nights and stormy shores.

And even when fancy fills our ear with the shrieks of the drowning, or shows us their imploring faces and dying struggles, the corpses that strew the beach, the wild grief of widows, the desolate home where the fatherless boy weeps at a mother's knee, and the infant, unconscious of its loss, smiles or sleeps upon her breast—what is that list of wrecks to that which were written, had we such a record, of the men and women who are year by year wrecked in their youth on the dangers and vices of our towns! Let the places of business, where employers show no regard to the welfare, but only to the work, of those in their service,—let the houses where no friendly interest is taken in their domestics, in the way they pass the Sabbath, in their company and associates,—let the scenes of public amusement, the haunts of drunkards, and the hells of vice, give up their secrets, as the sea does the drowned it casts on its beach, and we should have a roll like the prophet's, " written without and within with lamentation, mourning, and woe "—something more shocking than the shores which the tempest strews with wrecks, than fields which war covers with its horrid carnage, the writhing forms of the wounded and the mangled bodies of the dead.

We have always considered it a hard crook in the lot of many, that they require to send their children away from the virtuous influences of home at the very period of life which forms the character, and requires, more than any other, a parent's kind and Christian care. A dangerous transition, they pass at once from the shelter and genial air of a conser servatory to the blast of rude tempests, to the cold night and its biting frosts. Yet such is the trial to which many a youth is exposed. His boyhood past, the day arrives when he must leave the safe and happy home where, ever since she first clasped her boy to her bosom, a mother's eye has watched over him, and a father's steps have guided his to the house of God, and his voice has mingled in the evening psalm, and his knee bent in the prayers which hallowed that home. It is a dark morning in the house. Every face grave and sad, they meet to pray and then to part; and for the last time a father's voice, amid a mother's sobs, tremblingly commends the boy to God. But the trial is past; and, the quiet harbour left far behind, with no other than his own inexperienced hand on the helm, the youth finds himself among the snares and sins of the city—breakers a-head; roaring breakers on this bow and on that. He is beset with temptations; and has now means and opportunities of indulging in sin with which his principles and virtue have never yet been tried. At first shocked with what he hears and sees, the raillery and ridicule of the wicked fail to shake his virtuous resolutions.

For a while he finds guardian angels in those memories of home that are still fresh and fragrant in his heart; in the recollection of a mother's last look and a father's last touching, tender prayers; in the knowledge that it would wring their loving hearts should he consent when sinners entice him. But time wears on; and familiarity with vice softens its harsher features. It looks less shocking every day. He begins to doubt whether he is not too puritanical and precise. And now comes the struggle. The Philistines are on thee, Samson! The hour of fate has arrived. He has put his foot on a slide, down which, unless God interpose and help, he goes to destruction with growing, flying speed. Not altogether approving, but quieting conscience by promises not to repeat it, he consents for once to desert the house of God for some pleasure-party; to venture for once, but only once, into scenes where virtue breathes the air, and dies. That first act wherein he yielded to the enticement of sinners, and whereby he did violence to conscience, is, so to speak, the first parallel of the siege. The ground is not lost without many a sore struggle; yet step by srep, from trench to trench, the besiegers push on the attack; at length the last wall shakes, totters, falls, and a wide breach is made. Now, unless Christ hold it, unless, as the enemy comes in like a flood, the Spirit of God lift up a standard against him, unless God save at the uttermost, vain all further struggle, vain the effort of expiring virtue. Exhausted after some feeble strokes and show of resistance, she yields, and vice conquers; and after a while, parents who, forgetting and forgiving all, open their doors to a child returning to die beneath their roof, find nothing left to mourn over but a miserable wreck — their only consolation, perhaps, as they stand weeping by his grave, that the turf lies light on the breast of a penitent prodigal.

As the French proverb says, " It is not only the *first* step that costs." Against that fatal step — the beginning of evil — let me warn the young; for if Satan, to use a homely proverb, gets an inch, depend on it, he will take an ell. The beginning of sin, as well as that of strife, is like the letting out of waters —at first a drop like a diamond lies in a fissure, or hangs sparkling from a grassy tuft of the embankment; by and by, a succession of drops like pearls falling from a broken string; by and by, a thin crystal stream; then a gush; then a torrent; and then, hurling down the dike, a wide, thundering, resistless flood, carrying havoc and death before it. Watch, and pray, therefore; for safety lies in avoiding the approach as well as abstaining from the appearance of evil — all toying, all tampering, with temptation; in a prompt obedience to the apostle's advice, Flee youthful lusts. Fight not, but fee ·

or if fight you must, copy the old Parthians, who, seated on fleet coursers and armed with bow and arrows, shot from the saddle, flying as they fought. If you cannot flee, then in Christ's name and strength face round on the foe, and make a bold stand for God; and the virtues of youth shall rebuke the vices of age, and hoary sin shall go down before you armed with God's word, as did the Philistine before the young shepherd and his sling. Giving yourselves and the dew of your youth to Christ, so far as sin is concerned, be those maxims your rule— Touch not, taste not, handle not. When sinners entice thee, consent thou not; but, recalling tender memories of home, a father's authority, and a mother's love, follow the advice of Solomon, " My son, keep thy father's commandment, and forsake not the law of thy mother; bind them continually about thine heart, and tie them about thy neck. When thou goest, it shall lead thee; when thou sleepest, it shall keep thee; when thou awakest, it shall talk with thee. For the commandment is a lamp; and the law is light, and reproofs of instruction are the way of life.

XXIV

EARLY PIETY.—Part IV.

From a child thou hast known the holy Scriptures, which
are able to make thee wise unto salvation through faith
which is in Christ Jesus."—2 Tim. iii. 15.

SOME live fast; and growing old in constitution
while yet young in years, die before their
time—their "sun is gone down while it is yet
day." Others work fast. Animated by ambition,
and sustained by untiring energy, they win for brows
not yet touched by its silver the fortunes and honours of age. Alexander the Great, for example, ere he
was two-and-thirty years old, had conquered Greece,
Palestine, Egypt, Persia; fought I know not how
many battles, and gained I know not how many victories. Ere he had numbered half the years of human life, this remarkable man had earned the proud
title of the conqueror of the world; bestriding it
like a colossus, he covered it with his shadow, and
at death shook it by his fall. Leaving old to come
down to modern times, some half century ago, he
who guided the helm of this great empire had just

entered on manhood; yet amid a hurricane of revolution that shook ancient kingdoms and hurled monarchs from their thrones, he was hailed as the "pilot that weathered the storm." Nor is the history of the two greatest generals of our, or of almost any other, days, less remarkable; seeing that ere the sun of either had reached its meridian, or there was a gray hair in their heads, both had shaken Europe with their battles, and filled the whole world with their fame. It is in the early part of the season that trees make those shoots which the last months ripen: it is youth that lengthens the bones which future years mature and strengthen. Though they do not reach their vigour, most men and women reach their height before they are twenty; and so, as history shows, with some few and famous exceptions, the greatness of all distinguished statesmen, warriors, orators philosophers, poets, though age was required to bring their talents to perfection, has been blocked out in the season of their youth.

The history of most pious men presents the same features. Few people are converted when they are old; some are in manhood: but in most, the seeds of the new life, though they lie dormant for months, perhaps for years, are sown in the spring-time of life. When his persecutors set before the aged martyr a heathen altar and a stake, bidding him decide to sacrifice to the gods or burn in the fire, he boldly chose death, saying, I have served my Master too long, and loved Him too well, to forsake Him now ! And as, on the one hand, no man who, like him, remembered his Creator in the days of his youth, forgets, or is forgotten by Him when his head is hoary ; on the other hand, few have remembered their Creator in manhood, or old age, but those who were brought to Christ before mid-life. A pious old age following a youth of vice, and a manhood of worldliness and indifference to religion, is not the rule, but the exception—and a rare exception. There is a close analogy here between the phenomena of the material and the spiritual world ; conversions in old age, or advanced manhood, being as uncommon as a fine afternoon with cloudless skies and glowing sunset, unless the rain ceases, and the weather clear before twelve o'clock.

Look, for example, at the brightest names, the greatest saints in Scripture history. Almost all were examples of early piety. Look at David ! Called by Samuel in his boyhood to be a king, but ere that anointed with oil more precious than flowed from the prophet's horn, how young his years, yet how mature his piety ; and how wonderful the faith which accepted the giant's challenge, and entering the lists against a son of Anak, proved itself the strongest of the two ! Look at Josiah wearing the crown when eight years old ; the youngest king

20

who ever sat on a throne, yet swaying the helm cf state
with a firmness that astonished his oldest and ablest
statesmen.   It was a sight to see that child seated on
David's throne; robed priests and gray-haired
councillors bowing before him; and the boy, with a
hand that hardly grasps the round of the sceptre,
guiding it with a wisdom that would have saved the
kingdom from shipwreck had that been possible.
But the palace presented a still more illustrious
spectacle; this boy, belonging to a class that has few
kings in it, walking with God when his years were
only twelve, and his feet were surrounded by the
snares and temptations of a court.   More than that,
he was working for God—with the energy of a Luther attacking abuses, bringing out God's own Word
to the light of day, and pursuing the work of public
reformation with a zeal which has never been surpassed in the best periods of the Church's history.
Look also at Daniel and his three companions—the
captive youths who maintained their purity amid the
seductions of a heathen court, and, though borne
away into distant exile, unlike many of our youths,
remembered in Babylon the house of their God and
the land of their fathers.   With prayer, they sustained their faith, and sanctified their chamber; and
many a time the sentinels, as they walk d their nightly rounds, heard them singing—strange sounds within palace walls—the songs of Sion and of Jerusa-

lem, their chiefest joy. Unless piety had struck its roots deep when their hearts were soft, yet young and tender, and had grown with their growth, and strengthened with their strength, it had never endured their fiery trial; nor stood erect against a power that bowed the heads of the multitude before the royal image like reeds or corn before the wind. They grew up into the stoutest men, with frames of strongest bone and toughest muscle, who are not stinted, but well fed in youth; and to early piety those brave, ancient witnesses owed the faith that stood undaunted before the ravening lions, and the blaze of the fiery furnace.

In further recommending early piety, I observe that youth is the *best period for acquiring religious knowledge.*

This remark holds so true of all knowledge, secular as well as sacred, that in another country they use this striking saying, " What the boy does not learn, the man does not know." In powers of attention, if volatile, easily roused, in restless activity, an insatiable curiosity, enthusiasm, buoyant spirits, and a ready as well as tenacious memory, God has given to youth such an aptitude for acquiring knowledge that it may well be called the seed-time of life; and to this season let both parents and children, teachers and scholars, apply the wise man's advice, " In the morning sow thy seed." It is the young and tender root that penetrates the soil; it is when its fibres are delicate, that, entering the fissures and following all their windings, it passes into the heart of the rock; and the earlier the mind, brought in contact with religion, is turned on its great and greatest subjects, the better hold it takes of them; and though at first feeling lost in a maze of mysteries, the more thoroughly in after life will it comprehend, and, like a root warped around the rock, the more firmly will it hold them.

Of the advantage of a thorough religious instruction in early life, where could I find a better illustration than in my own countrymen—their faults, which I would rather correct than conceal, notwithstanding? Germany, while boasting of them, has to a large extent abandoned the faith of Luther and her other great Reformers. Geneva prides herself on having been the home of Calvin; yet his creed—not in any of its peculiar but in all of its broadest evangelical doctrines—is repudiated in most of her pulpits. Her pastors preach doctrines which his soul abhorred, and her people love to have it so. In other countries, what a diversity of religious opinions prevail, not among different churches only, but within the distracted bosom of the same church! —these lands, not merely in their ecclesiastical but in their doctrinal systems, wearing creeds of as many colours as Joseph's coat. Now why is it that notwithstanding the divisions in Scotland, her people, to whatever section of the Presbyterian Church they attached themselves, have clung with proverbial tenacity to their father's faith; and in the contest with Popery or Infidelity, Antinomianism or Socinianism, have stood as firm as her sons in bloody battles and on other fields? When other churches have left their old anchorage, and, " driven with the wind and tossed," have made shipwreck of the faith, how is it that during the last three centuries the people of Scotland have stood by the old truth as " steadfast and immovable " as the mountains that guard her glens, or the rocks that girdle her storm-beaten shores ? How is it that here, where we have our full share of ecclesiastical divisions, no minister of the gospel has lapsed into Popery, and hardly one of her people ?—not more, certainly, than will be found in every age flying off, at a tangent, into some religious absurdity ? How is it that Rome has made so few recruits here ?—that the Scarlet Woman has seduced so few with her music, painting, dramatic spectacles, and meretricious ornaments ? These are facts, and, though we say it in no spirit of boasting, very remarkable facts. Now, since there is no effect without a cause, there must be some way of accounting for this. Nor is it far to seek. The circumstances admit of an obvious and easy explanation.

When George Whitefield came to Edinburgh nothing struck or pleased him so much as the sound that rose in the church when he happened to quote a passage of Scripture—giving book, chapter, and verse. His hearers, as was their wont, had taken God's Word with them to God's house; and as they turned up the passage, the leaves of two thousand Bibles rustled, like the sound of the wind among trees, in his astonished ear. To their thorough Bible-knowledge instruction, illustrated by that anecdote, and given to her youth in the house and in all her schools, and to the complete drill and training which her children, young men and women, get in that Shorter Catechism which, the work chiefly of English divines, and a remarkable compend of theology, takes a hold of the mind singularly firm, Scotland owes it that, though a hundred storms have blown, and blown their worst, she rides to-day over the very ground where the Reformers dropped their anchor three centuries ago. The tenacity with which, in spite of all their faults, and differences, and divisions, my countrymen have adhered to their ancient and common faith, illustrates the effect—for to nothing else can it be ascribed—of a thorough religious training in youth. Rich stores of divine knowledge are then most easily acquired. Deep and saving impressions are then most easily made. It is young recruits that become the best soldiers, and young apprentices the best mechanics; and the best Christians, in like manner, are those of whom, trained by a Lois or a Eunice, a saintly mother or mother's mother, we can say, in St. Paul's words to Timothy, "From a child thou hast known the holy scriptures, which are able to make thee wise unto salvation, through faith which is in Christ Jesus."

In youth *the heart is most impressible.*

Children are emotional—as easily moved by anything calculated to make them weep or laugh, love or hate, be grave or gay, be sad or merry, as the surface of a lake by the breeze that sweeps over it. But the affections of childhood, having at that inexperienced and unripe age no sound judgment to direct them, resemble those pliant tendrils which are ready to attach themselves to any object whatever; to cling, to twine themselves as readily in close embrace around some broken branch that lies rotting on the earth, as around the tree on whose strong and stately stem they might climb to the skies. Besides being characterised by a want of sound judgment, childhood wants steadiness in its affections. They are easily transferred to new objects. The impressions made on its heart are lively, but not deep or abiding. How soon the infant forgets a dead mother; and with the arms it throws around her neck transfers its love to the nurse that fills a mother's place. Before the sod is green above his grave, the boys that wept a father's loss, and walked so pale and pitiful behind his coffin, have resumed their gaiety ; and, but that memory sometimes casts a passing shadow on their enjoyments, are as bright and buoyant as the happiest of their playmates Calamity passes through their hearts, not like a ploughshare through the soil, but a ship's keel through the sea ; the furrow soon fills up, and in a short while childhood retains hardly any more trace of trials in its heart than of tears on its cheek.

In manhood, on the other hand, the judgment is or should be ripe ; but what the intellect has gained in ripeness, the heart has lost in tenderness, in impressibility. Cooled by age as well as by contact with the world, it has lost the glow of early days ; and since religion addresses itself both to the judgment and the affections, both to the understanding and the feelings, as well to the head as to the heart, youth, since, lying midway between childhood and manhood, it possesses the lively affections of the first, and the somewhat matured reason of the second, is, therefore, of all the ages of life, the most favourable for receiving saving impressions and turning to God. At the mouth of our great valleys, on the shores of those noble estuaries where our largest rivers join the arms of the sea, there lie alluvial lands, flat and fertile. There, in former ages, vast floods that filled the glens and swept their hill-sides, deposited the rich soil they carried in their muddy waters. There now the husbandman raises his richest crops; not, however, unless in tilling the land, ploughing and sowing the fields, he seizes that auspicious time between the wet and the dry, when the clayey loam is neither hard nor soft, but between the two. Such a season youth offers for that higher cultivation, where the seed is the words of eternal life, the soul is the soil, preachers are the sowers, angels shall be the reapers, and heavenly, eternal blessings are the rewards of faith and patience, of love and labour. Once gone, this most auspicious period never returns. Once lost, it is never recovered.

The prayer, " Remember not against me the sins of my youth," no doubt holds out hope to such as have let slip this precious time. Thank God, they are not to despair. Still, though Almighty grace may work a saving change at a later, and even in the latest period of life, not only does the probability of that grow less with every year's, and indeed hour's delay, but the finest specimens of piety are found in those who were converted and called when, as in the case of the good King Josiah, their hearts were young and tender. The practice of sin, persevered in, and prolonged over a period of guilty years, so blunts the conscience that it never recovers the fineness of its edge; nor is the heart capable of receiving the most delicate and beautiful impressions of Christ's image, unless they are stamped on it while, like metals or melted wax, it is soft and tender—ere it has grown hard and cold.

And what so adapted to youth as religion; what offers so many, such suitable, and such noble objects to its affections? Youth is enthusiastic: and what field for the loftiest enthusiasm like the salvation of a miserable and perishing world? Youth is brave: and more courage is often required of the Christian than of him who throws himself into the life-boat, and pulls through the breakers to the sinking wreck. Men have found it a harder thing to stand up for Christ before a battery of ridicule than, dashing through the smoke of battle, to charge a battery of cannon! Youth is generous: and where such scope for the purest generosity as in the call to take up our cross, deny ourselves daily, and follow Jesus in living and labouring for the good of others? Youth is earnest and impetuous: and this is the very temper religion urgently requires; it calls us to give all diligence to make our calling and election sure, since we know not what an hour may bring forth; this, not another, being the accepted time; to-day, not to-morrow, being the day of salvation. The door is closing, and the grave is opening: haste, for your life, it says; leap into the ark; another day another hour, even another moment, may be a long eternity too late. Once more, youth is prone to love : and in all God's universe what object so fair, so lovely, so worthy of our warmest affections, as He, the dear divine Redeemer, to whose bleeding brows belongs the wreath that David wove for Jonathan's, " Thy love to me was wonderful, passing the love of woman !"

It is well to give Jesus even blighted affections and a broken heart ; it is well, when the world cannot fill our hearts, to turn our trembling steps from its broken cisterns to the fountain of living water ; it is well, when experience has taught us that earth has no pillow without its thorns, to go and lay the aching weary head on Jesus' bosom ; it is well when the battered ship, with sails blown to ribbons and masts gone by the board, makes through the roaring sea for a harbour of rest and refuge ; it is well when man turns from his shattered fortunes, and maids from their false lovers, and mothers from their sweet, pale, lifeless coffined idols, to throw themselves at the feet or into the arms of Jesus. But it is better still, seeking Him early, to give our youth to Christ ; with its glistening dews to bathe the Rose of Sharon ; to honour God with our first-fruits ; to assign the Saviour such a place in our hearts as His poor, mangled body found in Joseph's tomb—one where no man had been laid.

It is a grand testimony to religion to see a gray and bent old man standing by the door of mercy and with voice and hand, with loud and urgent knocking, imploring God to open and let him in; but much nobler the testimony, and finer the spectacle, while he is muttering of the world, " Vanity vanity, and vexation of spirit," to see a youth in the very flower and beauty of his age refuse her tempting cup; turn away his head from her alluring smiles; and, in happy ignorance of her forbidden pleasures, resolve to give himself to Christ and a life of high and holy virtues—saying, both of the fair tempter and her temptations, " My soul, come not thou into their secret; with them, mine honour, be not thou united!"

Youth, as securing him the best of our life, should be *consecrated to God.*

In old age, men offer Him but the dregs of the cup; and a wonder it is that any one is spared to have dregs to offer. When men employ their time and talents, their health, their strength, their genius, not to serve, but injure, the cause of God, and turning His gifts against the Giver, wound the very hand that blesses them,—one wonders at the long-suffering and patience of God; that He does not shake them off as St. Paul did the viper, into the fire. Who can think of the load of obligations under which daily mercies lay us,—on the care of

that ceaseless Providence, without which we would
expire any instant, our health would turn into sickness, our reason into madness, and our blessings into
curses,—and especially on what, in the person of
His beloved Son, God has done and given to save
us,—who can reflect on these things and not be
astonished at the base ingratitude which would put
Him off with the wretched services of old age; the
forced reformation and repentance of a dying bed?
Ingratitude and insensibility this, against which God
with a sublime majesty might appeal again to crea
tion, saying, " Hear, O heavens, and give ear, O
earth : I have nourished and brought up children,
but they have rebelled against me. The ox knoweth
his owner, and the ass his master's crib ; but Israel
doth not know, my people doth not consider. Ah
sinful nation, a people laden with iniquity, a seed of
evil doers, children that are corrupters ; they have
forsaken the Lord, they have provoked the Holy
One of Israel."

There are many formidable and fatal heresies.
Some deny the divinity of our blessed Lord, reducing the Son of God to the common level of humanity. Some strip the Holy Bible of its lofty claims
to inspiration, reducing it to the common level of
other books. Some repudiate the doctrines of the
fall of man, of the corruption of our nature ; of
the atonement; of the imputation of our sin to

Christ, and of His righteousness to us. But, with whatever horror we may regard such dangerous errors, there is no error more dangerous or fatal, more likely to sink a man into perdition, than the notion that it is sufficient to seek God at the close of a life devoted to sinful pleasures, and passed in worldly pursuits. Other heresies slay their thousands; this, I fear, its tens of thousands.

In His dear Son, God has given to us the best He had to bestow; and is He not entitled to the best of ours in return? Insult is harder to bear than injury and what more insulting to the kindness, love mercy, and majesty of our God than in effect to say, I will turn to Him when I can do no better; so long as I can sin safely, I will do it; so long as I can venture to despise Him, I will do it; so long as my portion lasts, careless of my Father's displeasure, I'll play the prodigal, nor seek His house till want sends me a beggar to His door—till the roar of the cataract warns me that to persevere will be to perish. I will sail down the stream of pleasure, nor heed the voice that entreats me to turn, crying, " Turn ye, turn ye, why will ye die !"

Suppose, then, it were as easy to bend a bough when its bark is hoar with age, as when it was green and young; suppose it as easy to stop the course of a stone when it is whirling, smoking, leaping, thundering down into the valley, as when, just loosened, it began to move from its bed; suppose it as easy to turn the river from its course, where it sweeps on to the sea, as the rill by its mossy fountain; suppose it as easy to mould the clay, when grown dry and hard, as when it will receive on its plastic surface the impression of a new-blown leaf; suppose you could expect to reap a crop from land neither ploughed nor sown till trees were bare and hills were white; suppose old age were a favourable time to be saved; —are the poor services that it can render such as this lost world needs—such as the interests of the Church of God require—such as the cross of Calvary deserves—such as He who gave His Son for us should receive at our hands? Let us reject the notion. How plainly is it rejected, how strongly condemned, in this touching expostulation: "A son honoureth his father, and a servant his master. If then I be a father, where is mine honour? and if I be a master, where is my fear? If ye offer the blind for sacrifice, is it not evil? and if ye offer the lame and sick, is it not evil? Offer it now unto thy governor; will he be pleased with thee, or accept thy person? saith the Lord of Hosts!" Rejecting a thought that equally insults the majesty of Heaven and the mercy of the Cross, let us offer the best, first-fruits of our life to God, and Remember our Creator in the days of our youth.

XXV.

RETROSPECT AND PROSPECT.

"The harvest is past, the summer is ended, and we are not saved."—JER. viii. 20.

IT is in the form of one bending beneath the weight of years, and advancing with feeble steps, that Solomon paints man travelling to the grave; and, though done with a trembling hand, how graphic and true his touches? "The keepers of the house shall tremble"—the arms that held the plough, or plied the shuttle, or wielded the sword, shake with palsy; "the strong men shall bow themselves"—the limbs, those pillars of the frame, shrunk and shrivelled, totter beneath its weight; "the grinders cease"—the teeth decay, and drop from their sockets, warning man that he himself shall soon drop into his grave; "those that look out of the windows be darkened"—the eye, that window where the soul sits looking out on the world, grows dim with years, and man enters the shadow of the tomb before he enters itself; "he shall rise up at the voice of the bird;—the sleep of the cradle is calm, that

(472)

of robust youth long and deep, but old age brings broken slumbers, and wakes with the birds that sing in the dawn; "the daughters of music shall be brought low"—deafness swells the train of infirmities, and amid the cheerful circle the old man, cut off while alive from communion with the living, sits with furrowed brow and snowy head in a solitude which only religion can cheer; "they shall be afraid of that which is high"—with heart enfeebled, he leaves others to breast heights and hills, and, staff in hand, creeps along the flat shore or the level sward; "the almond tree shall flourish"—his head is white as its blossoms, with the frost of age; "the grasshopper shall be a burden"—such his weakness, though as the tiny insect leaps from blade to blade, the grass hardly bends beneath its weight; and, last of all, "desire shall fail"—the very wish for pleasures dies with the power of enjoying them. A miserable existence, unless where holy desires survive the decay of nature, and the saint longs for the hour when the dissolution of his old, crazy, earthly tabernacle shall set him free for his flight to heaven!

So Solomon paints man, to use his own words, as going "to his long home." But instead of a gray, decrepit man creeping slowly along a shadowy vista, with a grave yawning to receive him, he might have introduced a beautiful, rosy, gleesome child, bounding on over the short course between its cradle and a tomb. The journey to the long home—one which we begin with life and are all engaged in—is long to some and short to others. The infant commences it before it has learned to walk; the old man continues it when his limbs are too feeble to bear him across the floor. It is one we carry on sleeping as well as waking—on Sabbath as on other days—on which we never halt, till we stumble into the grave which is dug at the end of the road. On this journey we go swiftly—flashing through the threads of life like a weaver's shuttle; we go incessantly—moving night and day, like the hands that circle round the hours; our heart beating on like a pendulum, till the clock, wound up to go a certain time, has run down, or accident stops its motion.

We all are on the way to the long home; and at this season of the year* our position is that of travellers who have reached the summit of a mountain range that parts two great valleys. Standing on one of Time's lofty watersheds, we have left one year behind, and the next, into which we are about to descend, lies stretched out before us. In such circumstances it is natural to do two things :—first, to look back, taking a retrospect : and, secondly, to look forward, and try to pierce the veil which, like

* This discourse was preached on the last Sabbath of the year.

a gray mist spread over the valley, conceals the future from our view.

The Retrospect.—One of the strangest things we
meet with is to see consummate wisdom so far as the
interests of this world are concerned, and consummate folly as to everything belonging to the next, in
one and the same person—just as in the bed of the
Rhone after it has received the turbulent Arve the
spectator sees two volumes of water that for a while
flow on side by side—the one foul, the other so beau-
tifully blue and pure that it looks like a liquid sky.
Once on a time a vessel, freighted with gold, was
wrecked in circumstances which left her crew no
chance of life but swimming to the distant shore.
Some had committed themselves to the deep; others
were stripping for the struggle; when one, turning
an avaricious eye on the treasure, seized the fortune
at his hand. Infatuated wretch! His fellows remonstrated, but in vain. Loaded with gold, he leaps
from the ship, and strikes out bravely for the shore.
But by and by his strokes grow feebler, quicker—
then a short convulsive struggle—and then, borne
down by the weight he carries, he sinks beneath the
wave. What a fool he was! We had not been such
fools!—so many say, and perhaps truly; and yet,
guilty of greater folly, they allow themselves to be
so engaged, and indeed engrossed with the pursuits

of time, whether of business or pleasure, as to neglect their salvation, and lose their souls.

The children of this world are wise in their generation! If a man is building a house, he takes good care, in the first place, to get a sound foundation. Is it a lighthouse, to stand with its tall form and burning head a lonely pillar amid tempestuous seas?—beneath the sand and shells that have flung on the fatal reef he goes down to the solid rock, seeking a foundation which cannot be moved. And after having secured a good foundation, in laying one course on another, in raising story over story, the work of examination keeps pace with the work of building. By square and plummet he proves his work; teaching us, even when we are resting, in the righteousness of Christ, on the Rock of Ages—in view of events which shall try every man's work, how we should bring ours to the test of God's holy Word.

This retrospect should embrace the way in which we have discharged our duty to *God*.

It is much easier to say what God has done for us than what we have done for Him. That opens up a vast subject; His bounty presenting the aspect of a majestic river, which, never frozen by winter nor dried by summer, winds full and flowing through the past. To reckon up the blessings which we have received at His hand would prove, in fact, a task as impossible as to number the dew-drops on the glittering sward, the leaves of a forest, or the sands of ocean. No doubt, as life is at the best but a chequered scene, we may have been afflicted; yet how far have our mercies outnumbered our miseries? Besides, who has not been afflicted less than his iniquities deserved? Besides, does not faith in the assurance that all things shall work for good to them who love God, and are the called according to His purpose, fling a bright bow on life's blackest cloud? —work such change on our trials as the branch which Moses cast in on Marah's waters, turning bitter to sweet and evil to good?

When God has done so much for us, nothing can be more reasonable than to inquire what we have done for Him; and anticipate by a few years, or days perhaps, the hour when He shall address to each of us these solemn words, Thou shalt be no longer steward; give an account of thy stewardship.

Opportunities of serving, honouring, glorifying, speaking for Him have occurred every day of the past year; and have they been improved, or neglected? Of our whole time He claims a seventh part—fifty-two days in every year, and therefore no less than ten whole years in the threescore and ten of human life—all this for His special service; communion with Him, and preparation for a world of which this is but the vestibule. How much work

for God might we have done in fifty-two busy **days?**
—how much has been done? Required to **do all**
for His glory—even in matters of eating and **drink-**
ing, can we recall any one thing we have done **for**
that end?—any one word we have spoken on behalf
of His cause, to the praise of His honour?—any
one effort we have put forth to be saved, or to save
others? Alas! on reviewing the past, the holiest,
the best and busiest of us have to acknowledge ourselves "unprofitable servants;" and as to others, with
a whole year misspent, abused, utterly lost, they
seem miracles of sparing mercy; nor does one know
whether most to wonder at their ingratitude, or admire His long-suffering who even yet delays to strike,
waiting to be gracious.

This retrospect should embrace the way in which
we have discharged our duty to *our own souls.*

It were sad if, on reviewing the past year, with all
its opportunities, we could come to no other conclusion than this—" The harvest is past, the summer is
ended, and we are not saved!" We may have increased our store of earthly comforts, we may have
clambered up some steps higher in society, we may
have added broad acres to our estate—hundreds or
thousands to our wealth; but, if we are not saved,
we have only increased the difficulties of our salvation and the terrors of death. Nor, should we die
now, have we any other sentence to pronounce on

our works than Solomon pronounced on his — I looked on all the works which my hands had made, and on all the labour which I had laboured to do; and behold all was vanity and vexation of spirit; and there was no profit under the sun. We have spent our money for that which is not bread, and our labour for that which satisfieth not: and, with more toil and care and trouble than had been required to build a bower in Paradise, we have been training up a green, dying gourd in the vain hope of finding beneath its leaves the happiness found only in Him who is as an hiding-place from the wind, and a covert from the tempest; as the shadow of a great rock in a weary land.

Happy those who did not see the old year die with unforgiven sins on its gray head, nor dread meeting it again at God's bar of judgment. Happy those whom it found in a state of enmity, and left at peace with God. Happy those who, on taking stock and striking a balance, if I may so speak, find themselves poorer in spirit and richer in grace— who, on examining into their position, find that though nearer the grave they are riper for heaven, nearer to glory; and that a year which, making many wives widows and children orphans, turning some hopes into fruit and blasting others in the flower, has wrought many changes, has changed them to the better—chastened and sanctified them: so that they

say, " we all, with open face beholding as in a glass
the glory of the Lord, are changed into the same
image from glory to glory, even as by the Spirit of
the Lord."

This retrospect should embrace the way in which
we have done our duty to *others.*

The Life of Jesus, the title of many good and
some bad books, has filled volumes. So full was
that life of gracious utterances, and so crowded with
works of majesty and mercy, that the evangelist St.
John says, " If they should be written every one, I
suppose that even the world itself could not contain
the books that should be written."   Yet the Life of
Jesus may be summed up in this one short sentence,
He went about doing good.   This brought Him from
heaven and nailed Him to the cross : for this object
He lived, for it He died.   Fancy our Lord on one
of those mountain tops, where, with the world beneath and the heavens above Him, He courted solitude, taking a quiet survey of one of His years—
looking back on all the works which His hands had
wrought, and on all the labour that He had laboured
to do.   How crowded the year with miracles and
mercies—sinners warned ; mourners comforted ; the
dead rising at His word ; the blind gazing on His
blessed face ; the deaf listening with rapture to His
words ; the dumb singing His praises and proclaiming His name and power ; more good crowded into

one short day of that life than is spread over long
years of ours !

Unless the same mind be in us that was in Jesus
Christ, we are none of His. So it behoves us to
consider what testimony, in good attempted or done
to others, the past year bears to the genuineness of
our Christianity. Whom have we warned ? In our
family, or in the circle of our friends or neighbours,
whom have we sought to bring to Jesus? What
hungry ones have we fed, what naked clothed ?
Whose wrongs have we sought to redress, whose
sorrows attempted to alleviate ? Whose cup has
been filled out of ours ? What widow's heart have
we made to sing for joy ? Of the two, a river that
fed of heaven and swelling beyond its banks spreads
its waters on the thirsty fields, or a whirlpool that,
moving around itself, and drawing all things to its
centre, swallows them up into its own greedy and
devouring vortex—which does our course most resemble ? In the year that is gone has the world
been the better or the worse of us ?

It behoves us to consider these things, nor go
recklessly on with such as, during the whole past
life, and indeed their whole past life, have never
given one hour of self-examination to a serious
review of their life. What recklessness is this ?—
in our circumstances, what madness ? Do we sail
a sea where there is neither storm, nor cross

21

tides, nor sunken rock, nor shifting sandbanks, that we go so merrily on with songs below, and dances on the deck; neither keeping watch, nor taking observations, nor heaving the lead for soundings? There were fewer souls, as well as ships lost, if men would use the means of safety. We shrink from examining ourselves; but if, when judging our own cause with a strong bias in our own favour, we cannot bear to examine ourselves, how shall we stand at the bar of divine judgment—how endure the searching eye of God? " If thou hast run with the footmen and they have wearied thee, then how canst thou contend with horses? and if in the land of peace wherein thou trustedst they wearied thee, then how wilt thou do in the swelling of Jordan?" Here, more than anywhere else, it is well to know the worst. None are beyond the reach of redemption, whom to awaken to a sense of their condition would only be to torment before their time. Men are going to ruin; but not like the boat that was seen shooting the rapid, and had reached a point above the cataract where no power could stem the raging current. To the horror of those who watched it shooting on to destruction, a man was seen on board, and asleep. The spectators ran along the banks. They cried; they shouted; and the sleeper awoke at length to take in all his danger at one fearful glance. To spring to his feet, to throw himself on the bench, to seize the oars, to strain every nerve in superhuman efforts to turn the boat's head to the shore, was the work of an instant. But in vain. Away went the bark to its doom, like an arrow from the bow. It hang a moment on the edge of the gulf; and then, is gone for ever. Suppose a man to be as near hell! —if I could awaken him, I would. The dying thief was saved in the act of going over into perdition. Christ caught and saved him there. And He who is mighty to save, saving at the uttermost, can save, though all our life were wasted to its last breath, if that last breath is spent in gasping out St. Peter's cry, " Save me, Lord, I perish !"

The Prospect.—Inspired of God, men have fore-told coming events; and so have others who were neither prophets, nor prophets' sons. To Kirkcaldy of Grange, then holding out Edinburgh Castle against the Protestant Reforming party, with whom he was once associated, John Knox (as I remarked on another occasion) sent a remarkable message from his death-bed. "Warn him," said the dying man, " not to trust in yon craggy rock, from which he shall be shamefully dragged to be hanged up in the face of the sun." And, improbable as to many at the time it seemed, it fell out as Knox had pre-dicted. He was dragged from his stronghold, like a ruffled eagle from her rocky nest, and ignominiously hanged in the face of day. The secret of the Lord, says the Bible, is with them that fear Him; and in regard to extraordinary communications of His will and mind, who shall limit the Holy One of Israel ? But the great Reformer made no claim to the gift of prophecy; and whatever powers were attributed to him in a superstitious age, those who honour his memory regard Knox as having been nothing more than a man of more than ordinary sagacity. Penetrating through the mask of false pretences into men's real designs, and reasoning from causes to their legitimate effects, he owed his fame, as one inspired, to the seer-like certainty with which he foresaw and foretold the natural issue of affairs.

History, in a sense, is prophecy; since, according to the words of Solomon, " that which is to be hath already been." It is so to a large extent in the kingdom of Nature; her sequences and her seasons being fixed by unalterable laws, each running year just repeats the past. And thus, though groves are mute and fields are naked now, we can predict that spring shall come with opening buds and singing birds; and summer come, her green lap filled with flowers; and brown autumn come, armed with the reaper's sickle and crowned with ears of corn.

Taking men in the mass, so is it in regard to their fortunes and destiny—to vary the mode but not the sense of the wise man's adage, That which hath already been is that which is to be. This does not apply to individuals; since many who lived last year three hundred and sixty-five days, shall not live this year as many hours. Nor does it apply to individual homes and households — the cradle shall give place to the coffin; the marriage last year formed, this shall dissolve; and, on the other hand, a tide of good fortune coming with the turn of the year, many before its close, taking their harp from the willow - tree, shall sit singing with Hannah, " My heart rejoiceth in the Lord; mine horn is exalted in the Lord; for the Lord killeth and maketh alive; he bringeth down to the grave and bringeth up." But though the fortunes of individual persons or single families, may vary much from year to year, it is otherwise with masses of men. In regard to these, the events of last year, whether they were good or evil, shall find their counterpart in this, and thus the retrospect becomes a prospect, and the past presents a magic mirror in which we can descry the future.

Thus some shall *continue to neglect salvation.*

A rope thrown to a drowning man, if well thrown once, does not need to be twice thrown. It needs no eloquent speaker on pier or bank to address the sinking wretch and persuade him not to " neglect so great salvation." Let it go spinning out within clutch of his eager hands, and how he grasps it;

and holds it with the grim gripe of death ! But it
is not once, or twice, or twenty times that salvation
in these last twelve months has been offered; and
to this day many have obstinately, madly refused to
accept it. By preachers and His providences, even
as a father pleadeth with his children, God has pled
with them; His Son has implored them; though
vexed and grieved by their obstinacy, His Spirit has
continued to strive with them—the year has brought
them a thousand opportunities of being saved; yet
it is gone, and they are not saved. Alas! in the
words of Scripture, " The harvest is past, the summer is ended, and we are not saved."

Give men an opportunity of escape—do literally
what Christ is figuratively said to do, " proclaim
liberty to the captive, and the opening of the prison
to them that are bound," disarm the warders, throw
open the cells—and what a rush for liberty ! and,
after a brief space of wild shouts and tread of hurrying feet, what a profound silence and perfect solitude ! Yet how often has the door of mercy been
thrown open ? With kindness in His looks, and
love in His heart, and His hand pointing to an open
door, how often has Jesus appeared to us, saying,
" Behold, I have set before you an open door ! ' and
turning over to the other side for a little more sleep,
how often have we dismissed Him with this reply,
" Go thy way for this time; when I have a conven-

ient season I will call for thee!" Is this to go on
for ever?—each year repeating the risk, the sin, and
folly of the past? The prospect looks even more
melancholy than the retrospect. There is less hope
for us each year and day we live in sin. Every hour
we are drifting out to sea — the helpless, helmless
barque is leaving the lessening shore farther and
farther behind. Our disease becomes incurable.
Like those stones which, though soft as clay on being
raised from the quarry, grow hard as flint through
exposure to the weather, our hearts are growing
harder day by day. Let such as have been delaying,
delay no longer; dare no more. The axe is raised,
gleaming, against the tree; and though it should not
fall before the year expires, before that God may be
provoked to withdraw His Spirit, and leave us to
our fate, saying, "They are joined to their idols,
let them alone."

Some shall be *converted.*

Like the loftiest snow-crowned peaks that tower
above the common Alps, there are periods and
events in history which are peculiarly marked and
memorable. Such a period in the history of the
world was that of the Deluge, when all mankind
were drowned but one family; and also that Christmas night when angels announced the advent and
sung the birth of the new-born King. Such a period
in the history of nations was that of the Hebrew

exodus, when Israel burst his bonds, and left the
land of Egypt; and that also when He who had
delivered His people by the hand of Moses summoned a woman to the rescue, and saved them by
the hand of Esther from the cruel wrath of Haman.
Such also was the era of the Reformation in our
Church, and of the Revolution in our country—
events whose influence, growing with time, and ex-
tending with distance, and widening out on all sides
like the watery circle that leaves the middle of the
lake to break in wavelets on its strand, is felt this
day on the shores of America and the plains of
Hindostan.

In the history of individuals also there are memorable periods—events on which turns man's eternal,
as well as his present, destiny. And of all his years
and days that is worthiest of a Christian's remembrance on which, passing from a state of nature into
one of grace, he was born again—he drew the first
breath, and in an earnest prayer, uttered the first
cry of a new life. Many usher in each new year
with revelry, and celebrate their birth-day as it
comes round with feasts, and songs, and dances, and
delights, who shall regret they were ever born—saying, " Let the day perish wherein I was born—why
died I not from the womb ?' But the last year shall
be one of everlasting and grateful remembrance to
all whom it found the enemies, and left the friends

of God; whom it found slaves and left freemen; whom it found on the way to hell, but, converted, washed, and sanctified, it left on the road to heaven. That which is to be is that which hath already been. Only let us pray that if the past year has witnessed thousands, this may witness tens of thousands of souls converted, poor sinners saved ; that if its fields yielded harvests of thirty, this, in a revenue of glory to God and good to men, may yield, not thirty, but sixty, even an hundred-fold. We cannot but hope that many shall be saved this year — plucked as brands from the burning. God is making up the roll of His elect; Christ is gathering the jewels of His crown; heaven is filling fast; and why should we see others enter in countless crowds, and be ourselves left out? The cry comes forth, "Yet there is room," room to spare ! While the door stands open, rush in—for that matter strive to enter in, and while a mouldering tombstone shall bear the date of your first birth, of the year on which you were born for the grave, let this happier year be engraven on your grateful and enduring memory as that on which you were born for God and glory.

Death shall *summon many to judgment*

Though, as he lies a-dying, every one feels as if he were alone in the valley, none but himself on that dark road, he is not a solitary traveller—a

2 1 *

great throng crowd the way, passing in at the gates of the eternal world. Men die in such numbers, that for every breath we draw some one breathes his last; with every beat of our hearts some heart ceases to beat. Let a knell be rung for every departing spirit, and that bell would toll on without a pause till Time's own knell was rung, and Death itself should die.

That which hath been is that which is to be. Willing or unwilling, fit or unfit to die, converted or otherwise, voyagers to a land of bliss or bound to misery, many in this have entered on their last year. Like time and tide, death—regardless of his convenience and deaf to his prayers—will wait on no man. If in past years God has set a mark on our houses, and turned the angel of death from our door, as by the blood in Egypt; that immunity cannot last for ever. The more the years of our life, this one is the more likely to be that of our death— the farther the tide recedes, the higher at the flow it throws its foaming waves on the beach; the longer the cloud is gathering, and thickening, and darkening before it bursts, the brighter the lightning flashes, the louder the thunder peals.

Since death is gain to the Christian, and through faith in Christ may be so to all, we should familiarize our minds with that event: beginning every year, and indeed every day, as if it were to be—

what it may be—our last. Joseph of Arimathea prepared himself a tomb, probably placing it among the flowers and delights of his garden, that the sight of the " long home " where he was to lie might keep him mindful of his latter end. One whom I knew, with the same object and from no contempt of death, had his coffin made, and studied the Bible with that memorial of our mortality standing up, tall and black, beside him. One of the greatest monarchs went further still. Having resigned the sceptre and retired to a monastery, he prepared a tomb for himself, and fixed a day for the ceremonies of his burial. The funeral procession is formed; and with the bell tolling for the dead, it takes its slow way to the tomb, the king himself bringing up the rear—a ghastly form attired in a long white shroud. He is laid in his coffin; round the body the priests go, sprinkling showers of holy water, and swinging incense out of golden censers. The service for the dead is chanted over him; the last prayer is offered; the last psalm has died away in solemn echoes; the candles, types of life's flame, are extinguished; and, closing the door, they leave the living man alone, stretched out in a coffin, enclosed within a tomb, to meditate amid its lonely and awful darkness on such subjects as this singular and terrible solemnity was calculated to suggest. Violent and revolting as such expedients seem, bet ter thus to be kept mindful, than live habitually forgetful, of our latter end, and leave death to break in on our fatal slumbers with the suddenness and surprise of a thief. Watch, is the word of Christ—watch, for ye know neither the day nor the hour when the Son of Man cometh. To be prepared for death—so prepared that it may be the happiest event that ever befell us, so prepared that we may show how calmly a Christian can die, so prepared that we may confront this king of terrors without the shadow of a doubt or any sense of fear, so prepared that, seeing the heavens opening above our heads and angels descending to carry us to glory, we shall be better pleased to go than to stay—let us make our calling and election sure. Let us work out our salvation with fear and trembling; looking to Jesus for pardon, and to God to work in us by His Holy Spirit both to will and to do of His good pleasure.

THE END.